The Sacred and the Sovereign

The Sacred and the Sovereign
Religion and International Politics

JOHN D. CARLSON &

ERIK C. OWENS, Editors

Georgetown University Press
WASHINGTON, D.C.

Georgetown University Press, Washington, D.C.
© 2003 by Georgetown University Press. All rights reserved.
Printed in the United States of America

10 9 8 7 6 5 4 3 2 1   2003

Library of Congress Cataloging-in-Publication Data
    The sacred and the sovereign : religion and international politics /
John D. Carlson and Erik C. Owens, editors.
        p.   cm.
    Includes bibliographic references and index.
    ISBN 0-87840-908-4 (pbk. : alk. paper)
    1. Religion and international affairs.   I. Carlson, John D. (John David)
II. Owens, Erik C.
BL65.I55.S33 2003
291.1'787 — dc21   2002013808

Politics will, to the end of history, be an area where conscience and power meet, where the ethical and coercive factors of human life will interpenetrate and work out their tentative and uneasy compromises.

—Reinhold Niebuhr
Moral Man and Immoral Society

Contents

Foreword

JEAN BETHKE ELSHTAIN

ANYONE OVER THE AGE OF FORTY who possesses a college degree no doubt has been imbued at some point along the way with the "secularization hypothesis," as it was called. This hypothesis, oversimply, held that culture moved one direction only—away from religion (sometimes equated with superstition, myth, or whatever was not subjected to stern rationalistic scrutiny) and toward a religion-free, secular society. The queen of the sciences—a throne once occupied by theology (of all things)—would now be rightfully and sensibly assumed by science itself. Authoritative claims would possess a scientific warrant, or they wouldn't be authoritative claims: that simple. The social sciences rushed to embrace a narrow science of verification and to try to derive laws of social life. A rift between the "hard" pursuits that admitted of empirical verification and the "soft"—those that did not—opened up and is yet to be healed.

As usually happens with confident predictions, grand hypotheses, and historic teleologies in general, however, the secularization thesis came a cropper. Stunningly, religious belief not only failed to go the way of the great dinosaurs, it came back from the (only apparent) brink of extinction. To be sure, many countries of western Europe exhibit religious faith in its thinnest form: faith that isn't faith at all but a "baptize, marry, bury" custom. In the United States, however—the sprawling, energetic country that has always represented the cutting edge of democracy and technological innovation—religion is powerful, publicly visible, and growing in strength (in some denominations or faiths) and diversity. In much of the rest of the world, old religions enjoy surprising strength where the matter of conversion is concerned—Roman Catholicism is a case in point—and relatively new religions are growing rapidly (two examples would be Mormonism worldwide and evangelical Protestantism in Latin America). A radically fundamentalist version of Islam that preaches theocracy and practices intolerance of all other faiths has triumphed in several countries and poses a challenge—most Westerners would say a threat—to many others. Islam now faces challenges of the sort Christianity confronted in the sixteenth century, and much of the future of humankind hinges on the outcome of that story.

So no matter how you slice it, religion—the sacred—is potent and visible, for many people the central source of meaning and purpose in their lives. The political implications of this situation are diverse, as the essays in this volume demonstrate. One implication is a challenge to, or chastening of, the claims and aims of sovereign dominion. The nation-state solidified by the Treaty of Westphalia (1648), a century after the Peace of Augsburg (1555) that aimed to quell unrest prompted by religious strife—this, at least, is the way the story usually is told—faces unprecedented challenges. This observation does not mean that the nation-state is a dying breed. There is no call to replace the failed secularization hypothesis with another dubious claim that is similarly bound to fail. But the nation-state is being transformed from within and without.

These transformations take place from within as nonstate actors, including religious bodies, make powerful claims on the sovereign state. They take place from without as forces of globalization, including universal religious bodies, organize and unite people across state boundaries. Sovereignty is spoken of as being divided, or pooled, or combined. No one quite knows how to capture the energies unleashed in our world conceptually. In some places, such as western Europe, the traditional signs and symbols of sovereignty, the literal coin of the realm, is now the generic euro, stripped of all particularistic distinction. The European Union can bypass many of the democratic procedures of states, pushing through highly controversial reforms absent popular referenda. In other places, such as the microstates that sprang up like so many mushrooms with unpronounceable names in the wake of the collapse of the Soviet Union, the trappings of sovereignty are newly acquired and are not likely to be abandoned anytime soon.

It is an exciting and difficult time to be alive and to be a scholar trying to grasp at least some of this unwieldy topic in argument, evidence, theory, and working concepts. That is what this excellent volume, edited and introduced with painstaking care, attempts. I join the editors in expressing the hope that all the voices collected here will make more subtle our understandings and more capacious our views.

Jean Bethke Elshtain
University of Chicago
Chicago, Illinois

Preface

THIS BOOK GOES TO PRESS at a time in which our vista onto international political life is colored quite bleakly by violent conflict, war, and threats of further war. We conceived this project when ethnic political strife was ripping apart Kosovo, as it had done throughout much of the Balkans at the end of the twentieth century. We convened the conference that would inspire this book in October 2000, one week after the second Palestinian *intifada* began; regrettably, the waves of violence consuming the Middle East outlasted the production of this volume. The writing and editing of many of these chapters culminated as the terrorist attacks of September 11, 2001, were visited upon the United States, followed by the U.S.-led military action in Afghanistan to unseat the Taliban. Thus did terrorism and the subsequent "war on terrorism" prompt many of us to revisit central themes, challenge previously held premises, raise new questions, and offer further responses. Throughout the manuscript production, disturbing warnings of further terrorist attacks against Americans continued; Pakistan and India squared off again over Kashmir in a conflict threatening to erupt into a nuclear exchange; and threats of an invasion to disarm Iraq of weapons of mass destruction crescendoed.

Many observers would demur at characterizing these conflicts primarily as "religious wars." Yet in all of these circumstances, religion is implicated in complex and worrisome ways — and rightly so; no one can doubt that religious differences aggravate other tensions and factors. This book is not primarily about the causes of "religious violence," nor do we explore in depth the religious differences of the many conflicting sides involved. We do, however, lift up the ways in which religious commitments and traditions call us to reflect upon urgent problems such as violence and war and telling political developments such as the changing face of state sovereignty. Offsetting the widely shared presumption that religion is politics' perennial nemesis, we set out to retrieve and survey the unique contributions that religious angles and perspectives bring to conversations about international politics and indeed how religious ideas and institutions, wittingly or not, shape international political life.

We first envisaged the subject of religion in international politics through the lens of "sacred and sovereign" during conversations about possible theological warrants for humanitarian intervention. A host of questions drove our inquiry then, as now: Is there a point at which injustice within a state's boundaries requires armed intervention by foreign powers? If so, on what grounds might such intervention be required? What do our religious traditions teach about violence in the service of peacemaking or about the demands of justice and care in this context? Do "crimes against humanity" justify intervention, or require it, or both? Are the human rights so wantonly violated in such crimes grounded in a theological understanding of human dignity, or must they be?

These questions about humanitarian intervention soon led to broader thinking about the directions and influences—moral, political, and religious—of sovereignty in the new century. What other legitimate occasions exist for military, diplomatic, economic, or other forms of "interference" in the internal affairs of sovereign states? When terrorism was thrust to the top of the agenda, we began to push this project in dramatically different directions that we had not previously conceptualized. Yet we also discovered that we had come full circle: Many of the themes raised in early discussions about humanitarian intervention were reappearing as we dwelled on terrorism. Thus, we moved to embrace a range of issues, still clustered around a common set of problems and tensions representing the most bracing features and prominent contours shaping the post–cold war topography of international affairs.

Scholarly collaboration is one of the greatest rewards of academic life, and we are fortunate to have worked with an exceptional group of contributors on this project. We thank this distinguished cadre for the time they took from their other important duties and demanding schedules to participate. We appreciate their willingness to review—in many cases amend, in other cases rewrite—their chapters following the attacks of September 11, 2001, and the attendant "war on terrorism." The book is better grounded and more relevant to current affairs as a result.

Two institutions and many other people also warrant praise and recognition for supporting this project. The University of Chicago Divinity School, using resources from the D. R. Sharpe Lectureship Fund, provided generous financial support for the aforementioned conference, which was titled "The Sacred and the Sovereign: Human Rights, the Use of Force, and Religious Pluralism at Century's Dawn" and was held on October 20, 2000, in Chicago, Illinois. That conference first brought together many of the contributors to this volume—renowned scholars, public intellectuals, and gifted leaders with expertise in theology, political theory, the media, military operations, and diplomatic affairs—for a rich conversation about "just war" theory, human rights, political sovereignty, and humanitarian intervention. That conversation continues in this book, and it has been enlarged by other contributors who joined the work after the conference to discuss war crimes tribunals, terrorism, and other issues. We hope to expand this conversation further as this book reaches readers who, like its contributors, work inside and outside the academy.

We thank the Divinity School for its unswerving administrative and institutional support throughout this process, which helped bring this project to fruition. We also would like to express our deep gratitude to Clark Gilpin and Richard Rosengarten, deans of the Divinity School, for the insightful guidance and prodding suggestions they offered along the way. The ideas presented in this volume are better formulated and more coherent than would have been the case without their input. Jean Bethke Elshtain shepherded us at key points throughout this process, from conceptualizing the conference to fine-tuning the lessons yielded in this book. She has been an exceptional mentor and colleague on this project (as well as many others), and we are profoundly grateful to her. Sandra Peppers, the Divinity School's business manager, deserves our heartfelt thanks for handling too many logistical and financial details to mention, without which this project never would have left the ground.

This book is published under the auspices of the Pew Forum on Religion and Public Life—an organization that seeks to promote a deeper understanding of how religion shapes the ideas and institutions of American society. We have long known that developments abroad and relations among states have profound and abiding effects on political life at home, although the events of September 11, 2001, brought this lesson home with alarming force. It seems especially fitting here, in a volume that explores shifting conceptions of sovereignty and the increasing permeability of national borders, to consider how American ideas and institutions influence—and are affected by—issues and events that often are lumped under the heading "international affairs." By probing the religious dimensions of such affairs, we hope to fill an important international niche that complements and enhances the many Pew Forum projects that focus on domestic issues. We are proud to follow in the footsteps of Luis Lugo, whose own work in this field (along with so many others) lent solid footing to our research; as director of the Religion Program at the Pew Charitable Trusts, he is responsible in large part for the financial and institutional support that made the production of this book possible. We thank, too, our colleagues at the Pew Forum—E. J. Dionne, Melissa Rogers, Staci Simmons Waldvogel, Amy Sullivan, and Kirsten Hunter—for their support and encouragement.

We would particularly like to thank Richard Brown, our editor at Georgetown University Press, for placing his faith in this project, for his patience, and for his clear-minded guidance throughout the editing and production of this book. We are fortunate to have worked with such a fine director and such a dedicated and professional staff.

Finally, academic projects such as this rely heavily on the support, encouragement, and understanding of loving family, fine colleagues, and caring friends. We save this special expression of our appreciation for last.

Contributors

R. SCOTT APPLEBY is professor of history and John M. Regan, Jr. Director of the Joan B. Kroc Institute for International Peace Studies at the University of Notre Dame. A historian of religion who earned his Ph.D. from the University of Chicago, Appleby is the author of *The Ambivalence of the Sacred: Religion, Violence and Reconciliation*. He codirected (with Martin Marty) the Fundamentalism Project of the American Academy of the Arts and Sciences, and he is coeditor, with Martin Marty, of *Fundamentalisms Comprehended*, as well as the four previous volumes in the University of Chicago Press series on global fundamentalisms.

JOHN D. CARLSON is project coordinator for the Chicago office of the Pew Forum on Religion and Public Life. He is also a doctoral candidate in religious ethics at the University of Chicago Divinity School. Carlson's research interests lie at the intersection of theology and political life, and his dissertation explores how understandings of human nature and transcendence shape our pursuits of justice. He is coeditor of the forthcoming volume *A Call for Reckoning: Religion and the Death Penalty* (Eerdmans) with Erik Owens and Eric Elshtain.

FRED DALLMAYR is Packey J. Dee professor in the departments of government and philosophy at the University of Notre Dame. He holds a doctor of law degree from the University of Munich and a Ph.D. in political science from Duke University. He has been a visiting professor at Hamburg University and the New School for Social Research and a fellow at Nuffield College in Oxford. He spent 1991–92 in India on a Fulbright grant. Among his many publications are *Dialogue among Civilizations*; *Achieving our World: Toward a Global and Plural Democracy*;

Border Crossings: Toward a Comparative Political Theory; Alternative Visions: Paths in the Global Village; The Other Heidegger; and *G. W. F. Hegel: Modernity and Politics.*

JEAN BETHKE ELSHTAIN is Laura Spelman Rockefeller Professor of Social and Political Ethics in the University of Chicago Divinity School, the department of political science, and the Committee on International Relations. As a political philosopher, Elshtain has showed the connections between our political and ethical convictions. Her books include *Public Man, Private Woman; Women and War; Democracy on Trial; Augustine and the Limits of Politics; Who Are We? Critical Reflections and Hopeful Possibilities; Jane Addams and the Dream of American Democracy* and, most recently, *Just War against Terror: The Burden of American Power.* Elshtain is cochair of the Pew Forum on Religion and Public Life, a fellow of the American Academy of Arts and Sciences, chair of the Council on Civil Society, a member of the board of trustees of the Institute for Advanced Study at Princeton University and the National Humanities Center, and serves on the board of directors of the National Endowment for Democracy.

ROBERT L. GALLUCCI is dean of the Edmund A. Walsh School of Foreign Service at Georgetown University. He began his career with the State Department in 1974 and until January 2001 served as special envoy to combat the proliferation of weapons of mass destruction. Previously he served as assistant secretary of state for political-military affairs and deputy executive chairman of the United Nations Special Commission overseeing the disarmament of Iraq. As ambassador-at-large (1994–96) Gallucci was responsible for, among other things, negotiating the nuclear nonproliferation agreement with North Korea in 1994 and leading the civilian rebuilding effort in Bosnia in 1996. He has taught at the National War College, Swarthmore College, and the Johns Hopkins School of Advanced International Studies. Gallucci was the recipient of fellowships from the Council on Foreign Relations, the International Institute for Strategic Studies, Harvard University, and the Brookings Institution, and he is the author of *Neither Peace nor Honor: The Politics of American Military Policy in Viet Nam.*

PAUL J. GRIFFITHS is Arthur J. Schmitt Chair of Catholic Studies at the University of Illinois at Chicago. His main intellectual interests are in Christian theology and philosophy, Indian Buddhist thought, and interreligious dialogue and apologetics. Griffiths' major publications include *On Being Mindless: Buddhist Meditation and the Mind-Body Problem*; *Christianity Through Non-Christian Eyes*; *An Apology for Apologetics: A Study in the Logic of Interreligious Dialogue*; *On Being Buddha: The Classical Doctrine of Buddhahood*; *Religious Reading: The Place of Reading in the Practice of Religion*; and *Exploring Religious Diversity*. He also has produced five other books as coauthor or editor, more than thirty academic articles, and numerous book reviews and translations.

REV. J. BRYAN HEHIR is president of Catholic Charities USA. He also serves as distinguished professor of ethics and international affairs at Georgetown University's Walsh School of Foreign Service. Fr. Hehir's teaching, research, and policy work in the church over the past thirty years have focused on Catholic social teaching, the role of religion in American society and world politics, and issues of ethics and foreign policy. Prior to joining Catholic Charities USA (in September 2001), Fr. Hehir served Harvard University as head of the Harvard Divinity School (1999–2001), professor of the practice in religion and society (1993–2001), and faculty associate at the Weatherhead Center for International Affairs and the Kennedy School of Government. From 1973 to 1992 he served in Washington at the U.S. Conference of Catholic Bishops and at Georgetown University (as Joseph P. Kennedy Professor of Christian ethics). He was named a MacArthur fellow in 1984. Fr. Hehir's publications include "Military Intervention and National Sovereignty"; "Catholicism and Democracy: Conflict, Change and Collaboration"; and "The Just-War Ethic Revisited."

JOHN KELSAY is Richard L. Rubenstein Professor of Religion at Florida State University, where he also serves as department chair. Kelsay's research focuses on topics in comparative religious ethics; his publications include *Islam and War*; *Human Rights and the Conflict of Cultures* (coauthored); and *Just War and Jihad* (coedited). In fall 2001, Kelsay served as Tuohy Professor of Religious Studies at John Carroll University. During 2002–03, he was Laurance S. Rockefeller Visiting Fellow at Princeton University's Center for Human Values, where he focused on the law of war in Islamic tradition. His work continues and is supported by the John Simon Guggenheim Foundation. He served as coeditor of the *Annual of the Society of Christian Ethics* from 1996 to 2001, and currently serves as coeditor of the *Journal of Religious Ethics*.

ROBIN W. LOVIN is Maguire University Professor of Ethics at Southern Methodist University (SMU). He has held deanships at the Perkins School of Theology at SMU and the Theology School at Drew University, and he has taught at Emory University and the University of Chicago. His writings include two major studies of twentieth-century Christian social ethics: *Christian Faith and Public Choices: The Social Ethics of Barth, Brunner, and Bonhoeffer*, and *Reinhold Niebuhr and Christian Realism*. He also is the author of *Christian Ethics: An Essential Guide*, and he has written extensively on religion and law and comparative religious ethics. Lovin was president of the Society of Christian Ethics for 1999–2000.

GEN. JAMES P. MCCARTHY, USAF (RET.), is Olin Professor of National Security at the United States Air Force Academy. During his thirty-five-year military career, General McCarthy held several operational command positions, including command of a fighter squadron in Vietnam (where he flew 152 combat missions), two bomber wings, and the 8th Air Force; he also served as Deputy Commander in Chief, U.S. European Command, where he had day-to-day responsibility for all U.S. forces in Europe. He served several assignments in the Pentagon, including director of legislative liaison with the U.S. Congress. During his military career, McCarthy became an authority on strategic planning, resource allocation, advanced technology application, and major program definition. He served as chairman of the Task Force for Kosovo Lessons Learned and as chairman of the Transformation Study for the Secretary of Defense. He also serves on the boards of many business, professional, educational, and nonprofit organizations.

JOSHUA MITCHELL is associate professor and chair of the Department of Government at Georgetown University. His research interest is in the relationship between political thought and theology in the West. He is the author of *Not by Reason Alone: Religion, History, and Identity in Early Modern Political Thought* and *The Fragility of Freedom: Tocqueville on Religion, Democracy, and the American Future*. His father, Richard Mitchell, was the author of *The Society of the Muslim Brothers* (recently reissued by Oxford University Press).

ERIK C. OWENS is a doctoral candidate in religious ethics at the University of Chicago Divinity School and a former research associate with the Pew Forum on Religion and Public Life. His research and writing focuses on ethics, political theory, and the intersection of law and religion; his dissertation examines civic education and religion in American public schools. He is a graduate of Duke University and Harvard Divinity School and is coeditor (with John Carlson and Eric Elshtain) of the forthcoming volume, *A Call for Reckoning: Religion and the Death Penalty*.

SUSANNE HOEBER RUDOLPH is William Benton Distinguished Service Professor of Political Science Emerita at the University of Chicago. She received her Ph.D. from Harvard University in 1955. Rudolph studies comparative politics with special interests in the political economy and political sociology of South Asia; state formation; Max Weber; and the politics of category and culture. She is the author of numerous books, including *In Pursuit of Lakshmi: The Political Economy of the Indian State; Transnational Religion and Fading States;* and *Reversing the Gaze: Amar Singh's Diary, A Colonial Subject's Narrative of Imperial India*. During 2003–2004 she will serve as president of the American Political Science Association.

MARGARET O'BRIEN STEINFELS was editor of *Commonweal* from 1988 at 2002. Her writing has appeared in the *New York Times*, the *Los Angeles Times*, the *New Republic*, and other publications. She is the author of *Who's Minding the Children? The History and Politics of Day Care in America*. Before joining *Commonweal*, Steinfels was director of publications at the National Pastoral Life Center and editor of its journal, *Church*. From 1981 to 1984, she worked as executive editor and business manager of *Christianity and Crisis*. She also has worked as a social science editor at Basic Books and as editor of the *Hastings Center Report*.

INTRODUCTION

Reconsidering Westphalia's Legacy for Religion and International Politics

JOHN D. CARLSON AND ERIK C. OWENS

A PROJECT AS EVOCATIVELY TITLED as this one is likely to arouse a range of reactions: suspicion, approbation, hopefulness, alarm, or even disdain. Whatever the response, taking on things sacred and sovereign in international affairs calls for careful explanation. A panoply of objections usually comes to mind whenever the topics of religion and international politics are broached together: worries over the commingling of church and state; trepidation about oppressive theocracies and militant fundamentalisms; and worst-case scenarios — of crusades or wars of religion. These were the ghastly spirits that modern secular politics, beginning in the sixteenth and seventeenth centuries, so arduously sought to exorcise — at least, that is the most common rendering of the story. As a result, we rightly worry when events seem to augur their return. Are there ways to broaden our idioms and understanding beyond associations with intolerance, prejudice, violence, and oppression that seem to follow whenever religion and politics are joined in international contexts? These assumptions are distinctly modern, born out of a history of religious strife and violence in Europe that was resolved — again, so the story goes — finally by erecting sovereign firewalls of statehood to contain conflict.

However, the modern arrangement of nations and states that has lasted for several centuries, including most of the twentieth century, has now begun to show signs of wear. Is it not appropriate to revisit some of the terms and foundational assumptions that have sustained our politi-

1

cal discourse for so long? The task before us here is not to reclaim and reinstitute premodern forms of thought but to expand and enrich the repertoire available to us for thinking about religion and international politics in the present and future.

In the post–cold war years, many scholars, journalists, political theorists, state officials, and citizens around the world began to take notice of the changing status of sovereignty, including its declining significance in international politics or at least its chastening as an absolute principle.[1] For better or for worse, the idea of a nation-state, sovereign over all affairs internal to its territorial borders, has been challenged by a host of factors and developments in the 1990s and early twenty-first century: the "pooling" of sovereignty by nations to form international political bodies (e.g., the European Union); the quickening pace of globalization evident in international commerce, technology, culture, and communications that obscures the traditional boundaries of states and the rules by which they govern; the swelling role and ambitions of transnational organizations, as well as the "spaceless communities" of adherents linked across oceans and land masses by various forms of shared moral, religious, and political commitments; and stepped-up efforts by the United Nations, human rights groups, and individual states to codify and enforce, through international law, norms that limit states' claims to unconditional "domestic jurisdiction." In each of these cases, many states have experienced and often acquiesced to the declining authority and control over the citizens and institutions within their borders, making them more subject to the intervention of a range of "outside" actors and agencies.

A few crucial political developments in particular draw our attention to the encroachment on territorial authority traditionally reserved to national governments. Most prominently, the 1990s witnessed a previously unknown attentiveness to the possibilities and realities of humanitarian intervention growing out of much earlier ideas about human dignity and universal rights. In the decades following World War II and the Holocaust, liberal democratic societies coming to terms with their commitment to human rights, in the wake of their incongruous failure to respond to such violations, took consolation in the mantra "never again." Yet in the 1990s, "it"—genocide—was indeed happening again, perhaps in less extensive forms, but equally brutal. On televisions around the world, specters of the Holocaust and other historical atrocities reappeared amidst humanitarian disasters in the Balkans, Africa, and east Asia. The Persian Gulf War (launched ostensibly to announce a "new world order" in which states' sovereignty could be assured and defended) would soon give way to new world disorder. In the ensuing years, a series of horrific events placed before liberal, democratic, and powerful nations the occasion to make good on their oft-stated commitment to political order, human rights, and basic moral decency: the murder and forced starvation of Somali citizens by unsparing clan warlords; the brutal genocide (often by machete) of 800,000 Tutsis in Rwanda; the gradual but systematic ethnic cleansing, rape, and mass murder of Muslims throughout the former Yugoslavia; and the violent expulsion of hundreds of thousands of East Timorese citizens to West Timor, following the colony's vote for independence from Indonesia. That some of these humanitarian atrocities were occurring in "sovereign" states seemed irrelevant to many people, despite repeated appeals of oppressive governments—joined by some voices in the West—to respect their national sovereignty and refrain from international interference or intervention.

By the end of the 1990s, the legacy of international intervention in these appalling episodes was decidedly mixed. Some observers proclaimed the 1999 NATO air campaign in Kosovo to be the first full-scale war waged by state powers for disinterested and purely ethical reasons.[2] Others noted the massive tally of victims elsewhere in the world (in Rwanda for example) who needlessly suffered, whether directly at the bloody hands of barbarism or indirectly at the clean hands of Western inaction. The sense of ambivalence and regret about the Western response was reflected in *mea culpas* from President Bill Clinton, UN Secretary-General Kofi Annan, and Dutch Prime Minister Wim Kok to atone for forgetting, once again, the lesson of "never again" as it applied to Rwanda and Bosnia.[3]

As part of the effort to regroup morally and politically and to respond to this averred shame (if only after the fact), focus shifted to bringing to trial individuals accused of inciting and perpetrating "crimes against humanity" and other egregious human rights abuses. If we couldn't (or didn't) stop them, at least we could punish them. This became the operative strategy for indicting war criminals from Rwanda and the former Yugoslavia, including former Yugoslav President Slobodan Milosevic, for crimes that no decent person or state could purport to defend. The perceived need to make a statement to the world for the historical record—and to prevent such heinous crimes from occurring again—spawned U.N.-sponsored international tribunals in the former Yugoslavia and Rwanda. True, states themselves were involved in efforts to prosecute wide-scale crimes that had occurred during the cold war (e.g., Cambodia's attempts to indict members of the Khmer Rouge and Spain and Chile's indictments of former Chilean president Augusto Pinochet). Yet those efforts often were overshadowed by the establishment of the International Criminal Court (ICC) in the Hague in July 2002 as a permanent venue of international justice. Under ICC terms of the Paris Treaty of 1998, nations retain "complementarity"—the right to try their own war criminals—but states (including those that did not ratify the treaty) that refuse to do so in accordance with international standards risk censure and punitive measures by the supporting states of the ICC.[4]

These humanitarian interventions and international tribunals, undertaken in the name of universal human rights, in many cases directly challenged the control that states and their leaders traditionally have enjoyed (or claimed to enjoy) over their territories. As such, these developments become important symbols and perhaps heralds of a distinctly different conception or era of sovereignty hovering on the political horizon. The Westphalian principles of nonintervention and domestic jurisdiction—so named for the 1648 Peace of Westphalia, which codified national sovereignty as the core premise of the nation-state system—served as the polestar that guided international relations and limited inter-state conflict for several centuries, including during the cold war years. Today, however, these Westphalian rules appear to be in a state of flux, prompting debate over what or who is the rightful authority and arbiter of supremacy in international politics. In other words, if state sovereignty is no longer *the* trump card in international relations, has some other authority or principle replaced it? Has the deck been reshuffled, a new hand dealt? This volume offers a range of perspectives on the changing face of sovereignty by exploring how religion and theology frame, clarify, or complicate issues surrounding the authority of nations in a global age marked by intensifying support for human rights. The contributors suggest that "religious" undercurrents, broadly construed, flow amidst the shifting tides of sovereignty and that attention to these eddies and currents deepens our understanding of many political trends operating on the surface of our globe. If there is a unifying thesis that this volume's contributors would all affirm, it is that *international politics cannot be fully or properly fathomed without addressing its embedded religious and moral dimensions.*

In the remainder of this introduction we seek to shed light on this claim and to provide the reader with a thematic chart for navigating the book. We do so in four sections. First, in explicating the key terms and describing the tension between "the sacred" and "the sovereign" (to which all of these essays in some way respond), we consider what resources religion brings to bear on political reflection. In the second section, we describe two "archetypes of sovereignty" that are helpful for showing how religious thought and institutions historically have been linked to patterns of sovereignty and how religion continues to be implicated at the threshold of a new era of sovereignty. Third, we sketch out the overall design of the book, introducing its contributors and their chapters. Finally, we suggest some overarching themes that integrate the contributors' thoughts and this project.

Coming to Terms with the Terms

At a basic level, "sacred" and "sovereign" serve as apt shorthand for the ways in which religion and politics converge, mingle, and conflict—or the ways they resist such encounters, as the case may be. Clearly, however, something more also is intended: We suggest that a tension exists between, on one hand, modern understandings of political sovereignty and, on the other hand, a supreme principle or set of commitments involving beliefs that are invested with sacred or religious qualities. Shifting understandings of sovereignty reflect a growing acceptance among citizens and political leaders alike (in the United States and abroad) that certain ethical principles and responsibilities, often articulated in religious terms, can trump prevailing values that traditionally have been associated with state sovereignty. We are not the first to hint at this possibility, but we do seek to explore and elaborate the stakes for political and religious realms of life when such a clash exists.[5]

In one sense, the terms of the debate are convertible, each signifying supremacy or ultimacy of some sort or another. *Sovereignty*, a multifaceted concept, connotes a wide range of attributes, including power, legitimacy, dominion, control, independence, autonomy, authority, legality, self-government, and preeminence.[6] Defining the term continues to be an important and evolving enterprise of political philosophy. To winnow the range of meanings, at least provisionally, we offer this conventional working definition: sovereignty as supreme and legitimate political authority within a defined territory.[7] Three elements of sovereignty follow from this definition. First, sovereignty involves the *authority* of political rule, including who or what form of rule governs, the authority by which a polity's legitimacy is known, and the ultimate appeal by which contested claims are adjudicated and resolved. In various moments and settings in political history, sovereignty over subject or citizen has been invested in monarchs, dictators, positive law, tradition, divine command, a constitution, or the general will of the people. Second and reciprocally, sovereign authority makes claims of *allegiance and obedience* on those who fall within its realm. To the extent that political rule and rulers enjoy the undiluted adherence of their followers, they or their states are said to be sovereign. Political allegiance also generates a shared sense of identity, grounded in ethnic, historical, or ideological commitments, which the nation or state often enshrines. Third, *territoriality* delineates the scope or reach of the sovereign's claims to which adherents are bound. In modern political history, the borders of nation-states generally have established the boundaries, laws, and terms of political authority and obedience.

For such a system to function, regard for the "internal authority" of nation-states requires mutual acceptance among states to refrain from exerting "external authority" over other states. To the extent that no supranational authority or world umpire governs the activities of states, international relations are said to be "anarchic" (from the Greek *anarchos*: no ruler). Anarchy in this context does not necessarily entail chaos; indeed, international law since Grotius has preserved this condition of "anarchy," mitigating chaos by prohibiting state aggression and affirming states' rights to defend themselves. Because international law generally does not designate enforcement authority to powers other than states, states remain sovereign, subject to the enforcement of other states in cases involving "illegal" actions.[8]

Although this understanding of sovereignty is widely recognized, particularly within the fields of political theory and international relations, it is by no means universally agreed upon. Contributors to this volume offer alternative conceptions of sovereignty, including critiques of the definition offered here. Consider the citizen of a nation who feels bound by claims—religious, political, or ideological—that undermine or countermand the actions, values, or pursuits of the ruling political order. Those who cite the power, dominion, and authority of God over all earthly matters, for example, may run the risk of idolatry if they invest such properties in the temporal powers of a state or its government. Appeals to something sacred or superior to politics would enter whether or not there is agreement over the specific character of these commitments. In various moments and movements, *the sacred* refers to that which is holy, sublime, universal, or true—a realm of ultimate reality, meaning, purpose, and significance that often is traced to the very source and power of this realm. Objects of sacredness often are invested with a transcendent quality, which cannot be reduced singularly to empirical terms. As such, the sacred accrues spiritual, divine, or heavenly qualities, including those that may supercede the claims of earthly affairs and of politics. Yet the sacred rarely is severed entirely from earthly concerns; ethical and religious norms of belief and conduct usually flow outward, placing upon believers a sense of awe or a feeling of dread that inspires allegiance and obedience, in *this* world, to such norms.[9]

This book contends that recent events in international politics demonstrate that some understanding of the sacred—however such notions are expressed in political vernacular or humanitarian law—rivals, contends with, and at times even upends the traditional rights and claims reserved for national sovereignty. Most central is the case for universal human rights, coupled with a growing concern for the innate dignity of the human person that undergirds such claims—whether rooted theologically or generalized in ways "ineliminably religious."[10] These beliefs often arch over the territorial borders claimed by states, while undermining the unlimited authority that states establish within them. Although a transnational regime of universal human rights (and, reciprocally, the designation of such transgressions as universal crimes) offers the starkest challenges to territorial sovereignty, there are other instances of transnational sacred activity. To mention only a few: the pilgrimages of African Sufis across sacred territory that straddle the boundaries of states;[11] the practices and teachings of the Catholic Church, which make certain supervening claims on its adherents without regard for their national citizenship;[12] and even global terrorist networks such as al-Qa`ida that appeal to sacred violence as an indispensable method for undercutting the legitimacy of Western and non-Western states alike, if not statehood itself.

Several strategies have been employed to "resolve" this tension between sacred and sovereign. One involves collapsing the authorities that each represents by making religious bodies—a church or a religious leader—sovereign over political affairs, as in a theocracy. Alternatively, the state and its leader may be elevated to the status of a deity, as occurred in imperial Rome. The worries over these strategies and their ill effects, alluded to earlier, do not bear repeating here. A second approach involves removing religion from the political equation, either by denying the existence of sacred claims or by explicitly delinking the relevance of religious claims to political life. Communism is the most extreme version of this "solution" (despite the religious fervor with which it espoused atheism); John Locke offers a milder version of this second "solution" in drawing "fixed and immovable" boundaries so as not to "jumble heaven and earth together."[13] In either case, the conscious attempt to sever the connection between religion and politics—by privatizing religion or eliminating it outright—also is problematic because it merely obscures the connection that inevitably persists. One result is that religion's effects on international politics are overlooked and poorly understood. If religious beliefs are perceived to be divorced from, or subsumed entirely by, the life of states, we are likely to neglect the role religion has played and continues to play in shaping and challenging structures of global political life. This formula is particularly dangerous when it is adopted by statespersons, foreign policy experts, political scientists, theorists, and journalists who then find themselves working without an interpretive framework that properly accounts for religious perspectives and their moral influences, good and bad.[14] Scholars of religion, for their part, often are reluctant to embrace the dynamics and interests of nation-states (e.g., power and coercion) as focal points for investigation and deliberation within religious studies: States are routinely subject to critical scrutiny, but an appreciation for the realities that institutions face, along with various warrants for their legitimacy, often is wanting.

In this volume we advance a third possibility that neither resolves nor removes but sustains the tension we identify here. This *via media* acknowledges the irreducibility of sacred matters to the life of nations, states, and their citizens and proposes a cautious yet deep engagement of religion and international politics. A combination of descriptive, critical, and constructive approaches taken up by this volume's contributors highlights the value and vitality of religion for bringing clarity to this task.

First, from a *descriptive* standpoint, religion for centuries has played an important role in shaping the structures of international political life. Theology and religious pluralism in the West are largely responsible for the Westphalian scheme of sovereignty that, with few exceptions, has endured since 1648. But what political, historical, and theological roles did religion first play in precipitating and shaping Westphalian principles of sovereignty? In the years before and after sovereignty fully established itself, how was the relationship of religion and politics construed? The descriptive axis of this project lends historical insight to these questions and dynamics, but it also brings into focus current arrangements among citizens, states, international institutions, and transnational organizations. Emerging political actors and moral-religious consciousness have begun to vie for space in the state-centric system of international relations that traditionally has defined itself in terms of power, security interests, and national loyalties: How, exactly, have these recent sociopolitical trends involving transnational "communities" and beliefs fomented a call to revisit the Westphalian settlement?

Understanding the empirical influences of religious institutions sharpens our shifting perceptions and expectations of politics and states. So too does a survey of religiously grounded traditions—especially those concerned with morality, politics, and the justifiable use of force. At times, religious traditions have reinforced the sovereignty of nation-states; today, however, these traditions are undergoing significant revisions in ways that also challenge the absolute authority of states. Consider Pope John Paul II's unyielding plea to the international diplomatic corps: "The principles of the sovereignty of states and of non-interference in their internal affairs—which retain all their value—cannot be a screen behind which torture and murder can be carried out."[15] The U.S.

Catholic bishops express the matter in a similar vein: "Sovereignty is in the service of the people. All political authority has as its end the promotion of the common good, particularly the defense of human rights."[16] Catholic as well as other religious traditions and institutions often have had a great deal to say, too, about the dignity of the human person, including the protection that human rights norms guarantee and the checks that accrue to states that threaten citizens within their borders. We should be mindful, though, that a challenge to the sovereign authority of oppressive states is contingent on the sovereignty of states that are willing to intervene (politically or militarily) on behalf of oppressed people. This assessment suggests that as we sketch out permutations and transfigurations of sovereignty, we cannot stop thinking about the continued importance of statehood. It could be that for all the recent challenges to the authorities and powers traditionally reserved to states, sovereignty remains, to steal a phrase from Daniel Philpott, "the struts and joists without which statecraft would not exist."[17] And at least for the foreseeable future, politics will continue to rely on sovereign states, and the international system that sustains them.[18]

Religious perspectives also afford an indispensable axis of *critical* interpretation that secular vantage points cannot provide. Critical reasoning that takes into account questions of ultimate meaning and higher purposes provides a more robust approach to politics than many forays in international relations are capable of mustering. If, as we have suggested, sacred aspirations and beliefs—whether couched in terms of universal human dignity, religious freedom to worship and pursue truth, or even the pursuit of peace—are never detached entirely from the everyday lives of citizens and believers, then why insist upon terms of debate that ignore this religious component? Many strands of religious thought call for faithful reflection upon, and engagement in, the political affairs of the world; as such, followers may be obliged to act not in spite of their convictions but because of them, albeit with the recognition that ultimate purposes and ideals hold out limits for earthly political arrangements. Of course, one part of this critical enterprise also calls us to recognize that religion has been and can create terrible problems for international politics.

Finally, religious perspectives move beyond critical analysis to adopt a *constructive* role when they show their unique resources for refining and resolving urgent political quandaries, including proposals concerning human rights, humanitarian military intervention, and the shifting tides of sovereignty. What sorts of burdens are incumbent on state, religious, and civic actors? Religious approaches respond by appealing to our most fundamental convictions and primary allegiances, not as internal barriers to political deliberation but as forces for responsible engagement, mutual respect, and reconciliation. For people who are open to the possibility, potent theological resources can undergird and guide fruitful political resolutions in ways that challenge certain prevailing assumptions about international politics yet affirm the stability, authority, and legitimacy that political institutions require for their efficacy.

In the following section, we consider past arrangements of sovereignty, with a focus on important religious aspects and insinuations. Drawing attention to how sovereignty has been informed by religion in the past serves as a resource for discerning the still-emerging character of sovereignty in an era of rapid global change.

Archetypes of Sovereignty

The conceptual history of sovereignty and the role of religion in its development have been well researched and skillfully presented by numerous scholars, and we do not attempt to recount that extensive narrative here.[19] Instead, in this section we describe what may be called two "archetypes of sovereignty"—the medieval and the modern—that have had important influences on Western civilization and have shaped our understanding of international relations. As their names imply, each of these archetypes is associated with a particular historical era, so in discussing their characteristics we present a sketch of their historical origins as well. The influence of each archetype has waxed and waned in different places and times, but evidence of both archetypes can still be found in current scholarship, including the chapters that follow. At the outset, we note that archetypes by definition are ideal types, conceptual categories that admit exceptions and elide precise historical details. The primary virtue of describing an ideal type is heuristic rather than historical, in that it provides a pattern for thinking thematically about the ideas and directions taken up throughout the book. With this caveat, we treat each of the archetypes in turn, attending to several categories of comparative interest between them, and then explore how features of each archetype are at work in contemporary international affairs.[20]

The current patchwork of nearly 200 independent, sovereign states that cover the globe constitutes such an accepted part of modern life that its existence often is taken for granted and assumed to be a natural, timeless, or perhaps inevitable arrangement of political authority.[21] Yet sovereign states as we now know them came into existence only in the sixteenth and seventeenth centuries in Europe (and later elsewhere); before that time, large-scale political life was governed by principles other than sovereignty, such as suzerainty (in ancient China), empire (in classical Rome), *respublica Christiana* (in medieval Europe), or theocracy (in early Islamic caliphates, as well as several Mesoamerican civilizations).[22] We can date the beginnings of state sovereignty—and some future historians no doubt will mark the decline of state sovereignty and the emergence of some other form of international political organization. Indeed, much of the current debate about sovereignty centers around whether a shift to a "postsovereign" international politics already is under way, and if so, what form or forms it will take.[23] Assessing earlier patterns of sovereignty will equip us to deliberate better about current shifts under way.

The Medieval Archetype

Before state sovereignty took shape during the sixteenth and seventeenth centuries, Europe was ruled by a complex association of political and religious leaders, none of whom had absolute authority in any given territory. Kings often reigned over disparate, noncontiguous lands, and their offices varied from place to place even within their own territory; the same person who was an "absolute" monarch in one place might be a constitutional ruler in another (as the Hapsburg kings were in Vienna and Brussels, respectively).[24] Feudal lords and leaders of religious orders owned land and had a limited measure of autonomy in those lands from their overlords and kings (who themselves had limited autonomy from the Holy Roman Emperor), but all were vassals to a higher authority. Atop this arrangement of overlapping jurisdictions sat the Holy Roman Emperor and the Pope, representing the "two swords" that defended the *corpus mysticum*—the metaphorical body of Christ formed by all believers scattered geographically but joined under common identity, purpose, and moral law.[25]

To the extent that there was a generally recognized "sovereign" of the medieval *respublica Christiana*, it was God. All of European Christendom fell under God's dominion, sealed by the coherence and comprehensiveness of the medieval synthesis, and political and religious authorities alike were understood to be the agents of God's sovereignty. Medieval peasants, priests, and rulers knew their place, well aware of St. Paul's admonition: "Let every person be subject to the governing authorities; for there is no authority except from God, and those authorities that exist have been instituted by God."[26] The "sovereignty" of God in this context connotes ultimate power or supremacy; thus, contemporary translations of Jewish, Christian, and Islamic sacred texts usually render the term "sovereignty" to denote this concept of God's supreme power and dominion over human affairs.[27]

Although in practice the lines of authority connecting the medieval peasant to emperor and pope formed more of a web than a pyramid with an apex, the idea of a direct hierarchical ordering of prerogative and privilege was widely accepted.[28] What unified the medieval *respublica Christiana*, however, was the belief that every person in the God-given social and religious order shared a common faith and obedience to the Christian moral law, regardless of one's rank or status.

Four aspects of the medieval archetype should be highlighted. First, religion unified politics under the overarching rule of God; in the medieval synthesis, faith and reason, religion and politics were cooperative partners, not antagonists (although antagonism was known to erupt concerning their respective spheres of influence). The archetypical medieval society aspired to a *sacrum imperium*—a single order capable of embracing at once the transcendent and the immanent, the ecclesiastical and the political, the divine and the human. Second, in this view political authority ultimately is derived from God, and obedience to political rulers comes from being a faithful Christian believer in God. Although the emperor and pope presided over separate temporal and spiritual realms, both acted in unison as regents of God's sovereignty on earth. Third, the structure of earthly rule was composed of intermingling authorities and overlapping jurisdictions; though usually imperial in nature, political rule in this archetype was dispersed, ambiguous, and not absolute. Fourth, in the medieval archetype the boundaries of civilization—and the identity of those who lived within these boundaries—were defined by religious belief; civilization ended where Christendom ended.

The Modern Archetype

Whereas in the medieval archetype of sovereignty religion is the unifying principle of political authority, in the modern archetype religion is understood to be a divisive and destructive force among political communities. The historical genesis of this archetype can be located in the prosecution and eventual settlement of the European wars of religion that pitted Catholics against Protestants in nearly constant warfare from 1530 to 1648. A brief sketch of the seminal religious and political developments in this period will help to clarify why the modern archetype represents such a distinctive alternative to its medieval precursor.

The religiopolitical unity of medieval Christendom, though never complete, fractured decisively by the early sixteenth century with the emergence of the Protestant Reformation in Germany. Protestant reformers, as diverse as they were, all rejected the Roman church's authority over local civil and ecclesiastical matters. Combined with the heretical claim that individuals could receive God's saving grace without the mediation of priests, the reformers' theological justification of local ecclesial independence provoked a quick response. Catholic princes allied with the Holy Roman Emperor and the pope led armed forces to quash the theological dissent; this conflict drove religious reformers to seek *political* sovereignty for their own states (that is, states governed by sympathetic princes) so that they might practice their faith without interference from Rome.[29] In other words, theological and political dissent became mutually reinforcing movements during the Reformation and Counter-Reformation. Religious freedom and the effort to throw off religious coercion became central to the formation of separate states whose citizens were free to believe and practice the state's religion.

In 1555, after a decade of destructive but inconclusive battles between alliances of German princes, Holy Roman Emperor Charles V reluctantly accepted the terms of the Peace of Augsburg. This treaty allowed individual rulers of the nearly 300 German states to choose either

Catholicism or Lutheranism as the official religion of that territory and to enforce that faith among their subjects as they deemed appropriate. Acceptance of local control over the state religion—a principle known as *cujus regio, ejus religio* ("whose the region, his the religion")—was a critical element of the broader emergence of state sovereignty expressed in the treaty as *Rex est imperator in regno suo* ("the king is emperor in his own realm"). As the first political settlement to confer sovereignty upon states, Augsburg represented a milestone in international relations theory, though in practice the agreement was never fully honored by its signatories. Many princes, the emperor, and the pope continued to intervene in the affairs of other states, and the religious and political animosity it sought to quell merely simmered in the region for sixty years before boiling over again in the Thirty Years' War (1618–1648).

From the outset, the Thirty Years' War was prosecuted for a mixture of political and religious reasons, so it is no surprise that its resolution — the Peace of Westphalia—and its legacy settled religious and political questions in ways that would keep these realms distinct and prevent their future entanglement. Harking back to the Peace of Augsburg, the treaties of Münster and Osnabrück that constitute the Peace of Westphalia reaffirmed *cujus regio, ejus religio* as a fundamental aspect of state sovereignty and the primary *modus vivendi* for managing the religious pluralism spawned by the Reformation. The Westphalian settlement did not formally dissolve the Holy Roman Empire, but by giving princes sovereignty over their territory, it sharply curtailed the political powers of the empire and the papacy alike. (This arrangement, predictably, was rejected by Pope Innocent X, who issued a bull denouncing the Westphalian treaties as "null, void, invalid, iniquitous, unjust, damnable, reprobate, inane, [and] empty of meaning and effect for all time.")[30] The treaty negotiations themselves exemplified the outcome: The parties to the settlement were equal representatives at the table, and the pope's emissaries were given no more authority than a local prince—a fact that undoubtedly contributed to its successful implementation.

To be sure, Westphalia did not transform the European political landscape overnight; it signaled not a dramatic break from the past but a consolidation and codification of a new conception of political authority. Just as (a few) sovereign states existed in the century before Westphalia, feudal empires would persist for a time after Westphalia. But the sovereign states scheme of international relations it formalized put a definitive end to the wars of religion among Christian states in Europe. The important point for our purposes is recognition of the religious origins of both the problem of pluralism and the solution to that problem. Although none of the early Protestant reformers explicitly took up the concept of political sovereignty (French philosopher Jean Bodin was the first to do so in systematic fashion, in 1576), by presenting a theological justification for local political and ecclesial autonomy they laid the foundations for the theoretical development and political manifestation of modern sovereignty. As political theorist Daniel Philpott has written, "Sovereignty, in substance if not in name, comes directly out of the very propositions of Protestant theology, in all its variants."[31]

Consider in particular four points of comparison between the modern and medieval archetypes of sovereignty. First, as noted above, the modern archetype treats religion as a divisive and destructive force rather than a unifying principle for political communities. As such, religious pursuits must be contained or confined to narrow purposes and specified realms within the political order. Second, in the modern archetype of sovereignty, political authority is no longer derived solely from God or from association with Christendom. In a Reformation variant of the modern archetype (Luther is among its most famous proponents), God is understood as having ordained certain vocations through which persons can fulfill their obligations to God and one another; unlike in medieval politics, one need not be a Christian to fulfill one's political vocation. (Contrary to a common misconception about the early Reformation, most of its instigators rejected strict notions of a "separation of church and state," although they certainly sought the separation of the *Roman* church from *their* state.)[32] In Enlightenment variants, in contrast to Reformation thinking, political authority is sheared entirely from God's domain, and is derived instead from the consent of the governed. Third, the structure of earthly rule is formed by a system of sovereign states, each of which has more tightly defined boundaries than the medieval archetype would allow but also unlimited authority and greater autonomy within those boundaries than was enjoyed by political rulers in the medieval *respublica Christiana*. Fourth, the modern archetype promotes the tethering of religious affinity and personal identity to the state, rather than an extranational or transnational religious authority such as the Catholic Church; instead of holding all states under a Christian umbrella, this modern innovation settled for relative "anarchy" among sovereign states.

How, then, do the foregoing archetypes of sovereignty provide insight into these and other developments in our own day? To begin, religion clearly plays both unifying and splintering roles in international politics — a fact we can appreciate better when we consider the differences between the modern and medieval archetypes. On one hand, certain extreme forms of religion and religious groups continue to foster and perpetuate violent conflict — exactly the situation modern state sovereignty was intended to prevent. Examples abound of places where religious beliefs contribute to political violence to some important degree: Sudan, Northern Ireland, Israel/Palestine, India, as well as the transnational terrorist organization al-Qaʿida. On the other hand, it is no less true — and here the medieval archetype enters into the picture — that religion or certain forms of "religiosity" can unite people through transnational communities, common commitments, and shared values. It is no longer the case that Christendom can be the source of this unity, but as several contributors to this volume argue, there is evidence afoot that a new postsecular global synthesis may be taking shape amidst an emerging "universal religiosity," ecumenism, or global concern for justice.

The authority of political rule also is a matter of contention between medieval and modern versions of sovereignty. The medieval archetype highlights the growing acceptance that nations must give up sovereign space and share authority with a host of other actors, including religious bodies and institutions. This account also admits that a universal ethic or regime of human rights (perhaps codified by international law) could delimit the sovereignty of states and hold them accountable to a higher moral standard than a minimalist anarchic system would allow. Nonetheless, the modern archetype demonstrates that political rule in most states remains grounded on secular authority — though as some contributors to this volume point out, this arrangement does not preclude an understanding that religion underwrites the authority of states and secular rulers.

The medieval and modern archetypes also offer contrasting perspectives on the very structure of earthly rule. Are we witnessing a new global *universitas* analogous to that of the medieval period, this time with more prominence given to international organizations such as the United Nations? Can the various claims of international monetary, political, and nonprofit organizations and the multiform claims of states be brought together to help synthesize some kind of unified vision of collective life? Or do the shifting arrangements of international and domestic political institutions represent a continuation of the modern *societas* of states?

Finally, sources of human identity and allegiance have been concretely affected by the changing roles of states and international institutions. Globalization has allowed persons and groups to form and maintain strong transnational religious, cultural, and ideological communities that resist or ignore national boundaries. Drawing on the medieval archetype of sovereignty, we can point to the current inability of many states to provide for all aspects of a citizen's identity, and thus for the need for citizens to identify with the goals of international or transnational organizations as well. Invoking the modern archetype of sovereignty, we also could point out that national identity nonetheless remains important and at times all-consuming—as surging nationalist movements in India and the Balkans or even fervent patriotism sweeping throughout the United States can attest. Although some relatively new sovereign states (such as Macedonia or Lithuania) attained sovereignty with a national identity already present, other new states (such as East Timor) are striving to create a national identity in spite of inhibited development after generations as a colony. In any case, the longing for autonomy, self-determination, and national identity that statehood brings is as potent as ever.

In sum, evidence of both archetypes can be witnessed today and in the chapters that follow. The modern archetype has held sway for almost 400 years, so we should expect its perspectives to continue to inform our thinking; more surprising is the persistence (or resurgence) of the medieval archetype. Although we have distinguished the two archetypes to clarify their differences, it is important to note that they remain closely related and that both may inform one's views on sovereignty at the same time. None of the contributors to this book, for example, would deny that states possess certain powers and resources that other institutions do not; nor do those who emphasize proper roles and responsibilities of states ignore the fact that nations increasingly must work alongside other authorities and organizations whose objectives are at odds with national interests, narrowly construed. As the following section demonstrates, contemporary responses to the challenges to sovereignty often involve a subtle combination of elements of these earlier patterns.

Structure and Design of This Book

This book is structured in three parts. Part I, "Religion and Armed Intervention," considers how religious perspectives and traditions construe the legitimacy and conduct of military interventions for humanitarian and other purposes, including strikes on terrorist organizations. Given its prominence and concreteness, humanitarian intervention serves as a pertinent case study to introduce the tension of the sacred and the sovereign. Arguments about the just use of force in defense of human rights or justice are among the most visible ways that religious viewpoints underwrite deeper claims that challenge the primacy of state sovereignty.

Fr. Bryan Hehir, a political ethicist and theologian, opens the inquiry in chapter 1 by describing a transformation in political discourse that has taken place over the past half-century that has created space for the incorporation of moral analysis and religious traditions into the study of international relations. As an ancient tradition of moral discourse rooted in a religious community, the "just war" ethic offers important insights about the crucial issues of war and peace—which, writes Hehir, "have been the most controversial arena of sacred-sovereign engagement." Indeed, the just war ethic "stands at the intersection of sovereignty and the sacred, adjudicating the claims of the former and the imperatives of the latter." The contemporary version of the just war tradition, however, has faced three distinct challenges over the past fifty years: nuclear weapons, humanitarian intervention, and terrorism. Hehir describes how, in each case, the tradition's attentiveness to the explicit and implicit interplay of religious conviction, moral analysis, and political-strategic discourse provides resources to guide both the national debate on public policies and the personal conscience of sovereigns, soldiers, diplomats, and citizens. With regard to terrorism, Hehir observes that the "transcendent dimension" of some terrorist claims can preclude the possibility of political negotiations and may signal the erosion of a sense of restraint regarding the means they employ. The world's military response to such terrorists nevertheless must be carefully limited and justified on a case-by-case basis to maintain just war's fundamental commitment to non-combatant immunity.

In chapter 2 General James McCarthy builds on, and works within, the themes and framework of the just war tradition set out by Hehir. McCarthy's perspective reflects thirty years of military operational experience, as well as crucial insight he gleaned while serving as chairman of the Secretary of Defense's Task Force for Kosovo Lessons Learned. He notes the moral possibilities of humanitarian interventions and discusses the challenges they pose to nations and the military forces that execute them. Like Hehir, McCarthy applies just war criteria to contemporary situations; McCarthy worries, however, that if Kosovo is a harbinger of interventions to come, they may not measure up to important just war principles. The violation of key criteria, he avers, rendered intervention in Kosovo problematic on several fronts: moral, diplomatic, and strategic. He urges renewed attentiveness to the particulars of military tactics and the diplomacy of force—practical dimensions of deliberation that were underanalyzed in many reviews of the Kosovo intervention. In particular, he points out that—in light of the strategy of gradual escalation of force, which caused considerable damage to Yugoslavia's civilian infrastructure—the *jus in bello* category of proportionality must be reconsidered to take into account that an *inadequate amount of force* could lead to unethical consequences in ways that usually are associated with the excessive use of force. McCarthy concludes that practical dynamics must reflexively shape and influence moral theory and the process of political decision making.

Margaret O'Brien Steinfels continues the discussion of Kosovo in chapter 3 while expanding on wider democratic processes and deliberation. Where General McCarthy explores the intersection of moral theory and military operations, Steinfels, former editor of the lay Catholic magazine *Commonweal*, considers the role of the media—and, by extension, the democratic citizenry the media informs—in the debates over intervention in Kosovo and elsewhere. She scrutinizes objections to interventions that are based on support for state sovereignty; yet she also affirms the Westphalian model by noting that Milosevic's Yugoslavia was a "failed state" that, in essence, had forfeited its claims to sovereignty. Drawing lessons from Kosovo, Steinfels goes on to argue that no uniform set of criteria can adequately direct political responses for every case in which intervention may be called for. She acknowledges that the just war tradition may be as good as any resource for mustering the kind of moral-political reflection that humanitarian disasters thrust before policymakers and informed citizens alike.

Jean Bethke Elshtain, a political philosopher who locates ethical concerns centrally to her task, ruminates in chapter 4 on the Persian Gulf War and the Kosovo air campaign. Echoing earlier concerns about proportionality, she criticizes the conduct of these interventions, though for different reasons than General McCarthy does. In both conflicts the just war tradition's moral complexity was siphoned off—often displaced by rhetoric quite foreign to principal claims of this rich ethical and political tradition. Drawing insights from many voices of political realism, Elshtain's appraisal finds its firmest footing by reclaiming realist roots of the just war tradition as understood by its great forefather, St. Augustine. Unlike classical forms of realism, the Elshtain/Augustine alternative of "just war as politics" is about more than power, war, and national interests: It is a way of thinking that refuses to separate politics from ethics.

For religious ethicist John Kelsay, humanitarian interventions provide formidable challenges to state sovereignty from several angles, including those of international organizations and other states. Challenging the notion that sovereignty was ever "sacrosanct," Kelsay notes in chapter 5 that justice has been a perduring feature of sovereignty, from the Westphalian focus on just international order to post–cold war emphases on human rights. For Kelsay, just war thinking proffers helpful resources for assessing the basis of a state's legitimacy and the factors that undermine this legitimacy, including the problematic "failed state" that worries Steinfels in chapter 3. Just war thought also provides purchase onto challenges to state sovereignty from substate actors, including people who embrace terrorism as an acceptable means to pursue their grievances of injustice. Yet how, exactly, does one adjudicate these simultaneous competing claims of justice? Within both the just war and Islamic traditions, Kelsay maintains, the legitimate authority of the sovereign, and the attendant moral conduct that sovereigns are to exercise, provide moral discernment about which side possesses the preponderance of justice.

Part II, "Human Rights, Political Authority, and Religious Commitments," moves outside the question of intervention, expanding the inquiry by probing other ways that religion is implicated in the sea change of sovereignty. Religious commitments, traditions, and institutions often exhibit a transnational character, the claims of which cut across state borders—and often against states' authority as well. But religious commitments also can undergird and legitimate the sovereignty of states, or at least certain responsibilities—for justice, order, the common good—usually ascribed to them. Contributors in this section appropriate several different religious outlooks to frame and respond to new features and configurations of sovereignty. Their undertakings hover at the intersection of human rights and political authority or power, illustrating how religious traditions and international institutions converge on such issues and, in so doing, open the field of view for political inquiry.

Political scientist Susanne Hoeber Rudolph opens the vista in chapter 6 by providing a descriptive survey of how religious beliefs and religious actors, operating in transnational space, stand in relief against the changing landscape of state sovereignty. Rudolph introduces and illumines a religious variant of transnational "epistemes"—formal and informal communities that share common worldviews and purposes. Religion once traversed transnational space behind the flag of imperial conquerors, Muslim and Christian, who hoped to make their religions hegemonic. Today, however, the new religious presence is *not* a universal church like the transnational Christendom of the Middle Ages (which was later fragmented by the emergence of the nation-state). Instead, as state sovereignty is attenuated and as national and cultural boundaries become more porous, another form of universal religiosity is emerging, shaped by adherents who eschew the thought of religious hegemony but embrace a social and intellectual process of ecumenization that reaches across and incorporates elements of different religions. This development raises questions of how best to preserve pluralistic religious beliefs. Thinking anew about freedom of religious practice and belief—the oldest of human freedoms, known even before rights were articulated as such—Rudolph raises critical concerns about the International Religious Freedom Act of 1998. Specifically, when one state or religion sponsors and dominates such a project—particularly a state whose nationals advance conversionary aims—the transnational initiative for universal religiosity can be undermined. Why? Because the nurturing of universal religiosity entails recognition that there is truth in all religions and that maintaining pluralistic vitality is a central requirement. A preferred alternative to defending religious freedom internationally, then, would involve a collaborative effort among states and transnational institutions.

Where Rudolph is vexed over the influence that states still exercise in certain domains of international affairs, particularly regarding the enforcement of religious human rights, theologian Robin Lovin warns in chapter 7 that institutions that take on powers and authorities traditionally reserved for states inevitably will develop interests that are distinct from—even opposed to—the people they ostensibly serve. Persuaded by the theological and historical insights of "Christian realism," Lovin argues that whatever system emerges from the present weakening of national sovereignty will have the same tendency toward injustice as the Westphalian system. Drawing from a historical analysis of medieval and modern archetypes of sovereignty, he charts a path for the future of sovereignty. Although he welcomes the escalating role of many international institutions, he suggests that their success will rest on their ability to revive important features of earlier conceptions of sovereignty. Prior to the modern notion of sovereignty that focused almost exclusively on a ruler's absolute control of coercive power, there were medieval sovereigns who, amidst the entangling jurisdictions in which their rule was located, understood that a people's awe and identity were crucial components of the sovereign's authority. If international institutions are to be effective in a post-Westphalian era, Lovin argues, they must be able to generate a sense of awe and emerge as a source of identity and loyalty among those who otherwise lack power within the nation-state system.

Where Lovin and Rudolph locate central dilemmas of modern political life within the pluralistic arena of competing state bodies and international institutions, historian Scott Appleby makes a close inspection of the pluralism of religious traditions in chapter 8. In particular, the most interesting debates, for Appleby, are shaped by the internal pluralism *within* particular traditions. Turning to the theme of universal human rights, Appleby argues that internal debates within Islam provide a crucial venue for an Islamic defense of basic human freedoms—a possibility that has come under repeated attack and suspicion following the terrorist acts of September 11, 2001. If religious traditions such as Islam, Christianity, and Judaism are able to locate within them the ability to promote human freedom without compromising religious beliefs, they advance the possibility of serving God and man alike. Moreover, a tradition's focus on its own "first-order discourse" of sacred beliefs and commitments better equips it to engage with other traditions in "second-order discourse" that is capable of promoting a transnational and transreligious regime of universal human rights.

Like Lovin and Rudolph, John Carlson works at the nexus of religious belief and international institutions. Like Appleby, Carlson considers the religious resources for affirming human rights, though his inquiry seeks a distinctively theological validation of political practices that uphold human dignity. In chapter 9 Carlson situates this project amidst quandaries involving crimes against humanity and the venues in which they should be tried. The decision to allow a sovereign nation to try its own crimes against humanity or to defer such judgments to an international tribunal, he maintains, must be juxtaposed against other crucial concerns: how to construe and preserve human worth; how to affirm the mandates of nations; and how to pursue the demands of justice. Asking what difference a theological understanding of the sacred and the sovereign brings to the table, he invites us to ponder the ultimate source of these "ultimate" claims. He refracts this issue through the lens of "moral anthropology," probing two views of human nature in the thought of St. Augustine and Immanuel Kant. The implications of these moral and theological inspections are freighted with emergent political implications about the appropriate forms, pursuits, and expectations of justice that can be achieved feasibly in the murky realm of international politics. Specifically, an understanding of the *imago Dei* as the source of human worth may call for unexpected ways to uphold human dignity in cases involving crimes against humanity. Carlson takes up the extradition of former Yugoslavian President Slobodan Milosevic to a UN war crimes tribunal and how this action foreclosed opportunities for more vigorous forms of justice than international venues may be able to provide.

Part III, "Sovereignty and Its Critics," continues the conversation of Parts I and II about intervention, human rights, political power, and religious allegiance. In so doing, however, it offers challenges to sovereignty as a primary category for reflection and moral clarity. Contributors in part III offer implicit and explicit reasons, articulated on political or religious grounds, why setting the terms of debate in the grammar of sovereignty impairs moral deliberation, political action, or religious belief. Clearly, many chapters in this book provide critically developed outlooks on sovereignty, often assessing its limits as well as rival values that may be underdeveloped or unappreciated when sovereignty becomes the reigning consideration. Whereas preceding chapters present sovereignty as a primary category of religious or moral deliberation or as an institutional reality in international politics, however, each of the final chapters in its own way denies that state sovereignty is an issue about which one should worry much at all.

In chapter 10, Robert Gallucci, a former high-level U.S. State Department official with more than twenty-five years of diplomatic experience, imparts an insider's view of statecraft and political realism. For Gallucci, *raison d'état* and power politics, classically conceived, are central features of any military intervention—even one with a humanitarian mission. Gallucci explores four detailed case studies illustrating the decision-making and policymaking process leading to approval or rejection of a proposed military intervention. In a forthright appraisal, he affirms that respect for a nation's legal sovereignty has rarely (if ever) been a primary concern in the U.S. government's decision to intervene. Instead, legal justifications and responses to concerns about sovereignty are developed only after "the right thing to do" has been determined on other grounds. In many cases, national interests traditionally understood are the primary causes behind U.S. intervention. Yet there are far-reaching moral dimensions even in these circumstances. In some situations—Somalia, for example (which Gallucci discusses in detail)—the moral issues prevail over narrowly political reasons for intervention. In particular, Gallucci argues, respect for sovereignty in the face of gross violations of human rights does not relieve the United States of its moral obligation to intervene. Gallucci concludes chapter 10 by offering four moral-political criteria for intervention that offer clarity for how and when the United States should respond to other nations' egregious violations of human rights.

Much of this book turns on how religious sources and perspectives—when brought to bear onto international political life—clarify, alleviate, or reconcile tensions with state sovereignty and political commitments. In chapter 11, however, moral philosopher Paul Griffiths admonishes that this supposed tension between the sacred and the sovereign may not be reconcilable at all. Griffiths insists that true religious allegiance is fundamentally incommensurable with the claims of sovereignty and states because political sovereignty makes claims on its citizens that often are at odds with the unsurpassable and comprehensive claims that religions make on their adherents. Griffiths warns that efforts to reconcile the religious and the political have failed (and always will fail), at great peril to the integrity of religion—by forcing on citizens a sacred reverence of the state, or a system of states, or by transmuting states into God. In short, one who affirms primary allegiance to God must forgo states' claims to sovereignty because, in the final analysis, the state is not of ultimate or abiding concern. On such a reading, the clash between sacred and sovereign is not resolved through politics. In fact, it is not resolved at all but eluded through the task of prophetic critique—even martyrdom.

In chapter 12, political philosopher Fred Dallmayr takes up his theological concerns about sovereignty through a narrative of Jesus' encounter with Pontius Pilate. Dallmayr, like Griffiths, takes issue with sovereignty talk and the limited framework of *suprema potestas* ("supreme power") that it imposes on political thought and discourse. Dallmayr traces the implications for different forms of supreme power and authority. The upshot of the shift from a medieval notion of sovereignty to the Westphalian model was that religious faith became privatized and co-opted by the state. Within Christianity, this trivialization of religious belief often met Gnostic and millenarian responses that called for destruction rather than transformation of "this" world. This insight is the springboard for Dallmayr's retrieval of Jesus' message: that of a "sacred nonsovereignty" that neither elevates political power at the expense of religious faith (as sought by imperial Rome) nor seeks to eliminate earthly politics altogether (as some religious militants aspire to do). Dallmayr goes on to consider more recent possibilities for, and latent philosophical proponents of, nonsovereignty.

Erik C. Owens brings the discussion to a close in his concluding chapter on sovereignty after September 11, 2001. Although some of the lessons to be drawn from September 11 will require a longer historical perspective to appreciate, Owens suggests that at least one lesson is already evident: Notwithstanding the many contemporary challenges to the modern archetype of sovereignty, September 11 teaches us that we ought to focus on strengthening the sovereign states system rather than undermining it. The dangers that weak and failed states pose to the world community have never been more clear; they provide fertile soil for a host of problems with international consequences: not only terrorism but also money laundering and the illegal trafficking of weapons, drugs, and people. Porous national borders, once considered a boon to commerce, only exacerbate such problems. Owens examines alternative approaches to the problem of weak and failed states and concludes first that states must be held accountable for fulfilling the responsibilities that accompany the rights of sovereignty (including the maintenance of minimal conditions of peace, security, and justice) and second, that states that cannot fulfill these obligations must be the site of sustained nation-building efforts by developed nations, despite the risk of "neoimperialism" that attends such efforts.

In the book's afterword, political theorist Joshua Mitchell reflects on how his own upbringing in the Middle East anticipated—yet was overturned by—the terrorists who attacked the United States and its symbols of commerce and politics on September 11, 2001. The pursuit of glory, which Mitchell praises and laments, is a universal human occupation, but this pursuit need not entail violence and destruction, especially of the kind ushered in by recent terrorist acts. At a minimum, key institutions in international relations must be affirmed by all nations: Civilizations and their citizens depend on the sustenance of sovereign nations and the vitalities of commerce to survive and thrive.

This book's contributors bring different approaches and backgrounds to this venture, but they are united in the belief that the present realities of global political life demand an urgent rethinking of the concept of sovereignty and the role that religion, morality, or both can or should play in it. By bringing together intellectuals and government officials, political experts and scholars of religion, this volume addresses significant and multifaceted issues that an account by a single author, methodology, or perspective would be unable to capture. The specific intersections of religion and international politics explored in this book are best told by several authors from different fields, callings, and traditions. The result is a spirited conversation that yields important differences and deep agreements while representing a breadth of views that respects the issues' complexity.

Themes and Trajectories

Having sketched out the structure and contours of this project, we offer seven broad considerations or arcs of inquiry. These overarching themes and animating currents are important categories of moral and political deliberation about international politics, especially in an age in which sovereignty is undergoing profound alterations.

Failed States

The problem of "failed states" is a preoccupation of several contributors to this book. Their reflections raise a host of questions: What does it mean to be a sovereign state, and when, if ever, do states lose their claims to sovereignty? What kinds of standards can or should underwrite legitimate statehood? Must all people and nations share such assumptions about state authority and legitimacy? Is sovereign authority a prerequisite for nations to intervene, including into nations that also claim to be sovereign? Several contributors furnish different responses to these questions: Margaret O'Brien Steinfels first raises the issue in considering the case for military intervention to stop ethnic cleansing in Kosovo; John Carlson considers failed states' inability to bring to trial their own "criminals of humanity" and the resulting role that international institutions should play; John Kelsay suggests how issues of sovereign authority and legitimacy should be construed in cases involving terrorism; Robert Gallucci reviews several cases of American intervention in which the question of sovereignty in political decision-making processes was all but absent because certain states in question had lost their legitimacy. Finally, Erik Owens argues that the international community must embark on a sustained program of nation-building to stabilize or reconstitute failed states.

Authority of Moral Norms

Integral to this discussion of "failed states" is a driving concern about moral norms: convictions and attendant practices that are—or that many people think should be—normative and universally binding, regardless of the particular circumstances and contexts in which they play out. The case for universal human rights provides the most notable evidence of this theme. "Crimes against humanity" have prompted intervention in cases in which "mere" human rights violations of a less malicious nature have not. Clearly there are other moral norms as well. Norms about the proper conduct of war seek to ensure that those who act on behalf of oppressed victims do not become oppressors and victimizers themselves — which, of course, rules out the methods of terrorists who specifically strike civilian and nonmilitary "targets." Such moral-political standards share a restriction placed on certain means and methods — to ensure that important ethical boundaries are not transgressed in the pursuit of certain ends. Universal norms most often are undertaken in global politics under the rubric of international law — an important facet of this discussion. In emphasizing the moral character of such norms, however, and not simply the legal dimension, we plumb deeper to consider the theological and ethical warrants for law and the conduct of states.[33] Scott Appleby delves into the religious consistency of "Islamic rights talk" with widely shared proposals for a regime of universal human rights. James McCarthy and Jean Bethke Elshtain each worry in practical and ethical terms about the violation of key norms or "rules" of war, such as noncombatant immunity and proportional use of force. Some important lines of inquiry here include the following: What is the relationship between moral norms and failed states? Are states that commit or sponsor crimes against humanity or give host to terrorist organizations in violation of moral norms? Must such norms be codified in international law or some other form of consensus to be valid, effective, and enforceable?

Justice and Sovereignty

Another thematic category that garners the attention of several contributors is the relationship between sovereignty and justice. Although this theme is related to dilemmas involving failed states and moral norms, the language and conceptual dimensions of justice prompt debates that are worthy of special focus. How has justice historically been construed in politics, both within traditions and countertraditions? What validates these particular conceptions of justice, especially when competing conceptions of justice vie for supremacy and legitimacy? What kind of presuppositions about human nature, God, earthly life, peace, and politics must be excavated to appreciate fully the workings and limits of justice? Fr. Bryan Hehir examines the shifting understandings of sovereignty within the enduring tradition of just war thought, with attention to far-ranging adaptations and innovations within boundaries established by the tradition. John Kelsay, also working within the just war tradition, poignantly raises comparative measures to appraise conflicting claims about justice and sovereignty. Robin Lovin cautions that states and international bodies will appeal to justice as they use their power to develop interests of their own; ironically, however, sovereignty (in the form of awe and respect) may be precisely what is needed to render more effective these and other pursuits of justice in the twenty-first century. John Carlson's chapter examines the "anthropological" and transcendent features of justice—how claims of human nature and understandings of the divine shape the aims and limits of different versions of justice and how sovereignty becomes formulated in turn. Fred Dallmayr discerns how Jesus' teaching, which was misunderstood as an authoritative challenge to earthly sovereignty, led to the unjust charges for which he was executed; this injustice, nonetheless, also sounded the call for a reign of radical "nonsovereignty"—a world transforming occurrence that made available boldly different possibilities for justice and politics.

Vigorous Religious Belief

Many of the contributors to this book worry about and work to maintain the integrity of religious commitments, skeptical that the language and machinery of political sovereignty can provide an adequate framework for sustaining authentic religious belief. Does the level of "ultimacy" for which states strive—and which the vernacular and institutional structure of sovereignty facilitates—create settings that limit religious believers from exercising the full range of their convictions? In short, is political sovereignty a religiously tenable ideal? Can "full-bore" claims about truth and ultimate meaning be brought to bear in a political system—whether state-centric or globally construed—that is agnostic, if not antagonistic, to those claims? Susanne Hoeber Rudolph scrutinizes powerful states' willingness and ability to nourish genuine religious pluralism, noting especially the implications when proselytizing aspirations drown out burgeoning but fragile new endeavors in ecumenism.

Paul Griffiths highlights how seductive efforts to reconcile religious and political allegiance often trump or adulterate deep religious belief. Dallmayr highlights problems with several attempts to bring scriptural injunctions into complete conformity with earthly politics, either for the dilution of religious conviction or for the violent reactionary response that accompanies this kind of approach.

A Preference for Traditions

Interwoven throughout the book are appeals to various intellectual traditions with religious origins and dimensions—traditions that either locate politics centrally within them or provide insights into politics' pursuits. In showcasing the religious character often concealed in these traditions, we demonstrate that religion woven together with law, morality, national interests, and power relations represents the warp and woof of international political life. These long-standing traditions provide critical distance and potential for assessing the actions and undertakings of states and other political actors, while offering constructive proposals that can chasten ambitious expectations of politics as well as nudge political projects to take more seriously matters of faith and morals. In some cases, the survival of a tradition is linked directly to its ability to evolve, adapt, and speak to changing global political conditions. Coincident to this task is an appreciation and embrace of moral truths and norms that, over time, have been revealed to us and that establish sure-footed political approaches and ongoing patterns of continuity.

What innovations are necessary for these traditions to serve as sturdy ships as we navigate the shoals of a new era of sovereignty? What insights does a tradition-based approach proffer that "tradition-less" thinking does not? How can particular traditions speak to those outside the tradition? These and other questions are appropriate to bear in mind while traversing the chapters presented here. Hehir provides an in-depth account of just war thought's historical development, grappling with issues ranging from conflicts between sovereign states to humanitarian interventions and military strategies to uproot terrorism. McCarthy and Steinfels exemplify how religious traditions provide vital frameworks for practical thinking about force, particularly as such considerations pertain to the military or to lay citizens reflecting on the moral duties and civic responsibilities of their government. "Christian realism" is another tradition that revives fresh resources for judgment and appraisal, evidenced by Elshtain's reading of just war and by Lovin's attentiveness to the pragmatic elements of power and self-interest that suffuse all forms of political process. Clearly, however, global politics today cannot be hemmed in by Western traditions alone. Appleby and Kelsay probe key tenets and movements in Islam's rich tradition, mining for reserves that render cogency to dilemmas about human rights, violence, and political strife.

The Role of Institutions

Several contributors assume vantage points in which institutions (e.g., nation-states, international governmental organizations, transnational religious and civic organizations) constitute essential structures of global political life. Renewed attention to the life of institutions is warranted given the vast authorities, claims, and allegiances that this overlapping institutional network generates. More analytical work is needed to understand the newfound prominence of nontraditional institutions, particularly religious nongovernmental organizations (NGOs), and their ability to work cooperatively within—while pushing the boundaries of—traditional state-centric frameworks. Secular NGOs—such as those specializing in issues of civil and human rights, the environment, and economic development in underdeveloped nations—also extend across national borders, gathering the attention and support of citizens of many countries. These and other transnational causes solidify global "communities" of sorts with loyalties that compete with, even supercede, loyalties traditionally enjoyed by states: Global causes become more sacred than—if not incorporated into—the national interests of sovereign states and their citizens. Increasingly, there are more possibilities that these borderless communities will become bound by shared beliefs that take on a religious character, broadly construed. Should one welcome such occurrences? How can regional distinctions be maintained in the move to affirm transnational norms of state conduct? Rudolph's chapter explores one facet of such developments in her proposal for a "universal religiosity," shared by members of many nations, religions, sects, and creeds.

These new institutional possibilities also bring new perils, however, and Lovin homes in on this likelihood. International institutions will flounder unless they are able to reflect critically on their own propensity to misuse power and limit pretensions to righteousness. Nor are states—or any institutions—likely to give up powers they have long exercised. In many cases, some observers would argue, states should be hesitant before signing on to such enterprises as the International Criminal Court. Carlson draws back from ceding too much authority to international juridical bodies, and what this might mean for the mandates of nations and the collective responsibility of their citizens. Owens' concluding chapter highlights the special accountability of states in countering terrorism, and Joshua Mitchell's afterword argues that, in the wake of massive devastation wrought by terrorism, the institution of the nation-state itself must be preserved. What modifications must nations embrace to survive in a world in which transnational organizations, including international terrorist organizations, seek to check or subvert the influence and power of states? What standard, if any, will test the legitimacy and authority of non-state, transnational actors? Will their institutional integrity depend on their complete independence from the affairs and interests of nations?

Realist Presumptions

Finally, the contributors to this book are not bound by ideological commitments that diminish the relevance of their ideas for concrete proposals in politics. In making this assertion, we seek to counter a common assumption that anyone who invokes religious or ethical concerns is a naïve idealist, untutored in the hard-nosed realities of political power and state interests. Although the contributors draw their traditions and approaches from different wellsprings, they are bound across disciplines and vocations by a shared commitment to rigorous dialogue and examination of the moral and religious dimensions embedded in "real-life" political processes. Elshtain, Hehir, and Steinfels appreciate fully that force plays an essential albeit tragic role in world affairs—though this role is far less tragic than pacifist commitments would oblige of them. Gallucci argues that national interests will always form the fulcrum upon which state actions pivot, but moral concerns are vital to how such interests are portrayed and interpreted. Lovin's brand of realism responds as an explicit rejection of an overly optimistic political agenda for the world—one that, historically speaking, was poorly grounded and, theologically speaking, was incapable of taking root in the soil of earthly ambiguity.

We hope these themes, and this book as a whole, will spur serious reflection on — and perhaps a reappraisal of — pressing issues involving religion and international politics today. The contributors describe deeply influential historical and contemporary developments, interpret them critically in light of traditions of religious and ethical reflection, and offer constructive proposals to remedy persisting problems or to extend the moral efficacy of existing political arrangements. By drawing attention to the uncertain future of how sovereignty will be arranged and appraised in coming years, the book as a whole argues that religion is a crucial resource for understanding forces of global political life. One of Westphalia's legacies was to remove religion from conversations about the affairs of states; this project seeks a post-Westphalian recovery to reclaim religion's spot at the table as an imperative conversation partner for politics. Although we hope this book will be a substantial resource for academics working in the areas of religion, politics, and ethics, we believe readers outside the academy also will benefit from the views presented here.

Notes

1. See, for example: Gene Lyons and Michael Mastanduno, eds., *Beyond Westphalia? State Sovereignty and International Intervention* (Baltimore: Johns Hopkins University Press, 1995); Luis E. Lugo, ed., *Sovereignty at the Crossroads? Morality and International Politics in the Post-Cold War Era* (Lanham, Md.: Rowman & Littlefield, 1996); Susanne Hoeber Rudolph and James Piscatori, eds., *Transnational Religion and Fading States* (Boulder, Colo.: Westview Press, 1997); Jean Bethke Elshtain, *New Wine and Old Bottles: International Politics and Ethical Discourse* (Notre Dame, Ind.: Notre Dame University Press, 1998); Jonathan Moore, ed., *Hard Choices: Moral Dilemmas in Humanitarian Intervention* (Lanham, Md.: Rowman & Littlefield, 1998); Robert Jackson, ed., *Sovereignty at the Millennium* (Oxford: Blackwell, 1999); Charles W. Kegley and Gregory A. Raymond, *Exorcising the Ghost of Westphalia: Building World Order in the New Millennium* (Englewood Cliffs, N.J.: Prentice Hall, 2001).

2. Vaclav Havel, "Kosovo and the End of the Nation State," trans. Paul Wilson, *New York Review of Books* 46, no. 10 (10 June 1999): 4–6.

3. See Scott Peterson, "The Bigger Picture: An Age of Apologies," *Christian Science Monitor*, 24 March 2000; Rod Nordland, "Dutch Courage" *Newsweek*, 29 April 2002; Marlise Simons, "Dutch Cabinet Resigns over Failure to Halt Bosnian Massacre," *New York Times*, 17 April 2002.

4. The Rome Statute of the International Criminal Court (ICC) has been the subject of intense debate in American foreign policy and international law circles since it was adopted at the UN Diplomatic Conference in July 1998. President Clinton demonstrated his ambivalence about the treaty by signing it just hours before the signature deadline (December 31, 2000) but refusing to submit it for Senate approval or recommend that his successor do so; his successor, George W. Bush, made his views clear in an unprecedented "unsigning" process whereby the United States notified the ICC that it did not intend to become a party to the treaty. For lucid arguments for and against the treaty and the concept of universal jurisdiction it represents, see Henry A. Kissinger, "The Pitfalls of Universal Jurisdiction," *Foreign Affairs* 80, no. 4 (July/August 2001): 86–96; Kenneth Roth, "The Case for Universal Jurisdiction," *Foreign Affairs* 80, no. 5 (September/October 2001): 150–55.

5. See, for example, Drew Christiansen and Gerald Powers, "Send in the Peacekeepers: Sovereignty Isn't Sacred," *Commonweal* 124, no. 4 (28 February 1997): 16–18; Peter Ford, "Few Sacred Borders to New U.N.," *Christian Science Monitor*, 29 September 1999, 1; R. C. Longworth, "Human Rights May Now Trump Sovereignty," *Chicago Tribune*, 9 December 1999.

6. Two excellent historical surveys of the concept of sovereignty are given by Daniel Philpott, "Sovereignty: An Introduction and Brief History," *Journal of International Affairs* 48, no. 2 (winter 1995): 353–68; Robert Jackson, "Sovereignty in World Politics: A Glance at the Conceptual and Historical Landscape," *Political Studies* 47 (1999): 431–56. Philpott's historical study of sovereignty is combined with a theoretical argument about "international constitutions" in his crucial contribution to this field: Daniel Philpott, *Revolutions in Sovereignty: How Ideas Shaped Modern Institutions* (Princeton, N.J.: Princeton University Press, 2001).

7. This is the working definition used by Daniel Philpott in "Sovereignty," 353–68.

8. For a classic argument for the anarchic nature of international relations, see Hedley Bull, *The Anarchical Society: A Study of Order in World Politics*, 2d ed. (New York: Columbia University Press, 1995 [1977]).

9. Scott Appleby's discussion of the sacred is helpful for framing the discussion here. See R. Scott Appleby, *The Ambivalence of the Sacred* (Lanham, Md.: Rowman & Littlefield, 2000), 28.

10. For a probing consideration of whether human rights discourse inevitably bumps up against religious ideas, see Michael Perry, *The Idea of Human Rights: Four Inquiries* (New York: Oxford University Press, 1998).

11. Susanne Hoeber Rudolph, "Introduction: Religion, States, and Transnational Civil Society," in Rudolph and Piscatori, *Transnational Religion and Fading States*, 11.

12. This remains true despite the fact that the Catholic Church, as one of the oldest transnational organizations, has adapted to the nation-state system by locating its leadership in its own sovereign country.

13. John Locke, *A Letter on Toleration*, ed. James Tully (Indianapolis: Hackett Publishing Co., 1983), 33.

14. For studies that take seriously the place of religion in foreign policy analysis, see Douglas Johnston and Cynthia Sampson, *Religion, The Missing Dimension of Statecraft* (New York: Oxford University Press, 1994); Elliot Abrams, ed., *The Influence of Faith: Religious Groups and U.S. Foreign Policy* (Lanham, Md.: Rowman and Littlefield, 2001).

15. Pope John Paul II, "Address to the Diplomatic Corps," *Origins* 22 (4 February 1993), 587.

16. U.S. Conference of Catholic Bishops, "The Harvest of Justice Is Sown in Peace," *Origins* 23, no. 26 (9 December 1993); also available at www.nccbuscc.org/sdwp/harvest.htm.

17. Philpott, "Sovereignty," 354.

18. Anne-Marie Slaughter's seminal article "The Real New World Order," *Foreign Affairs* 76 (September/October 1997): 183–97, makes this point nicely.

19. Among the recent works that take up the religious dimensions of sovereignty as the concept developed in Europe and took root around the globe are Philpott, *Revolutions in Sovereignty*; Jackson, "Sovereignty in World Politics"; Daniel Engster, *Divine Sovereignty: The Origins of Modern State Power* (DeKalb: Northern Illinois University Press, 2001); Kegley and Raymond, *Exorcising the Ghost of Westphalia*; and Hideaki Shinoda, *Re-examining Sovereignty: From Classical Theory to the Global Age* (New York: St. Martin's Press, 2000).

20. Our conception of "archetypes of sovereignty" owes a debt to Daniel Philpott's account of the three "faces of sovereignty" and the "revolutions in sovereignty" in his book of the same name. We take our account to be complementary to his.

21. As of November 2002 the U.S. Department of State recognized 192 independent states and 62 "dependencies and areas of special sovereignty" (e.g., American Samoa and Western Sahara) that are administered by sovereign states. See www.state.gov/countries.

22. Jackson, "Sovereignty in World Politics," 432; Paul J. Weber, "Theocracy," in *Encyclopedia of Politics and Religion*, ed. Robert Wuthnow, vol. 2 (Washington, D.C.: Congressional Quarterly, 1998), 733–35.

23. For an overview of recent scholarly debate on the future of sovereignty, see the special issue of *Political Studies* (vol. 47, 1999) devoted to "Sovereignty at the Millennium," which includes an excellent introduction by Robert Jackson.

24. Jackson, "Sovereignty in World Politics," 436.

25. The "two swords" doctrine, pronounced by Pope Gelasius I (P.P. AD 492–496), described the joint rule of the *regnum* (earthly territorial rule) and *sacerdotium* (religious authority, whose pinnacle is the Bishop of Rome).

26. Romans 13:1 (New Revised Standard Version).

27. See, for example, in the Hebrew Bible, Daniel 2:44 ("And in the days of those kings the God of heaven will set up a kingdom which shall never be destroyed, nor shall its sovereignty be left to another people"); in the Christian New Testament, Acts 4:24 ("And when they heard it, they lifted their voices together to God and said, 'Sovereign Lord, who didst make the heaven and the earth and the sea and everything in them . . .'"); and in the Muslim Qur`an, al-Hashr, 59:23 ("He is Allah, than Whom there is no other God, the Sovereign Lord, the Holy One, Peace, the Keeper of Faith, the Guardian, the Majestic, the Compeller, the Superb").

28. Philpott, *Revolutions in Sovereignty*, 78.

29. Ibid., chapter 6.

30. Cited in ibid., 364.

31. Ibid., 108.

32. Martin Luther, for example, vigorously affirmed the Pauline principle that political rulers were ordained by God to govern for the good of society; he therefore supported the local princes' right to appoint priests and to help govern the local church as they saw fit. The prince, Luther wrote, is the "mask of God" who administers God's justice in temporal affairs; temporal authority is rightly given to the state to preserve peace (by suppressing religious dissent if necessary), punish sinful acts, and restrain the wicked from further misdeeds. Martin Luther, "On Temporal Authority: To What Extent It Should Be Obeyed," in *Luther's Works*, vol. 45, trans. J. J. Schindel (Philadelphia: Muhlenberg Press, 1930), 81–129.

33. Enforcement of international law is limited quite often by the fact that, in some arenas, only states possess the resources and influences to check their own conduct or that of other states.

PART I

Religion and Armed Intervention

1

The Moral Measurement of War:
A Tradition of Change and Continuity

J. BRYAN HEHIR

THE CREATIVELY CHOSEN TITLE OF THIS BOOK, *The Sacred and the Sovereign*, echoes the dictum of Jesus when he was challenged about the relationship of his teaching and the imperial power of Rome. His response, "Repay to Caesar what belongs to Caesar and to God what belongs to God" (Matt. 22:21), seemed crystal clear in intent, yet has been endlessly debated since it was uttered. To analyze sovereignty and sacredness is to continue a millennial narrative in the Christian tradition. Beyond the confines of that tradition, sovereignty gets much more analytical attention than the sacred. For centuries a staple in the study of political philosophy and international relations, the concept of sovereignty in an era of globalization and in a world of multiple international institutions is an abiding topic across disciplinary lines of politics, economics, and law. Although these disciplines dominate the study of sovereignty, the focus of this book has solid lineage. Historically and analytically, "the sacred" has been the source of both legitimation and limitation of sovereign power. Well before a time when the sovereign state had assumed the form and the importance it now has, individuals holding political power sought support from, and had to contend with, traditions and institutions claiming higher moral authority than the political order possessed.

This book drives us back, therefore, to the relationship of religion, ethics, and politics, and in doing so it reflects a broader movement of ideas and themes at work in the contemporary international system. To capture the significance of these intersecting ideas we can use the period since the end of World War II. The experience of that conflict (its causes, its destruction, and its outcome) produced two distinct and to some degree diverse responses. In the study of world politics, the dominant response was the revival of classical realism, focusing on the power and the interests of states and questioning—or at times denying—the relevance of normative issues in world politics. In the arena of diplomacy, the creation of the United Nations—a second try at world order—embodied the tension between an institution based on states (including explicit attention given to the interests of major states) and a philosophy that sought to subordinate sovereign state claims (regarding war and human rights) to a normative framework shaped by the charter of the United Nations and international law. For the first twenty years of the postwar era, the dominance of the realist proposal made it difficult to provide space in policy discourse or public argument for the moral assessment of state power. The period from the mid-1960s to the mid-1980s, however, produced three realities in the world that invited and compelled a return to normative analysis: the Vietnam War, the human rights movement, and the nuclear debate. Each had its distinctive roots, but none could be analyzed in the exclusive terms of power and interest. The consequence of the debates surrounding each of these topics was the revitalization of arguments and movements (particularly nongovernmental organizations of all kinds) that focused on ethics and international relations. This topic and the multiple subthemes it encompassed became an accepted part of the landscape of the study of world politics and the making of foreign policy. A stream of books, articles, and journal articles testifies to the continuing dynamic of the dialogue between politics and ethics.[1]

The return of moral argument, however, did not include significant attention to the role of religion. Moral analysis in international relations, like the analysis in the distinct but burgeoning field of bioethics, was cast primarily in the language of moral philosophy. Some of this analysis had historical roots in religious traditions, but they were not a continuing source of ideas. The return of the sacred—of religious ideas, institutions, and communities—as the object of analysis beyond the boundaries of religious traditions themselves was a product of the post–cold war period. Although the role of religion in political change was evident in the last third of the twentieth century, systematic analysis began in the final stages of the cold war and then expanded significantly in the 1990s. The relevance of religious belief, traditions of moral analysis inspired by it, and the role of religious communities precisely as a challenge to sovereign power was evident across a range of issues: the use of force, human rights, political change, and economic justice; regionally the role of religion in Latin America, Eastern Europe, the Middle East, and South Africa was clear to all.

The result of this double transformation in political discourse over the past fifty years, incorporating both moral analysis and religious traditions, creates the setting for a new assessment of the sacred and the sovereign in a new century. The focus of this chapter is the place where war fits between the claims of sovereignty and the imperatives of the sacred. Except for the theme of the legitimacy of temporal power itself, issues of war and peace have been the most controversial arena of sacred-sovereign engagement. These issues also demonstrate the interplay—explicit and implicit—of religious conviction, moral analysis, and political-strategic discourse. My intent is to sketch how one ancient tradition of moral discourse rooted in a religious community has developed, and then to examine three distinct challenges that the contemporary version of the tradition has faced over the past fifty years.

The Just War Ethic: A Pluralist and Developing Tradition

Analysis of war and strategy in moral terms is not confined to a single moral theory. A full discussion would range across very different perspectives and arguments about the morality of war as a dimension of politics. My focus is on a single contribution to the wider debate: the just war ethic, understood as a religiously grounded but now distinct and independent moral vision concerning issues of war and peace. Because this ethic has a religious foundation, some analysts continue to stress the interplay of religious and moral ideas. Because it has acquired a distinct status, others use the tradition without much reference to its religious lineage.[2]

In spite of its pluralistic lineage, the just war ethic has evolved over centuries as a coherent normative position. In describing this evolution, philosophers tend to stress the outcome—the elements of systematic coherence—whereas historians, attuned to the complex array of sources for the synthesis, tend to stress the evolution of the journey the ethic has followed.[3] Although the just war ethic is a blend of theology, morality, law, and custom, it is best understood in its contemporary form as a normative doctrine—an ethic that takes its place at the intersection of war and politics. It stands also at the intersection of sovereignty and the sacred, adjudicating the claims of the former and the imperatives of the latter.

At the foundation of the ethic stands a theological anthropology (a conception of human nature and a reading of human history) and a basic moral conviction from which the systematic ethic proceeds. The anthropological foundation is captured in the Augustinian insight that war is the result of sin and the remedy for sin. Augustine was a realist, but he was not a Hobbesian; he was vividly aware of the fallibility of human nature, including the sense that aggression was an ever present possibility in interpersonal and social relationships. Hence the conclusion that at the root of war stood a confirmation of the Christian doctrine of original sin—an abiding structural flaw in human history.[4] At the same time, Augustine's understanding of the role of grace in history preserved his conception of human nature from the stark Hobbesian thesis of the war of all upon all. Augustinian anthropology has been the subject of debate for centuries; in the past century theologian Reinhold Niebuhr used a version of Augustine to ground his Christian realism with a consequent ethic of war that was an analogue of the just war ethic but not simply an endorsement of it.[5] Niebuhr found the classical just war ethic too rationalist—too sure of its distinctions and careful line-drawing in politics and history. Whereas Niebuhr found the theological account basically convincing, political scientist Kenneth Waltz found it less analytically useful; its analysis was so deeply rooted (in human nature *ut sic*) that it failed to account for less profound but more influential factors that produced the constant threat of war—factors such as the "anarchical" structure of world politics.[6]

Distinct from Niebuhr and Waltz, the consensus position of just war reasoning accepted Augustine's insight (namely, that war is possible but not inevitable) and set out, in the words of John Courtney Murray, S.J., "to condemn war as evil, to limit the evil it entails and to humanize its conduct as far as possible."[7] In maintaining this position the just war ethic stands between sovereignty and the sacred, defining the sovereign's rights and roles and defending the sacredness of human life. Contrary to the pacifist position, it holds that because war is a permanent possibility, it should be contained within the moral universe, not simply declared to be immoral. Conscious of the need to limit recourse to war, it locates the right to use force with persons who hold responsibility for governance. Aware of the ambivalence of sovereign power, it then restricts the right of the state to resort to force.

In a process that has been both continuous and circuitous, this moral tradition has been based on two key convictions. First, in a world that is limited and sinful, conflicts of interests, purposes, and values cannot be expunged from human affairs; second, conflicts—even those rising to violence—can be analyzed, differentiated, and judged, so that legitimate and illegitimate uses of force can be identified. Essentially, the tradition affirms that sovereignty must be restrained and the sacredness of life protected.

Reduced to its bare essentials, the moral tradition holds that morally legitimate use of force must be limited use, and limits are to be imposed on purposes, methods, and intentions. Why war is fought, how war is fought, and the motives of war are all subject to scrutiny. The moral doctrine is an intricate combination of normative traditions. It involves a substantive theory of justice that yields categories of just cause or purpose in war. It sets limits on means by invoking consequentialist and deontological criteria, ruling out all direct killing of combatants and assessing other consequences by the category of proportionality. It is a tradition that focuses on acts of war, but it also is agent-centered in its attention to motive and intention. It provides legitimacy for sovereign power, endowing it with rights beyond those of individuals, but it holds states to standards of proof to justify behavior. Specifically, it grants the state the power to call citizens, as a matter of duty, to defend society, but it also instructs citizens on the limits of obedience to state power.

The tradition denies the central claim of the modern doctrine of sovereignty—the right to declare war purely on the basis of national interest interpreted by the state—by establishing tests of "just cause," "right intention," and "last resort." It also rejects the concept that the logic of strategy is immune from critique or moral control. Finally, the tradition refuses to accept the seemingly natural assumption that war should be fought from motives of hatred or denial of the humanity of one's adversary; in this tradition war occurs within an abiding moral community: The adversary can never be reduced simply to the enemy.

The tradition therefore is not "realist" in the sense of insulating sovereign power and strategic discourse from moral analysis, but it is realist in the sense that it seeks to understand, engage, and even complement the state in its role of defending the political community up to and including the use of force. This tradition seeks dialogue and debate with sovereign power and with strategic discourse. It is a practical moral tradition that is designed both "to set the right terms for national debate on public policies bearing on the problem of war and peace" and to guide the personal conscience of sovereigns, soldiers, diplomats, and citizens.

The conversation the tradition has cultivated across the lines of politics, strategy, and ethics can be traced over 1,500 years. The meaning of sovereign power has changed, but the essential nature of the moral argument has been sustained. The tradition originated in the Roman Empire, was adapted by canonists and theologians to the medieval *Respublica Christiana*, came to terms slowly with the modern sovereign state in the sixteenth and seventeenth centuries, and entered the twentieth century unprepared for what Raymond Aron called the "century of total war" yet capable of adaptation and renewal. The renewal did not begin until after World War II; the first half of the twentieth century found the tradition marginalized by its heirs and by state practice.

The renewal of the moral tradition, led appropriately by theologians, has been carried forward by their successors—now joined by moral philosophers, historians, lawyers, and policy analysts. The renewal of moral argument parallels but is not identical with the tradition of positive international law; it also is parallel to but not embodied in political-strategic analysis. It must be kept alive, sharpened, corrected, and expanded continuously, or it will again be marginalized. In the past fifty years the renewal of the tradition has had to engage the sovereign state, now encompassed within the political-legal framework of the charter of the United Nations and the broader context of international law that flows from the charter. It also has had to confront a technological revolution in the use of force (led by weapons of mass destruction, but not limited to them) that has posed qualitatively different challenges for an ethic of means from anything encountered in the previous fifteen centuries of change in strategy and tactics. The full story of this engagement of sovereign power and sacred tradition is beyond this chapter. The outlines of the encounter can be found, however, in a summary account of how the tradition has adapted when it has faced three challenges: the nuclear age, humanitarian military intervention, and terrorism.

Three Challenges and Change: A Synthetic Statement

I attempt here the outline of an argument; each distinct challenge has generated a substantial literature that is not reducible to a single response. Like the broader tradition itself, the address to these three complex challenges exhibits pluralism and the need for further development. This outline concentrates on the nature of the challenge posed for moral tradition, the adaptations it has generated, and conclusions I draw from use of the theory in these designated cases.

The Nuclear Age and Weapons of Mass Destruction

The death and destruction caused by two world wars constituted a compelling call for a reassertion of moral limits in warfare — but one that stood in direct continuity with previous instances of warfare. The continuity was broken and the empirical challenge to the moral tradition changed with the use of atomic weapons against Japan in 1945. These primitive versions of weapons of mass destruction opened the nuclear age. The unique challenge of the nuclear age — still with us today — involves its original form, its cold war history, and its continuing legacy.[8] Nuclear weapons directly challenged the heart of the just war ethic: An ethic committed to multiple limits now confronted the potential of unlimited violence. Strategists recognized the novelty of the challenge before moralists did. Bernard Brodie captured the problem succinctly and with compelling force in 1946: "Thus far the chief purpose of our military establishment has been to win wars. From now on its chief purpose must be to avert them. It can have almost no other useful purpose."[9]

Other strategic analysts came to echo Brodie's prediction, although a persistent view held that these new technological advances could be fitted into the traditional logic of war. Implicit in Brodie's quote lies the logic of deterrence—not escape from the nuclear age but a way of containing and managing its awesome danger. Developing that logic into a viable strategy, which involved "living with" nuclear weapons but not using them, engaged the resources of three generations of strategists, governments, and military establishments.[10] The task involved not only coming to grips with a quantum leap of destructive capability in the hands of sovereign states but also paradoxical changes such power introduced into the logic of strategic planning. Secrecy—a long-treasured resource of states—was no longer useful; effective deterrence required that one's adversary know one's capabilities exactly. Superiority of striking power contained its own ambivalence; if it seemed to threaten the deterrent of the other side, it could induce preemptive use by the weaker state. Sovereigns sought not superiority but stability. Defense against attack—the defining rationale of military establishments—seemed neither attainable nor, in some forms, desirable.

None of these propositions went uncontested, but all retained a basic validity. The strategy of deterrence was fashioned in the political context of the cold war; by the late 1960s the terms of the argument were established, and the succeeding twenty years involved variations on the main themes.

For the most part, moralists did not join the argument until its basic themes about deterrence and use (and the complex connections between them) were well defined. From the late 1950s through the 1980s, the moral response to the nuclear age took shape. Like the strategists, the moralists could use traditional concepts, but they had to refashion the moral argument in a new context.[11] The ethic of war had been focused on conduct in warfare; the nuclear age required an ethic of use (in war) and an ethic of deterrence (the way of keeping the peace). Strategically, if deterrence was to be credible, use had to be possible and effective. Morally, use had to fit within the twin criteria of discrimination and proportionality, neither of which seemed secure if nuclear war began and escalated. Moralists in the just war tradition predominantly followed the strategic position of seeking to draw as wide a barrier against use as was feasible without totally denying its possibility in some form. The morality of nuclear peace, the condition of mutual deterrence, stretched the moral categories to the limit. A pure consequentialism could abide effective deterrence, but the traditional ethic had never been purely consequentialist. Faced with this fact, some moralists moved to nuclear pacifism (denying legitimacy to any form of use or deterrence); others eroded the status of noncombatant immunity and accepted a consequentialist version of the just war ethic.[12] The moral stress involved in such a move was captured eloquently in the now-famous dictum of Michel Walzer in *Just and Unjust Wars*: "We threaten evil in order not to do it, and the doing of it would be so terrible that the threat seems in comparison to be morally defensible."[13]

Those who found deterrence tolerable—even necessary, if not morally attractive—but could not square the tradition with a dominant consequentialist position faced the arduous task of granting some legitimation to use (enough for credible deterrence, but restricted to the few possible options that met the demands of discrimination) and conditional endorsement of a deterrent posture. This position was always tied to a commitment to arms control and a tenuous hope for political change that would erode the nuclear dilemma.[14] That hope, never clearly defined by either strategists or moralists, was at least partly realized by the sudden collapse of the Soviet Union and the process of ending the cold war.

The demise of the cold war has not solved the legacy of the nuclear age. This third stage of the nuclear narrative is what confronts us in the twenty-first century. The danger faced for forty-five years by the superpowers and the world as a whole—the danger of a nuclear catastrophe of unprecedented destruction—has been radically reduced. The agreement signed in May 2002 by U.S. President Bush and Russian President Putin to reduce nuclear arsenals to less than 2,200 weapons symbolizes the dramatic change in world politics since the cold war. Yet neither the existence of weapons of mass destruction nor the knowledge of how to produce them has disappeared. The heart of the nuclear dilemma for forty years—superpower conflict—has been substantially eroded but is now replaced by the multidimensional challenge of proliferation.

Preventing the spread of weapons of mass destruction has been a part of arms control policy since the early 1960s. The Nonproliferation Treaty (1968) has been the cornerstone of this effort. Negotiated at the height of the cold war, it sought to locate control of nuclear weapons in the hands of the superpowers and the other nuclear states. The problem of the treaty—from both a policy and an ethical viewpoint—was reflected in its text. The existing nuclear states were far more interested in preventing the expansion of the nuclear club than they were in committing themselves to a serious effort toward nuclear arms control or disarmament. Nevertheless, the treaty played a useful role throughout the cold war. The post–cold war problem of proliferation is both more important than ever and more difficult than its earlier versions. The end of the cold war contributed to a new set of proliferation issues: "loose nukes" in the former Soviet Union; more difficulty maintaining control of fissionable material; nuclear scientists who are no longer useful to their governments. Although some states (Argentina and South Africa) have reversed their budding nuclear programs, others (Pakistan and India) have become members of the nuclear club (with few safeguards), and other states (Israel) are capable of rapid nuclear deployment.

In this new context for proliferation policy, two large policy questions pose strategic and normative problems. First there is the linkage of proliferation with terrorist groups—nonstate actors who are neither pledged to restraint nor even easily identifiable. Proliferation among states is a difficult but well-defined problem; inducements and sanctions can be used to prevent or encourage states not to pursue development of weapons of mass destruction. Terrorist groups—by definition, entities that cannot field large-scale military deployments—regard weapons of mass destruction as a quick fix with potentially massive payoff. Often dedicated to goals that are both political and suprapolitical, they are not easily bribed or deterred. Second, nonproliferation policy today often is tied to proposals for military intervention in threatening states (e.g., North Korea or Iraq). These proposals should be sharply differentiated from the problem discussed below, humanitarian military intervention. Intervention to prevent proliferation threatens the standard realist case for nonintervention, the attempt to reduce interstate conflict except in cases of aggression. It also raises a host of questions about how threatening a state's posture or policy must be to constitute a "just cause" for intervention. Is possession of nuclear weapons just cause for intervention? The intent to produce such weapons? Their deployment? Or are other supporting reasons, such as possession plus a record of aggression or menacing behavior, needed to meet the just cause criteria?

The nuclear ethics of the cold war, which focused on preventing cataclysmic damage between the superpowers, does not address many of the issues we encounter today. Regulating superpower behavior assumed a status of equality; the arsenals and strategies of the actors were well known; the ethical issues concentrated on reinforcing the nuclear taboo, probing the targeting strategy for deterrence, pressing the imperatives of arms control, and continually reminding the protagonists of their systemic responsibility to avoid catastrophe.

The dominant characteristic of the ethics of nonproliferation today is the inequality of the parties. Advocates and enforcers of the treaty are the possessing states that seek both to deter proliferation and to persuade nonnuclear states to endorse a system designed to freeze the status quo. The inequality—present and future—is justified in terms of systemic safety; a world of multiple nuclear powers greatly increases the chance of miscalculation, accident, or escalation. Systemic safety is a justifiable policy goal, but it must meet two objectives: States usually seek weapons of mass destruction because of local or regional conflicts, and possession of nuclear weapons conveys a certain leverage for any state in world politics. Making the systemic safety argument persuasive requires big-power reductions in weapons and efforts to relativize the auxiliary benefits that seem to flow from membership in the nuclear club. Depriving a policy of moral merit because it is based on inequality is too simple in this case, but moral support for nonproliferation must include arguments for ameliorating the effects of inequality and, I believe, presumptive opposition to military intervention as an assumed method of enforcing nonproliferation. The case must be made in great detail why preemptive action should be taken.

Humanitarian Military Intervention

The redefinition of nuclear policy was one result of the end of the cold war. A second was the challenge posed to international law and state policy by cases of intrastate chaos and conflict resulting in massive loss of life and human rights violations, from central Africa to southern Europe. Analytically, it is difficult to identify a causal connection between the end of the cold war's imposed discipline and the eruption of violence and fragmentation of states that followed throughout the 1990s, but the correlation is clear. The cases are well known, encompassing the entire decade after the fall of the Berlin Wall: Bosnia, Somalia, Rwanda, and

Kosovo were the dominant examples, but Sudan, Liberia, East Timor, Sierra Leone, and Haiti also were part of the narrative. The story began in the early 1990s with debates about whether Bosnia was a civil war or an interstate conflict. That ambiguity, which was a factor in delaying response to the situation, stood in sharp contrast to the blatant instance of genocide in Rwanda[15] and the sharply defined question of Kosovo— described by Adam Roberts as "the first time a major use of destructive armed force had been undertaken . . . to bring a halt to crimes against humanity being committed by a state within its own borders."[16] The progression of decisions from Bosnia through Africa and back to Kosovo involved large arguments about politics, law, strategy, and morality. The essential problem that the 1990s presented was one of international jurisprudence. The law and politics of the question were all too clear, embodied in the provisions of the UN charter against intervention in affairs of domestic jurisdiction and complemented by the received tradition of international law. Against law and politics stood events and moral demands: Large-scale violence and killing (reaching the technical definition of genocide) made observance of the law seem irresponsible and inhumane. Case by case, governments and international organizations made their choices with little evidence of consistency or settled policy. The results were mixed, and the century drew to a close with little consensus at the international level and no clear policy about intervention within the major states, particularly in the United States. The lack of consensus at both levels of world politics was rooted in normative assumptions, the policies of states, and weak international institutions.

Normative Assumptions

The phrase *normative assumptions* is potentially misleading because it is broad enough to encompass legal norms and moral norms. In fact, as I indicate above, they were not complementary in the case of intervention. The tradition of positive international law, which grew out of the just war ethic in some respects, is rightfully protective of nonintervention as a basic rule of world politics. The rule arose partly from the experience of the sixteenth and seventeenth centuries, when interventionary politics drove the wars of central Europe. The rule corresponds also with classical realism—a theory of politics that is at home with war but not promiscuous about fighting for anything short of "vital interests." Legal and political conviction framed the rule to reduce instances of interstate conflict; it was a maxim of order designed to tame the state of war. As noted above, its functional utility is attested to in prevailing conceptions of international law and in the UN charter. Military intervention can occur under the auspices of the charter, but only with the authorization of the Security Council. Such action must pass a double test: The United Nations is inherently conservative about overriding the non-intervention rule precisely because of the fears of small and weak states with long memories of imperialism, and key large states possess a veto in the Security Council. The combined effects of these distinct restraints provide opponents of intervention with normative support for opposition that is rooted either in principle or in a conception of interest.

Policy of States

Certain conceptions of principles and interests contributed to the hesitation of major states to respond to calls from the media, from non-governmental organizations (NGOs), and from suffering populations for outside assistance to stop the killing and violence in the 1990s. The United States, given its role and resources, is the prime example (but not the only one) of a major state devoid of direction on humanitarian intervention in the 1990s. The Clinton administration, after campaigning on a moderately interventionist policy, hesitated on Bosnia, took casualties in Somalia, and then—as a result—took a pass on Rwanda. Partly in reaction to this chain of abstention, the United States invoked the doctrine of humanitarian intervention in Kosovo, which some moralists would argue posed more serious legal obstacles than some of its predecessors.

This reading of Clinton policy—a critique of late or little response to chaos and violence—is very different from the one its political opponents made. Republicans in Congress and George W. Bush in his presidential campaign depicted the Clinton policy as far too expansive on intervention. Their opposition to intervention was based on a quasi-theory of the U.S. role in the world. Essentially, it had echoes of the nineteenth century about it: The United States should learn from the successful Great Powers of that era. The role of the Great Power, its contribution to world politics, is to maintain the macrostability of the international system. In brief, Great Powers are to be concerned with the policy of other similar powers and not be diverted into expending resources in marginal conflicts that, however significant their human suffering, do not affect the global balance of power. On this view, the corollary drawn on intervention is the classical realist position: Interventions should be rare, carefully chosen, always successful, and determined only by the vital interests of the state.

When this position—or even the less absolute but still cautious Clinton policy—is placed in the context of the post–cold war international system, its consequences are direct and substantial. One effect of the collapse of the cold war was the disappearance of the idea that U.S. interests are geographically global. For fifty years the prevailing conception had been that every continent and virtually all states outside the Soviet bloc were part of the vital interest of the West and the United States. The author of containment, Ambassador George Kennan, always contested this universalist view (as he would contest an interventionist position in the 1990s), but he usually lost the argument. With the collapse of Soviet power, however, many states could be defined in material terms to fall outside the sphere of U.S. vital interests. Basically, they could not harm us, they held no major economic interest, and they had little or no leverage on U.S. policy. If "vital interest" was to be the criterion for intervention, the cases of the 1990s did not meet that standard. This view of policy, combined with the foregoing normative assumptions, tended to provide a guide and a justification of sorts to abstain from humanitarian intervention.

International Institutions

Although the United Nations clearly is cautious about intervention, in its norms and its role in the world there is a basis for it to be the repository of concern for cases like those of the 1990s. The UN charter's caution about intervention must be read in conjunction with human rights law that emerged from the United Nations and now constitutes a significant aspect of international affairs.[17] These human rights norms at least challenge an expansive reading of domestic jurisdiction. In addition, when major powers define their responsibilities narrowly, the deficit of leadership creates opportunities and obligations for the United Nations. Indeed, the early Clinton policy envisioned the United States playing a collaborative role with the United Nations; this policy collapsed, however, with the defeat in Somalia. From a purely theoretical perspective, the United Nations should be the principal focus for decision making on intervention and for coordinating appropriate action. The clear evidence of the 1990s, however, is that there is a gap in institutional capability between the potential United Nations role on these issues and its ability either to authorize or to provide adequate forces to undertake interventionary action.

In the face of these interlocking restraints on humanitarian military intervention, what is the role and direction of the traditional moral doctrine in the face of the conflicts of the 1990s? Historically, the moral tradition, with its religious foundations and expansive conception of human solidarity and duty, has been more interventionist than the legal tradition. The original rationale of the just war tradition, typified by Augustine, grounded the right to use force in the duty to defend people under attack. The moral tradition came to terms with the modern sovereign state, but it never lost the perspective that states exist in a broader human community, and a fabric of rights and duties binds that community prior to the authority of the state. This moral perspective can accommodate the rule of nonintervention, but not one held in an absolute fashion. The rule—like its correlate, the doctrine of sovereignty—has only relative moral standing; both can be overridden by moral imperatives to save lives and prevent systematic violations of human rights. But the just war tradition is not dismissive of the role nonintervention plays in an "anarchical" world of sovereign states. The moral doctrine in its own right seeks to reduce the causes of war; in that sense it finds a certain convergence with the nonintervention rule.

How, then, to accord the rule a limited but necessary role without allowing conflicts within states to be immune from outside action? Elsewhere I have tried to develop the lines of an ethic of intervention that is based on the logic of the just war ethic for interstate behavior.[18] Essentially, such a view establishes a presumption against intervention but defines a range of exceptions that override the presumption. The experience of the 1990s, in my view, should expand the exceptions beyond the standard case of genocide. Policies short of genocide—on display in Somalia, Sierra Leone, Bosnia, and Kosovo—constitute sufficiently serious violations of law and morality to legitimate intervention. Expanding legitimation for intervention (just cause) places pressure on the other criteria. Intervention is more difficult to contain and restrain than war. The reason lies in the always debatable cause standard (never as clear as aggression across a recognized frontier) and in the process of rationalization that historically has accompanied interventions.

Authorization therefore plays a crucial role in assessing interventions; some form of multilateral authorization is required. This standard is lower than that in the UN charter, which restricts such authorization to the Security Council. As Kofi Annan acknowledged in a 1999 address to the UN General Assembly, however, the veto can prevent such authorization when the facts call for it. It is useful, therefore, at least to test the possibilities of regional authorization in extreme situations.

Although the other just war criteria (intent, last resort, proportionality) can be useful in shaping a final judgment on intervention, the experience of the 1990s highlights the centrality of the just means principles (discrimination and proportionality). As Adam Roberts observes, "In the long history of legal debates about humanitarian intervention there has been a constant failure to address directly the question of the methods used in such interventions."[19] From Somalia to Kosovo, the evidence of the past decade is that justifiable intervention must attend to the means question. This assessment should not be difficult for the moral tradition; the dominant emphasis of the twentieth century has been limiting the means of warfare. From the intricacies of nuclear debates about targeting, declaratory and use policy, and first use to the close attention paid to means in the Persian Gulf War, the ethics of war has focused on limiting the use of power.[20] It has been the intervention debates that have brought the *Jus ad Bellum* questions of cause, authority, and last resort back into the moral arguments.

This essay does not allow for detailed casuistry about the means used in the cases of the 1990s, but two characteristics can be noted. On one hand, the historical trend line since World War II has been in the clear direction of severe public scrutiny of the means of warfare, and corresponding attention to precision in targeting and use by the U.S. military. On the other hand, one cannot ignore Nicholas Wheeler's comment that 6,000 to 8,000 Somali civilians[21] are the estimated casualties from U.S. tactics, nor can one avoid probing the implications of Mary Robinson's judgment that "in the NATO bombing of the Federal Republic of

Yugoslavia, large numbers of civilians have been incontestably killed, civilian installations targeted on the basis that they are or could be of military application, and NATO remains the sole judge of what is or is not acceptable to bomb."[22]

To return to the original proposition, the structure of the problem of international jurisprudence remains; there is not yet a consensus about how to accommodate the moral demands of responding to internal conflict within the existing fabric of international law and the UN charter. The principle issue is the *jus ad bellum* question of legitimating intervention, but the *jus in bello* questions of the past century are a necessary element in designing justifiable intervention.

Terrorism

Neither the dangers of the nuclear age nor the chaotic choices about intervention prepared the world for the events of September 11, 2001. Terrorism is not a new phenomenon in world politics, but the scale and scope of the attacks on the United States and the symbolic significance of striking New York and Washington gave those events a worldwide significance. In the United States, the immediate response was focused on providing a sense of security and stability in the country and meeting the urgent needs of victims, their families, and the cities where the attacks occurred. Once that process had begun—when the dead were buried, the search for the missing was organized, and the funds were collected to meet multiple needs—the difficult analytical work of seeking to understand the long-term significance of the attacks began.

By 2001 the policy and academic communities had been at work for a decade seeking to define the structure of power and patterns of political, economic, and strategic interaction that followed the collapse of the familiar cold war universe of bipolar competition. Multiple proposals contended for primacy, but no single striking conceptual framework had captured the day. Neither the traditional schools of political analysis— realism and liberalism—nor attempts to recast the analytical framework completely by substituting civilizations for states or by installing economics as the guiding category of world politics were able to win consensual support.[23] Pluralism dominated the analytical world, while multiple proposals for reorganizing U.S. military forces were debated in specialized circles in Washington and the academy.

In all of these analytical debates, there always was a bow to terrorism as one factor in world politics. The effect of September 11 was to locate terrorism as the prism through which all other elements of power and politics were assessed. By itself, of course, the concept of terrorism does not have the scope and depth to be an integrating category of analysis; the world in its constituent dimensions is too complex to be collapsed into terrorism. But the urgency of responding to the fact of terrorism has given it at least the temporary status of *primus inter pares* as a category of analysis and planning. Other issues—such as proliferation of weapons of mass destruction, failed states, and the need to provide economic assistance to poor and chaotic societies—all came to be assessed in light of their relationship to terrorism.

Part of the difficulty of raising the analytical and political importance of terrorism to this status is that no single definition of terrorism commands universal agreement. Certain characteristics—that terrorism is a crime, that it is indiscriminate violence designed to provoke widespread public panic, and that it is a means to political objectives—create broad agreement but something less than concise analytical support. Given this unsettled intellectual context, I offer a definition of terrorism, as reflected in September 11, that highlights the challenges this use of force poses for the just war ethic.

From this perspective, terrorism can be analyzed in terms of its *agency*, its *methods*, and its *motives*. The most striking characteristic of the attacks of September 11, 2001, was their source: a transnational network of actors who demonstrated their capability to launch a sophisticated, coordinated attack in the very heart of the world's most complex and powerful nation. To put this question of agency in perspective, one must relate it to the fact that the rise of transnational movements and organizations has been a major aspect of international relations since the 1970s. For the past thirty years scholars have struggled with the question of how to weigh the relative role of transnational actors against the classical analysis that has focused on the power of the state. Early versions of this research highlighted the transnational organizing capabilities of corporate power; in the late 1980s, attention shifted to other transnational networks that often pursued normative goals such as human rights, conflict resolution, and economic development. On the whole, transnationality came to be regarded as a source of complexity in world politics but also a hopeful development that could restrain state power in some instances and complement it in others. The attacks of September 11 highlighted what had been recognized but not sufficiently emphasized: that transnational capabilities could be placed in the service of a murderous strategy. Like the state, transnational actors could be beneficial or deadly forces.

Transnational terrorism—like most terrorist groups—focuses on "soft" targets; these targets usually involve civilians. A more discriminating historical review would need to acknowledge instances when terrorists avoided attacking civilians, but the dominant character of terrorist attacks involves primarily civilian targets. As noted above, a double dynamic lies behind this strategy: First, terrorist organizations are incapable of sustaining "conventional" military operations; second, civilian casualties contribute directly to a principal terrorist objective—creating pervasive fear in the general public.

Terrorists usually have specific political goals and objectives; where this is the case it can help in analyzing the nature of the group and even determining whether any politically viable option exists to solve the conflict with terrorists. The September 11 attackers seemed to be motivated in part by political issues in the Middle East. It is very likely, however, that politics does not exhaust either their objectives or their worldview. There is a transcendent dimension to some terrorist claims and strategies—a realm of ideas, objectives, and goals that transcend the political order and politics cannot meet. Such a perspective can be a mix of religion and politics or some secularized ideology that is not reducible to the normal conception of politics. When such a transcendent vision is at work there are two consequences. First, it is difficult to conceive of negotiations or compromises that would satisfactorily meet the terrorist's goals. Second, transcendent purpose often relativizes any restraint on means. The perceived value of the ends erodes a sense of restraint or tends to legitimate any means in pursuit of the transcendent goal.

Each of these dimensions of terrorism poses a challenge for the traditional just war ethic. The transnational character of the actors requires accommodation by an ethic that, at least in the modern era, has focused on the role of states and international institutions. Therefore, like governments, international lawyers, and the United Nations itself, just war ethics must decide how such groups are to be classified as actors (e.g., the proper authority criterion), what distinctions should be made between civilian and combatant status among them, and who has the legitimate right to use force against them. In addressing these questions, the long and varied history of the just war ethic may provide resources. Prior to the modern era, with its clear delineation of sovereignty, the just war ethic functioned in the medieval polity of multiple political actors and overlapping lines of authority. Although none of this applies to terrorists as such, it does offer some background for addressing nonstate actors with systemic capabilities.

In addition, one strain of just war thinking sought to analyze what the claims of "just revolution" would look like. Clearly one criterion is that such actors would have to observe an ethic of means and could not resort to terror as a tactic. The categories of just revolution, however, provide a way to test the claims of nonstate actors against an established polity. Transposing this analysis to the international level would be a formidable task, though not wholly different from previous experience in the tradition.

However, the second characteristic of terrorism—its conscious, purposeful, indiscriminate violence—must weigh heavily in any assessment of the status of terrorists. Just causes are never enough in the just war tradition. The need to hold firmly to the noncombatant immunity criterion is fundamental for this traditional ethic. It applies with equal stringency to states and nonstate actors. To erode this principle is to lose the most effective barrier between limited use of force and murder.

In addressing the claims of transcendent terrorism, the just war ethic brings lessons from its history. Through the Middle Ages, the tradition justified war for both political and religious purposes. In adapting to the era of the sovereign state and seeking to accommodate the lessons of the religious wars of the sixteenth and seventeenth centuries, the just war ethic withdrew legitimation for any form of religious *casus belli*, restricting just cause to the legitimate needs of the political community. The experience of the just war ethic, properly adapted, may be of particular value in addressing the political-religious relationship. Unlike most secular political analysis, it is sensitive to the role of religious beliefs, convictions, and communities in the political process. It also has learned from difficult experience, however, that justifying military force with a religious rationale distorts both politics and religion.

The moral analysis of and judgment on terrorism also must include moral assessment of actors that seek to defeat terrorism. The "war on terrorism" fought in the name of protecting moral values must be judged by the traditional moral standards of war. Again, a detailed casuistry is not possible here, but the direction of how the moral assessment should proceed can be indicated. In describing the response to the terrorist acts of September 11, the United States has roughly distinguished a two-phase response. The first phase, directed against al-Qa`ida in Afghanistan, has been under way for several months at this writing; the second is the pursuit of terrorists (al-Qa`ida and others with global capability) beyond Afghanistan.

The response of the United States and allied states to the attack of September 11 clearly fell within the moral category of just cause. The attack itself and subsequent statements from Usama bin Ladin threatening future terrorist action gave rise to the right of self-defense—one of the basic moral categories and a right rooted in Article 51 of the UN charter. Two questions have been raised about this argument based on self-defense. Because terrorism is a crime, some observers have asked whether the best response is to pursue terrorists through a combination of police and legal measures. Others have raised the issue of whether the last resort criterion had been tested in the U.S. response. Both questions are useful precisely because the understandable sense of loss and vulnerability in the United States produced very few arguments about whether a military response was needed. The crime versus war question is a very useful distinction for the long term but not a reason for withholding an initial military response targeted on al-Qa`ida in Afghanistan. The struggle with terrorism will be a long, multidimensional effort. The meaning of the "war on terrorism" will be much closer to that of the cold war than to that of the Gulf War. In this effort police work, legal strategies, and collaboration with other governments on several fronts will be much more prominent than military power. Yet al-Qa`ida posed a direct military threat, and as the fighting showed, they are a battle-hardened adversary. The government of Afghanistan was unwilling or unable to take action against them. The conditions of Article 51 were fulfilled, in my view, and the strategic need to dismantle the main corps of al-Qa`ida troops required the use of force. These arguments also are the basis for my judgment that last resort in the case of Afghanistan was met. Measures short of force would not have dislodged al-Qa`ida in Afghanistan.

That leaves the just means test. As noted above, the issue of means has been the dominant ethical question in the nuclear age and the predominant point of debate regarding U.S. action in the Persian Gulf, in Somalia, and in Kosovo. It certainly will remain a central question in the struggle against terrorism. Precisely because terrorists are criticized for not observing any means test in war, states that oppose them must be able to defend their response in light of the just means test. At this writing, the data are not comprehensive enough for a final judgment on U.S. strategy and tactics. As in the wars of the 1990s, there is evidence that the United States used rules of engagement that did not involve the direct targeting of civilians. There also were solid reports that civilians were killed by U.S. bombing. Some of the questions raised in Kosovo and the Gulf War were raised again; these questions have less to do with the conscious targeting of civilians than with how much risk to civilians the United States was willing to allow and whether proportionality in civilian areas was observed. Final answers to these questions and good comparisons among these diverse conflicts require more detailed studies. My sense is that just cause clearly was met in Afghanistan, and just means were a goal of the strategy—but that goal was not always met.

Stage two of the war on terrorism will raise a different range of questions than the fighting in Afghanistan raised. First, the just cause question cannot be assumed to be answered if the struggle moves beyond Afghanistan. The Bush administration has cited sixty countries as possible targets; just cause would have to be demonstrated in each case. Second, just means will require a differentiated test. Identifying a terrorist organization in a society is one thing; the question of whether the government is actively engaged with the terrorists or is tolerating or unable to restrain them must be determined. Even if the terrorists and the government are allied, the civilian society cannot be swept into the struggle as a target. Third, in analyzing the overall strategy for fighting terrorism across the globe, a question of proportionality must be raised. As the world's leading military power, the United States has unique positive responsibilities, but it also must observe unique restraints. To some degree this position drives the question back to nonintervention. The intervention contemplated in President Bush's address to West Point graduates in June 2002 is not humanitarian intervention but the kind of Great Power intervention that legal restrictions seek to restrain. That restraint is argued in light of the need for order among states and in the name of containing imperialist impulses. Terrorism is a direct threat to order within and among states, but resistance to it cannot be pursued in such a way that the United States itself becomes a threat to the order of world politics. At this writing, it is not clear that U.S. policy has a sense of necessary limits to correlate with its sense of urgency to combat terrorism.

The ethic of war in this new century cannot focus exclusively on any of these three large questions. Nuclear danger remains; humanitarian intervention very likely will be needed again; terrorism must be resisted, but means will be as important as ends in this struggle. The ancient ethic has the elements to respond to these questions, but—as in the past—it must be shaped and structured to meet new demands.

Notes

Themes developed in this essay also appear in Bryan Hehir, "International Politics, Ethics and the Use of Force," *Georgetown Journal of International Affairs* 3, no. 2 (summer/fall 2002): 17–23.

1. A sampling—illustrative of a much broader collection—would include Stanley Hoffman, *Duties Beyond Borders* (Syracuse, N.Y.: Syracuse University Press, 1981); Michael Walzer, *Just and Unjust Wars: A Moral Argument with Historical Illustrations* (New York: Basic Books, 1977); Terry Nardin and David R. Mapel, eds., *Traditions of International Ethics* (Cambridge: Cambridge University Press, 1992); David R. Mapel and Terry Nardin, eds., *International Society: Diverse Ethical Perspectives* (Princeton, N.J.: Princeton University Press, 1998). See also the journals *Philosophy and Public Affairs* and *Ethics and International Affairs*.

2. James Turner Johnson, *Just War Tradition and the Restraint of War* (Princeton, N.J.: Princeton University Press, 1981); Paul Ramsey and Stanley Hauerwas, *Speak Up for Just War or Pacifism* (University Park: Pennsylvania State University Press, 1988); cf. Walzer, *Just and Unjust Wars*; Joseph S. Nye, Jr., *Nuclear Ethics* (New York: Free Press, 1986).

3. Johnson, *Just War Tradition and the Restraint of War*, represents the historical perspective; for the philosophical perspective see James Childress, "Just War Theories," *Theological Studies* 39 (1978): 427–53.

4. Frederick H. Russell, *The Just War in the Middle Ages* (Cambridge: Cambridge University Press, 1975), 16*ff*.

5. Reinhold Niebuhr, "Augustine's Political Realism," in Robert McAfee Brown, ed., *The Essential Reinhold Niebuhr* (New Haven, Conn.: Yale University Press, 1986), 123–41.

6. Kenneth Waltz, *Man, The State and War: A Theoretical Analysis* (New York: Columbia University Press, 2001).

7. John Courtney Murray, *We Hold These Truths: Catholic Reflections on the American Proposition* (New York: Sheed and Ward, 1960), 270.

8. See McGeorge Bundy, *Danger and Survival: Choices about the Bomb in the First Fifty Years* (New York: Random House, 1988).

9. Quoted in Fred M. Kaplan, *The Wizards of Armageddon* (New York: Simon and Schuster, 1983), 31–32.

10. See Harvard Nuclear Study Group, *Living with Nuclear Weapons* (Cambridge, Mass.: Harvard University Press, 1983).

11. See Nye, *Nuclear Ethics*, and Walzer, *Just and Unjust War*; Paul Ramsey, *The Just War: Force and Political Responsibility* (New York: Charles Scribner's Sons, 1968); John Finnis, Joseph M. Boyle, Jr., and Germain Grisez, *Nuclear Deterrence, Morality and Realism* (Oxford: Clarendon Press, 1987).

12. Nye, *Nuclear Ethics*, reviews a spectrum of positions in response to the nuclear age. See also David Hollenbach, "Ethics in Distress: Can There Be Just Wars in the Nuclear Age?" and William V. O'Brien, "The Failure of Deterrence and the Conduct of War," both in William V. O'Brien and John Langan, eds., *The Nuclear Dilemma and the Just War Tradition* (Lexington, Mass.: D. C. Heath and Co., 1986).

13. Walzer, *Just and Unjust War*, 274.

14. National Conference of Catholic Bishops, *The Challenge of Peace: God's Promise and Our Response* (Washington, D.C.: U.S. Catholic Conference, 1983).

15. Samantha Power, "Bystanders to Genocide," *The Atlantic* 288 (September 2001): 84–108.

16. Adam Roberts, "NATO's Humanitarian War over Kosovo," *Survival* 41, no. 3 (autumn 1999): 102.

17. Catherine Guicherd, "International Law and the War in Kosovo," *Survival* 41, no. 2 (summer 1999): 19–34.

18. See J. Bryan Hehir, "Intervention: From Theories to Cases," *Ethics and International Affairs* 9 (1995): 1–13; and idem, "Military Intervention and National Sovereignty: Recasting the Relationship," in Jonathan Moore, ed., *Hard Choices: Moral Dilemmas in Humanitarian Intervention* (Lanham, Md.: Rowman and Littlefield, 1998), 29–54.

19. Roberts, "NATO's Humanitarian War," 110.

20. See J. Bryan Hehir, "The Just War Ethic Revisited," in Linda B. Miller and Michael Joseph Smith, eds., *Ideas and Ideals: Essays on Politics in Honor of Stanley Hoffman* (Boulder, Colo.: Westview Press, 1993), 144–61. Ramsey's entire effort—

unmatched in volume by any single author—focused on limits in use; see his *The Just War.*

21. Nicholas J. Wheeler, "Humanitarian Intervention after Kosovo: Emergent Norm, Moral Duty or the Coming of Anarchy?" *International Affairs* 77, no. 1 (January 2001): 116.

22. Quoted in Roberts, "NATO's Humanitarian War," 114.

23. See Stanley Hoffman, *World Disorders: Troubled Peace in the Post-Cold War Era* (Lanham, Md.: Rowman and Littlefield, 1998).

2

Ethical Implications of Kosovo Operations

GEN. JAMES P. McCARTHY, USAF (RET.)

T HE PURPOSE OF THIS CHAPTER is to provide an assessment of the ethical implications of the North Atlantic Treaty Organization's (NATO) campaign in Kosovo against Serbian forces. I offer this perspective as someone who has flown in combat and commanded combat forces, although I also gained many insights during my visits to Kosovo and the countries supporting the combat operations there while serving as chairman of the Secretary of Defense's Task Force for Kosovo Lessons Learned. In this chapter I articulate my personal view that NATO acted in an unethical manner with respect to certain just war considerations. Before I discuss my judgment about the ethics of NATO tactics and military conduct, let me be clear that the United States has set the standard in the Western world for conducting effective military actions. Although I am critical of NATO's strategy and its policy implementation, my overall assessment is that Kosovo military operations were performed very effectively, with a high regard for avoiding civilian casualties. Our professional military people can be very proud of what they accomplished, even though my focus here is on our nation's and NATO's errors.

NATO's decision to intervene in Kosovo evoked arguments for and against. On one hand, NATO had the tacit consent of the international community. There was legal precedent for humanitarian intervention, and many observers argued that there was a moral obligation to intervene to stop the genocide and ethnic cleansing of Kosovar Albanians and the mass destruction of property. The arguments against intervention also are well known. State sovereignty always is an issue; many lawyers argue that there is no basis in international law for intervention, given long-standing precedents of nonintervention assumed in international relations. Moreover, interventions were not undertaken in other circumstances that may have been even more horrible and inhumane. So why intervene in Kosovo?

The just war tradition offers strong and widely shared principles for moral deliberation concerning the use of force. The religious and moral roots of this tradition run deep and are discussed in several other chapters in this book (see especially chapters 1 and 5). I direct my comments on just war to the moral dimensions of the tactics, strategy, and diplomacy that NATO and the United States undertook in Kosovo. I acknowledge that one may make a moral argument to intervene in Kosovo. If one is an advocate of intervention and recalls some of the tenets of just war theory—just cause, right intention, prospects of success, and legitimate authority—I judge that these tenets were met. My criticism is based on the preliminary analysis that NATO's political and military actions leading up to and during the Kosovo operations were inconsistent with just war principles in two primary areas. First, military intervention should always be the last resort, and this was not the case in Kosovo. Second, the incremental application of power in the air campaign was less effective than it could have been; furthermore, the specific rules of engagement seemed to be inconsistent in their application. The incremental approach and limited rules of engagement had a direct impact on the application of military force and the proportionality criterion of just war thinking. Thus, I focus my critique on last resort and proportionality.

Last Resort

America's push for a revolution in military affairs and use of precision technology has had a significant impact on U.S. military decision-making processes and has given NATO and the United States an increased number of alternative courses of action. Unfortunately, these military options are better developed and often appear to be more easily implemented than diplomatic or economic options, especially in complex and intractable political or ethnic conflicts. Technological advancements, particularly by U.S. military forces, make it appear as though we are capable of quick and clean skirmishes. That expectation—supported by standoff weapons capability, the lethality of small units, and precision strikes—increases the military options and the type of forces that may be selected for operations.

In the past, the time required for a military build-up was used by decision makers to explore other means to resolve a conflict. Now U.S. forces have been trained and equipped for rapid deployment and do not require a lengthy period to prepare for military action. The military option is so convenient that the time before engaging in operations is not always used to best advantage. Other options should be more thoroughly explored, but if the military option is chosen, the time before engagement should be spent clarifying objectives and the ability to meet them with a planned course of action. My argument is that in Kosovo operations, NATO did not use this time to plan a coherent course of action—which brings me to my first critique involving the *ad bellum* consideration of last resort.

The operations in Kosovo clearly illustrate the point that NATO trapped itself in a policy box. NATO's threats to use force as a way to achieve a negotiated settlement with Slobodan Milosevic created a box that left no alternative to the use of force when Milosevic declined to accept its terms. Focusing entirely on using military threats to achieve its objective, NATO failed to use other tools of statecraft that might have prevented the war. After the United States and NATO raised the stakes with the threat of force, it was, as we say, "sundown at the OK Corral." Being trapped in this policy box led to a major miscalculation: NATO was so convinced that Milosevic would capitulate that it was unprepared to conduct sustained combat operations. Political leaders were so optimistic about the success of the Rambouillet negotiations that military leaders were not permitted to (and thus did not) plan a major military campaign. When the first military operations started, only fifty-one targets had been selected for the air campaign, given the expectation that Milosevic would capitulate and that the operation would be completed in two days. When the desired outcome was not achieved, a reassessment came back that the war certainly would be completed in ten days. Only as the operations continued was there gradual recognition that this was going to be a relatively long war, especially if NATO did not change its military strategy.

Milosevic was so convinced that NATO would never agree on combat operations that he attempted to call NATO's bluff. NATO sent many mixed signals—particularly through comments rejecting the use of ground forces, which conveyed to Milosevic an apparent lack of will and caused him to make major miscalculations. Further miscalculations on both sides led to an ill-timed initiation of the war and then prolonged combat operations. This miscalculation created more loss of life and physical damage that seriously affected the lives of most Serbians living in the bombed areas—and would continue to affect them long after the air campaign ended.

So what are the consequences of that particular policy box and its miscalculation? Political circumstances leading to hostilities precluded NATO from taking any action other than war because both sides would have judged anything less as NATO demonstrating a lack of resolve. This ill-conceived political approach early on, in my view, placed the military in a position of not having a strategy and of not planning a decisive military campaign to which NATO member nations could agree. NATO—representing 570 million people with 56 percent of the world's gross national product (GNP)—went to war against a nation of 22 million people with less than 1 percent of the world's GNP. NATO's combined military power carried out 38,000 aircraft sorties, using 820 aircraft; NATO forces fired more than 300 cruise missiles and dropped 23,000 bombs. In the end, it took 78 days to achieve very limited military objectives—hardly a compelling victory! In my view, it also led to the moral problems I discuss below.

Proportionality

The second major critique concerns the gradual escalation of force as it relates to the *in bello* principle of proportionality. NATO member nations began the conflict with no shared political or military plan of how to fight; they lacked a strategy on the use of ground forces and had no agreement on targeting policies. Disagreements communicated a lack of solidarity and a loss of momentum that led to political actions designed primarily to demonstrate NATO solidarity and resolve rather than to achieve specific combat objectives effectively, which further increased the limitations on the warfighters as the conflict progressed.

To summarize a very complex issue: Many observers believed that the way to bring the conflict to a quick conclusion was to strike at the heart of Serbia and its military capability, as well as to destroy other targets to diminish political support for Milosevic. Of course, this strategy also had significant negative effects on the Serbian people.

Those who were appalled by what was happening in Kosovo attempted to defeat a very astute adversary and stop the ethnic cleansing from the air during the worst weather conditions in the Balkans for probably a century. This action placed NATO's air forces in a very difficult and tenuous situation, exacerbated by the fact that even military leaders could not agree on the proper strategy for conducting the operation. The public announcement of "no use of ground forces" gave Milosevic crucial opportunities for his forces to operate and survive and, hence, to continue ethnic cleansing while significantly increasing the difficulty of NATO's task and undermining its effectiveness. This policy judgment was carried to an extreme when the Supreme Allied Commander Europe (SACEUR) was not permitted to establish a ground component commander element to advise him on how to conduct operations against Serbian forces in Kosovo; the justification was that the public would perceive the move as planning the use of ground forces. In the end, NATO had no consensus on strategy; the desire to demonstrate resolve as well as other events drove strategic decisions.

One important lesson that the United States learned in Vietnam was that an escalatory approach with a slow application of military power prolongs conflict and increases the damage not only to people but also to the infrastructure of a nation. In fact, gradual escalation actually stiffens people's resolve over time because a nation can adjust to a gradual worsening of conditions under the incremental application of power by an adversary. Instead of ending the conflict quickly, the effect is to prolong the war and increase the damage. In Kosovo, we repeated this mistake. By gradually escalating force, we actually undermined the just war principle of proportionality. The *in bello* criterion of proportionality demands that the means used and the harm that comes from them should be commensurate with the aims they intend to achieve. Generally, proportionality is designed to prevent excessive use of force. Although I reaffirm the ethical importance of proportionality, I want to convey the concept that insufficient or tepid use of force also can be quite destructive and can erode the ethical imprimatur of a just war.

I add to this discussion of proportionality the matter of target selection. NATO target lists generally are developed on the basis of an analysis of what is called *effects-based warfare*. If the objective is to remove the enemy's use of a communications system, for example, key nodes can be destroyed to achieve the desired military effect yet permit fairly easy restoration after the war ends. The desired effect—eliminating use of the enemy's capability—can be achieved with limited but precisely focused means of force. Whereas in World War II "dumb bombs" were dropped in large numbers and destroyed entire facilities, during the Persian Gulf War the United States was able to apply precision strikes to oil refineries and other targets in Iraq. For example, we learned that we could shut down an entire facility's operation by destroying a set of controls in the southeast corner of a certain building. The amount of damage done to the facility might have been 1 or 2 percent, but the *effect* was that the facility was rendered nonoperational until new controls could be procured from the West and installed.

Yet in Kosovo, because the NATO approval process effectively permitted any nation's leadership to withdraw a target from the list, the target sets were relatively ineffective strategically. If a key target was taken off the list, NATO—continually looking for ways to demonstrate its resolve—had to find other targets to hit instead. Striking these lower-priority targets may have been more destructive and less effective than would have been the case had NATO leaders allowed military forces to strike the original targets. Military leaders respect the right and rationale of nations and political leaders to establish the parameters for military operations, but the consequences of politically withholding individual targets can be significant because it reduces operational effectiveness and increases the number of targets required to achieve the desired effect. NATO's compromises on targeting also undercut its political and strategic objective—which was to shorten the war and minimize the damage as just war theory advises (and effects-based warfare allows).

In my judgment, proportionality works two ways. We all understand that too much force can be applied—force that would be disproportionate to accomplishing the objective. However, too little force, or force that is improperly applied—particularly with significant political limits to maintain a consensus of the publics among the NATO countries—increases physical destruction and human casualties. It is not easy to judge or analyze this outcome, but I believe that NATO's combined political and military actions prolonged the war and made Serbia and Kosovo's efforts—as well as NATO's—to rebuild the war-torn nation unnecessarily difficult.

Furthermore, because Slobodan Milosevic failed to capitulate in the early days of the war, NATO leaders saw the need to escalate their efforts and build momentum by deploying more combat aircraft than were needed and increasing the number of targets struck each day. The result was more risk to NATO forces and increased damage to Serbia. Obviously, this course of action was less successful than if sufficient military force had initially been properly applied.

Finally, there also were weighty operational consequences—the worst, from my standpoint as an aviator, was delayed decision making about the operational flight cycle. Some "withholds" of targets were decided so late that the aircrew had already started engines when it was notified of the mission cancellation. As a result, the "flight integrity" of the formation could not be preserved. Formations of combat aircraft that had briefed together and depended on each other for mutual support and protection were launched partially, thereby increasing the risk to each aircrew and jeopardizing the missions. Better policy decisions could have obviated these unnecessary risks that were forced on many pilots.

Some Other Ethical Considerations

My final point is much more difficult to resolve. The increasing restrictions on forces conducting military operations have consequences for both sides: One side's limitations may work to the other side's advantage. In some ways, Milosevic won the information war, in that he was able to exploit NATO forces' commitments to restrictive rules of engagement by making NATO appear ineffective and attempting to undermine its legitimacy. The military should always be accountable for its actions, during and following combat operations, and the media provides an important role in that accountability. I am not arguing against political or ethical constraints as such. However, I cite some examples of how NATO changed the rules of engagement as a result of Milosevic's tactics, which exploited the political and ethical constraints under which U.S. and NATO forces chose to operate. These constraints, in turn, put U.S. and coalition forces at increased risk and created ethical dilemmas for both our forces and the nations involved.

A military term—*center of gravity*—identifies a focal point for the energies of a military force. The air campaign started when U.S. intelligence sources indicated that Milosevic was going to send a large force into Kosovo. When he did so, the Serbian tactical formations en route to Kosovo became vulnerable targets under the guidance of NATO Joint Surveillance Targeting and Reconnaissance System (JSTARS) aircraft. After NATO attacked those forces, however, Milosevic dispersed his troops quite effectively so that the ethnic cleansing in Kosovo was carried out at the company or platoon level rather than in large tactical formations. This dispersal increased the number of targets, making them individually less vulnerable. This dispersal also increased the difficulty of targeting Serbian troops—especially because they were dispersed among civilians. Military convoys were interspersed with civilian vehicles; in many cases, civilian vehicles were commandeered to move military supplies and equipment. So it was very difficult to end or disrupt ethnic cleansing from the air.

This analysis also demonstrates how the Serbs attempted to exploit civilian casualties as U.S. center of gravity. The most effective way for Milosevic to defeat U.S. and NATO forces was to undermine their legitimacy by inducing substantial collateral damage and forcing a withdrawal. Milosevic used schools, hospitals, and mosques to protect his forces because he understood that the United States and NATO would—and did—take great care to avoid collateral damage to these structures. For example, when I was in Kosovo looking at targets that had been destroyed, there was a tank sitting right up against the wall of a hospital. The tank had been positioned within a foot of the wall to discourage coalition forces, bound by the rules of war, from targeting it. In the end, thanks to advanced laser-guided munitions, the tank was successfully hit without damaging the hospital. The Serbian forces also understood which targets were high priorities to NATO and when attacks on those targets were likely to occur. Serbian soldiers used civilians as human hostages by locking them inside these target areas, anticipating that within a relatively short period a NATO weapon would destroy it, along with the people inside. When this happened, they would quickly drag the press over to observe the casualties. Thus, NATO faced a dilemma: The U.S. military has always attempted to minimize collateral damage, but the consequence of doing so in this situation effectively encouraged Milosevic to engage in more of these actions. How should one handle that moral dilemma?

There is no easy answer to this question, and some other considerations add to this issue. Fighter pilots facing moral dilemmas need to know where the target is located, as well as the rules of engagement. As civilians become a center of gravity, avoiding collateral damage becomes an extremely important rule of engagement. Consider the burden placed on a fighter pilot flying at approximately 700 miles per hour, who not only must find the target and destroy it within the few seconds he has in this terminal targeting phase but also must do the following: confirm the identity of the target as the correct one; ensure that the ordnance he is about to employ meets the target's requirements; and calculate that there will be little or no collateral damage. To the pilots' credit, several of them returned to their bases saying, "I could not make all those judgments." However, that choice also meant that the mission was not completed successfully. Combat restrictions also had the effect of requiring "eyes on target"—either through an electro-optical sensor such as the Predator or Hunter unmanned aerial vehicles (UAV) or someone in another aircraft who could assess the situation and radio back to the other pilots that the targeting requirements could be met. All of these requirements introduced a significantly greater risk to those conducting the operation.

One effect of these conditions and restrictions was that military commanders asked for smaller and smaller weapons. Recall the story of the television tower in downtown Belgrade. The commander, recognizing the rules of engagement, said, "OK, I must take down this tower, and I cannot affect the top floor where civilians work." Whether the coalition forces should have struck a dual-use communications tower is another issue, but how does one destroy the target? A 2,000-pound bomb would have taken down the tower in a moment, but with much collateral damage. The commander requested that the high explosives be removed from bombs, so the bombs could be dropped with concrete in them. This action would take the tower down by using kinetic energy, without destroying the building, and would have worked very effectively. However, it would have taken several weeks before the nonexplosive "bombs" were ready. In the end, a tactical cruise missile was used. It approached from a precise direction at a precise altitude, hit the tower, knocked it down, and avoided collateral damage. That is a fairly difficult and expensive way to kill a target, but the goal was achieved. The bottom line coming out of Kosovo was that commanders asked for smaller weapons because such precise weapons permit the destruction of a target while minimizing collateral damage.

Conclusion

My judgment of the air campaign in Kosovo is that NATO had a just cause, the right intention, a good prospect for success, and legitimate authority. All of that is good, but I would argue that with regard to the criteria of last resort and proportionality, NATO failed to meet the test. This failure was not because coalition forces acted immorally but because the issues and ethical challenges were complex, and we have not yet learned how to grapple with them effectively.

So what can be done? Preliminary findings coming from the Kosovo war must be considered within an ethical context. Some of the ideas presented here will require statistical analysis. For example, does a prolonged and escalated approach truly cause more damage than a forceful and quick approach taken at the onset? I think the answer is "yes," but the question certainly warrants sustained and careful treatment.

We also need to expand the moral and ethical discussion by bringing it to the more practical levels of strategy and tactics. What are the dilemmas, and how should we deal with them? I think that most military leaders—at least when I was in command—take just war considerations or other ethical concerns into account. We need to broaden that understanding, along with our education; we need to write about and discuss these issues further. Yet while we talk about educating our military leaders, in my mind the principal problem in Kosovo was policy leadership. Educating policymakers about the implications of their political constraints certainly is a difficult challenge, but not an impossible one.

The political changes in Serbia are a wonderful outcome of NATO's decision to intervene in Kosovo. Most observers applaud the relatively peaceful transition that removed Slobodan Milosevic from power. I think these events demonstrate support for those who argue that NATO should have intervened. That rationale, however, does not change the arguments that I have made about *how* we chose to intervene.

In sum, the ethical lessons learned from our operations in Kosovo are twofold. First, military force should always be the last resort, after all other courses of action and tools of statecraft have failed to achieve our political objectives. Second, once a decision to intervene militarily has been reached, military force should be applied proportionately but with effective and sufficient force to bring the conflict to a close as rapidly as possible; doing otherwise may cause greater damage and place one's own forces at unnecessary risk. The interdisciplinary dialogue this book seeks to initiate can broaden the understanding and increase appreciation of these and other moral challenges of humanitarian military operations.

3

An Editor's View of Kosovo: Dilemmas and Criteria for Humanitarian Intervention

MARGARET O'BRIEN STEINFELS

WHERE FR. BRYAN HEHIR HAS RENDERED a certain degree of moral judgment in his chapter and General James McCarthy has rendered a certain degree of strategic criticism, what I do, as a magazine editor, is render opinions—and we know how ephemeral those can be. Decisions about humanitarian intervention ultimately depend on people: the citizens of this country and others coming to understand what it is that is going on in a given country or conflict and ultimately affirming—or not—the policies of their government. I tackle my subject as both an editorial writer and a citizen by asking and answering five questions.

What Is *Commonweal* Doing When We Write Editorials?

Briefly, I regard an editorial as a concise expression of opinion on a pressing issue of the day, written primarily to persuade our readers of the magazine's views and conclusions on the subject. We have been doing this at *Commonweal* since 1924. Our readers are accustomed to a fairly elaborate but compact editorial analysis containing information and argumentation, put forth in a limited amount of editorial space. With regard to Kosovo, as with most issues having to do with war and peace, the magazine has applied exactly the criteria that Hehir, McCarthy, and other contributors to this book talk about: just war criteria. Strictly speaking, these criteria represent a philosophical-ethical-political framework, rather than a religious argument, for justifying—or not—the turn to armed conflict. Nonetheless, this framework is integral to my understanding of the Catholic tradition's approach to issues of war and peace. *Commonweal* has never been a party to the view "my country, right or wrong," which had a strong presence in the Catholic community through the Vietnam War; nor are we pacifists, who also have a vigorous and growing presence in the Catholic community. (As long as I was at *Commonweal*, we did not fall into either camp, though views can change—and they do, even in the Catholic Church and even at *Commonweal*.)

In the case of Kosovo, our position was shaped by the just war tradition, and it reached the following conclusions regarding *ad bellum* and *in bello* criteria. As the crisis developed, a genuine effort had been made to settle the outstanding issues through negotiations. The killing and expulsion of the Albanian population called for intervention in Kosovo. The goal of returning these refugees was legitimate; force became necessary when Slobodan Milosevic refused to concede and began to expel Albanians from Kosovo. The bombing appeared to be measured. Civilians were not purposely targeted, though destruction of roads and electric power plants certainly would affect the civilian population in the long run. Moreover, the United States and its European allies were ready to negotiate a cease-fire at the first sign from the Serbs. *Commonweal* opposed a ground war on just war grounds: We did not think it would succeed or that it could avoid serious civilian casualties. Recognizing how elusive conditions for a just war may have been in the Kosovo intervention, I raise some questions in this chapter about where that tradition fits, given the kinds of conflicts we face in a post–cold war world.

What Did the Editors of *Commonweal* Actually Know When They Were Writing Editorials on Kosovo?

Editors often know a little about a lot of things. From longevity and experience, we also may come to know a lot about a little. The magazine's previous positions on matters of war and peace (on Bosnia in particular) probably were the most powerful influence on *Commonweal's* position in favor of intervention in Kosovo. We had long urged armed military intervention in Bosnia by U.S. and European forces. It was clear to us, as it was to many active and informed citizens, that the UN peacekeeping troops posted there were an obstacle to both peace and war. The presence of lightly armed soldiers restricted from active defense — even of themselves — made them ready hostages for all sides, creating a political and military paralysis that permitted killings, torture, and a high degree of material destruction and ultimately implicating the peacekeepers in human rights abuses and genocide.

Events in Srebrenica in July 1995, when thousands of Muslim men and boys under the protection of UN peacekeepers were seized and murdered by the Serbs, remained etched in peoples' memories, though the full details of the savagery emerged only after military intervention in Kosovo had ended (in a November 1999 UN report). Attentive observers, editors included, saw in Kosovo a potential replay of Bosnia. We were not alone. President Clinton, in his national address announcing intervention in Kosovo, evoked the images and events in Bosnia, as did many journalists and commentators. What people had seen happen in Bosnia was a critical factor in the call to do something about Kosovo. Attentive citizens knew from Bosnia that Milosevic and his special police were capable of any atrocity.

Who were the special police, who were the militia, who were the gangs, and who were the military in Yugoslavia? At the time, there was a certain ambiguity about who was responsible, who was giving orders. What was clear, however, was that Slobodan Milosevic, president of Yugoslavia, was a ready and willing partner in ethnic cleansing, rape, murder, and genocide in Bosnia. Why wouldn't he do the same in Kosovo? And what of the Serbian people themselves — citizens of a democratic nation who had elected Milosevic? They seemed to be more than ready to support their leaders, to support the military and the militias. They seemed to tolerate just about anything in the name of preserving their nation and culture. This assessment raises the question: How responsible are whole-hearted civilian supporters of a regime such as this? There are, of course, just war strictures against targeting of civilians. Since the war in Vietnam, where the military paid a high price for civilian casualties, these strictures have become a genuine consideration in U.S. military targeting policies. Distinctions become blurry, however, when dual-use facilities, such as bridges and electric power systems, are targeted. Michael Ignatieff, in his look at the war in Kosovo, claims that the single most effective attack against Serbia occurred on May 24, 1999, when NATO forces bombed the transformer yards that supplied the Yugoslav power grid. "Once the power went off in Belgrade the regime's days were numbered: . . . such civilian support as it had began to ebb away." Yet as Ignatieff admits, "the most effective strike of the war was also the most problematic."[1] We can assume that this issue will continue to vex politicians and military planners, especially in cases of humanitarian intervention.

There are other ways of knowing as well. There often is a strong sense of connection to people from other nations working at the same tasks. *Commonweal*, like most other magazines of our kind, followed the events of central and eastern Europe—especially in Poland and Czechoslovakia—very closely in the 1980s and 1990s. *Commonweal* itself had close ties to *Todgodny Prozsnesky*, the Polish Catholic newspaper published in Krakow. Its editors and writers visited us in the 1990s, and we visited them.

Another way we know things is through direct personal experience. For example, I visited Sarajevo in 1968 with a group of French students—a visit that has always colored my sense of what the society was like. We were taken to the spot where, in 1914, Gavrilo Princip assassinated Archduke Ferdinand of Austria-Hungary. A sculpture of Princip's footsteps was embedded in the walk near the bridge where he fired the fatal shots. The Serbian guide described to our French translator the "patriot" who assassinated the archduke and thereby precipitated World War I. The description was relayed back through the group. By the time it reached the middle, the word "patriot" had become "assassin"; by the time it arrived at the end of the group, where I was standing, the word was "terrorist." This incident provides a sense of the layered history and complex understanding of how the Serbs saw themselves and how a group of French students saw the Serbs.

Commonweal's understanding of Kosovo was colored by the knowledge that under Tito, nationalism rather than communism held the country together. The tension and long struggle between Yugoslavia and the communist block colored the life of Yugoslavia and, one would have to say, the afterlife of Yugoslavia. Books that described the events in Bosnia also were an important influence on us.[2] Finally, the superintendent of my apartment building in New York—a former Yugoslav citizen from Macedonia who opposed intervention in Kosovo—kept me fully informed of relevant discussions on the World Wide Web.

There also were the images such as those shown on CNN. Despite the immediate power of television imagery, my impression is that print news reporting ultimately influences how people think about such events. John Burns, reporting from Bosnia for the *New York Times*, certainly had a great influence on how we at *Commonweal* saw the war. Burns was indefatigable in tracking down the Bosnia story. Steven Erlanger and Carlotta Gall did some of the same thing in Kosovo. Although *Commonweal* does not have access to Central Intelligence Agency or military intelligence services, we do have a broad range of information.

When we were writing editorials supporting military intervention, we knew about the decade-long resistance of Ibriham Rugova and the Albanian Kosovars. We knew that for ten years there had been a movement of peaceful resistance to Serbian control of the Albanian Kosovars. This resistance had its own civil infrastructure, which included separate educational and health services, as well as a system of political consultation and informal taxation (these institutions resembled the "parallel institutions" that had been so important a form of resistance in Czechoslovakia and Poland under the communists). The fact that the Albanian Kosovars made a strenuous effort to achieve their ends by peaceful means must be thrown into the hopper of how we saw what was going on in Kosovo. This form of resistance began to fail as Serbia tightened its military hold and the Albanians began to support the emergent Kosovo Liberation Army (KLA).

Commonweal editors knew that Americans and western Europeans had stood by in the early 1990s as the situation deteriorated. When James Baker served as George H. W. Bush's secretary of state, he famously remarked about Bosnia, "We have no dog in this fight." Indeed, American national interests—defined in classically narrow terms of secure borders and material survival—were not at stake in 1991, and most of Europe held the same view. So Yugoslavia ripped itself apart while the West stood by. The shelling of Sarajevo by the Serbs was the most infamous of the crimes televised around the world, but that was not the only city destroyed. Nor were Muslims and Croats the only victims; Serbs also were driven from their homes. The carnage became intolerable, all sides were exhausted, and finally the United Nations intervened. There followed the 1995 Dayton accords, masterminded by Richard Holbrooke with the acquiescence of Slobodan Milosevic.

We knew that the failure to deal with Kosovo was a serious flaw of the Dayton accords, which brought a peace of sorts to Bosnia. The Kosovars had hoped that a settlement of the conflict in Bosnia would include them. Those who read Holbrooke's *To End a War* can appreciate the difficulties negotiators would have faced had they taken up Kosovo.[3] It could have meant no end to the war in Bosnia because the passions that drove the Serbs and Milosevic over Kosovo would have destroyed Dayton.

Unlike many commentators, *Commonweal's* editorial board did not see the struggle in Kosovo primarily as a religious conflict between the Orthodox and the Muslims, although religious and cultural differences obviously color how the Serbs and Albanians see each other. (As a Catholic, I confess that the worlds of Islam and Eastern Orthodoxy are a mystery to me insofar as they function as religious institutions and as established or national churches. As an American Catholic who lives with the benefits of the First Amendment—particularly the separation of church and state—I have little sympathy for this amalgam of religiosity and nationalism.) In any case, in the course of the conflict Orthodox and Muslim religious leaders alike protested the violence on both sides. Though we at *Commonweal* did not think this was a religious conflict, I recognize that those who conclude that it was have at least this background fact of religion and nationalism to support their thesis.

In the fall of 1998, we also were aware that in Kosovo unarmed observers from the Commission for European Security were being harassed by the Serbs and manipulated by the KLA. We were conscious of the fact that there were many internecine conflicts and complex struggles going on within Kosovo before it emerged as a full-blown crisis. We knew that Albanian Kosovars were being expelled from their homes and communities, although they were not necessarily being expelled from the country itself. Finally, we were aware of the emergence of the KLA as an armed force in the struggle. Chris Hedges, writing in *Foreign Affairs*, described the KLA as a combination of terrorists, hard-line communists, drug-dealers, and smugglers.[4] That portrait was not wholly accurate, as we learned after the fact, but the notion that the KLA was a disciplined and cohesive fighting force seemed to be far-fetched (though it may have become so as a result of the war). It also is clear that the KLA played a very important role in bringing international attention to Kosovo in a way that Rugova's peaceful politics did not. The media must reflect on the attention-getting role that violence plays in comparison with the minimal attention garnered by people trying to carry out an alternate policy in a peaceful manner.

The negotiations at Rambouillet are discussed in this book by General McCarthy (who knows far more about the details than I), and I refer the reader to his chapter. At the time of the negotiations, Secretary of State Madeline Albright was subjected to a great deal of mockery because, it was said, she had overcommitted the United States and herself to a certain outcome, and that outcome didn't happen. Perhaps the negotiations at Rambouillet were a mistake or the proposed outcome was unrealistic. At the time, it seemed to be a reasonable effort to help end the conflict by peaceful means. Albright and many Americans thought that the problems in Kosovo could be resolved if the principals could meet in a Dayton-like negotiating situation. Was there any positive outcome from Rambouillet? I don't know. Perhaps the eventual French participation in the Kosovo intervention was influenced by the fact that these talks had gone on in France (it obviously was a major subject in French newspapers), and perhaps the French began to appreciate the downside to their traditional and uncritical alliance with the Serbs.

What, Finally, Was *Commonweal*'s Position on Intervention?

I confess that the issues of this book—"the sacred" and "the sovereign"—never came up in editorial discussions at *Commonweal* about Kosovo. These issues function at a level of abstraction that doesn't ordinarily interest editorial writers, whether at *Commonweal* or the *New York Times*, and probably does not influence military officers or state department officials either (as Robert Gallucci suggests in chapter 10).[5] In fact, I was astonished to encounter in the autumn of 1999 a professor of ethics and international law who issued a condemnation of NATO—which, he argued, had broken international law by violating the sovereignty of Yugoslavia. I was dumbfounded. In my view, Yugoslavia was no longer a sovereign state: It was in a state of devolution. Slovenia had left; Croatia had left; Bosnia had tried to leave and a war ensued—and now, here was Kosovo. To talk about violating the sovereignty of Yugoslavia seemed to me to avoid the real challenge of "failed states." Rather than defending sovereignty, perhaps philosophers and professors of international law ought to turn their attention to studying and defining the failed state and devising criteria by which others could calculate the prudence of intervention or nonintervention. (For a discussion of how the unjust conditions within failed states can legitimate foreign intervention—and, conversely, how a just order legitimates a state's sovereignty—see chapter 5.) What lessons and guidance do failed states such as Yugoslavia, Somalia, and Rwanda provide the international community?

At *Commonweal* we knew that just war criteria assume a notion of sovereignty. We discussed the issue of proper authority to declare war and who holds it (a matter that UN Secretary-General Kofi Annan took up in his September 2000 address to the UN). Our reading at *Commonweal* was something like this: If the UN cannot do anything about Kosovo, is there any other way something can be done? Who has the authority? Those who claim and exercise it—in this case, NATO? Bryan Hehir proposes in chapter 1 of this book some notions about how this just war thinking could be carried out in a more formal manner.

The most troubling questions for the *Commonweal* editors focused on civilian immunity and proportionality. Serb civilians in Serbia and Kosovo were given the benefit of these just war criteria, and rightly so. Yet these criteria are under pressure in a world in which nations are increasingly democratic and civilians very often are active proponents and supporters of armed conflict—no people more so than the Serbs. Slobodan Milosevic was democratically elected; he long had the support of Serbia's citizens because he was willing to use force to protect what the Serbs regarded as their territory and their legitimate interest in retaining parts of Croatia and Bosnia—and, of course, all of Kosovo.

The proportionality question (namely, whether the means—that is, the bombing—are in proportion to war goals) and questions about a reasonable chance of successfully ending the war are difficult to answer; perhaps they never will be answered. Did the NATO bombing cause the expulsions? Did the bombing bring about the very consequence it was intended to prevent? To date, I have seen little evidence that the bombing initiated or caused the expulsions, which had been going on internally for some time. Whether one considers accounts of "Operation Horseshoe"—the reputed Serbian plan to expel the Albanians, reported in the international press before war broke out—to be information or disinformation, it is clear that the Serbs were prepared to expel the Albanians. Perhaps the bombing simply provided a convenient excuse for the Serbs to continue what they had already begun, though we cannot be certain.

The *Commonweal* editors also spent a good deal of time on the question of the proportionality of a ground war. We were opposed to it. Nonetheless, I think that General McCarthy and Jean Bethke Elshtain are correct in arguing in this book (see chapters 2 and 4) that it was a strategic mistake for President Clinton to declare from the start that there would be no ground war. This announcement may have made the Serbs overconfident in their capacity to prevail. In any case, it seems to me that the deaths and destruction brought on by a ground war would have been out of keeping with the primary goal of the intervention—namely, returning the Albanian refugees to Kosovo. What we know about Serb abuse of civilians in Bosnia and Kosovo (including using them as shields and hostages) would have made it difficult for U.S. or European infantry to confront and fight Serb forces. The Serbian army put civilians on and in front of military convoys. What would have stopped them from tying people to tanks when confronted by other tanks? To me, a ground war seemed to be dangerous, destructive, and compromising of NATO forces.[6]

In Retrospect, What Have We Learned about Intervention?

To intervene or not, when to act and how to act: These are complex questions in a world in gradual transition from the inviolability to the permeability of the nation-state—a change fostered by instant communications and a slowly growing international consensus that human rights should trump national sovereignty.[7] International interventions *can* work, but they won't work everywhere, particularly at the current level of international development and cooperation. When they do work, they may require long-term commitments of resources and personnel that are difficult to sustain. At this stage of development, I don't think we can formulate a set of principles that will answer every question about when and how to intervene. Perhaps at this point in history, just war criteria (various versions of which are presented in this book) are as useful as any principles; they can help shape our thinking as we struggle to formulate and test a consistent set of principles about intervention. There are many theories—including conspiracy theories—about why interventions are undertaken, or not, and why they are successful or not. Instead of taking up the subject only at moments of crisis, we would do well to examine the causes and consequences of intervention—and, as a corollary, the conditions under which intervention ought not be pursued—in a serious and systematic way.

For example, does an intervention's effectiveness depend on the depth of a nation's internal political development? In South Africa, international intervention—consisting of economic sanctions; international isolation; and political, social, moral, and religious pressures—was successful over the long term: Apartheid came to an end. It was not a military intervention, but it took advantage of practically every other way to influence or coerce a society—in this case, a white society still capable of feeling moral and religious pressures, and a black society willing to live with the deprivations and rigors that sanctions brought. Black South Africans understood what was at stake; they understood political struggle and organization. They not only deployed various resistance strategies internally, they encouraged the international community to do so as well. These efforts turned out to be morally compelling, in a way that the sanctions against Iraq, for example, never can be.

Also in contrast to the situation in Iraq, a decent civil society ultimately may be put back into place in Serbia because the latter has elements of a well-developed political culture. Serbia has a history of being able to organize itself as a nation-state and a democratic society. Now that Milosevic is in the hands of the international tribunal at The Hague, the citizens of Serbia may be able to come to terms with the atrocities committed in their name and resume the life of a "normal" society. (See chapter 7 for further consideration of how to involve citizens in the prosecution of crimes against humanity.) Iraq, on the other hand, does not have a highly developed political culture; it remains, to all appearances, a society ruled by tribal and familial standards of loyalty. The most powerful tribe, though a minority, controls all of the means of violence. Until these conditions change, it is unlikely that sanctions or nonmilitary interventions in Iraq will succeed.

Rwanda, Sierra Leone, and other central African states have seen sporadic and generally ineffectual interventions by international organizations and other nations. What is to be done about these failed or collapsing states? Concerns about protecting or honoring sovereignty should not obscure the problems that arise when sovereignty ceases to be a coherent political description of a country.

Obviously, intervention always comes at a cost. William Shawcross's *Deliver Us from Evil: Peacekeepers, Warlords and a World of Endless Conflict* sets forth all the problematic issues that any policymaking process must take into consideration when an intervention, military or economic, is undertaken.[8] Shawcross's examples—including East Timor, Somalia, Cambodia, Rwanda, and Bosnia—make utterly clear that unintended consequences are the general rule of intervention, rather than the exception. There is no neat and tidy way to end military interventions, especially where two (or three or four) internal factions continue to struggle for control. Nor is secure, long-term care for refugees an unalloyed blessing: The longer refugees live in camps run by international organizations, the less likely they will ever go home or be permanently resettled; they easily can become another source of political instability.

What Do I Conclude from This Editorial Experience?

As an editorial writer, my dilemmas may be said to be the dilemmas of any good citizen who pays attention to international affairs. One needs good information, a decent amount of background knowledge, and the ability to see the intended action from several contrasting points of view. It always helps to listen to people who disagree with you. During the 1999 Kosovo crisis, *Commonweal* published—in the form of letters, articles, and book reviews—possibly every conceivable point of view to be

taken on Kosovo. I take that to be one of the important roles of a journal of opinion—not only to display the editors' views but to offer readers
a forum where they will find and declaim their own points of view.

What of Yugoslavia today? I think it is appropriate to celebrate that
things more or less went right—although, as General McCarthy says,
Yugoslavia still has a long road to recovery ahead. The war crimes trials
of Milosevic and other Serbian political and military leaders may bring
a welcome and necessary closure to certain issues and raise the stakes
for leaders elsewhere who might be tempted to follow their bad example.
Nevertheless, ethnic flash points remain in the Balkans: The status of
Kosovo is still to be resolved; tensions in Macedonia have led to violence
(though this time the situation has received immediate attention from
the European Union); Serbian nationalism could come to the fore
again. Nonetheless, the prospects for peace in the region are better established now than at the beginning of the 1990s. Will the citizens of
these new "entities" take advantage of the peacekeeping forces in their
midst to actually make peace? That remains to be seen.

Whether as editor or active citizen, each of us must make it our business to stay abreast of what is going on in Kosovo—and other trouble
spots—because we may be asked someday to support intervention or to
understand why, in a given case, it is good or bad policy. Finally, we citizens of the last superpower always have the responsibility of carefully
scrutinizing our own leaders' political and military policies—whether in
the Balkans, in Central and Latin America, or in the free-floating arena
of the war on terrorism. If there is one lesson to be learned from the demise of Yugoslavia, it is that citizens are not wholly innocent when their
elected leaders choose violent means to impose national policies.

Notes

1. Michael Ignatieff, *Virtual War: Kosovo and Beyond* (New York: Picador USA,
2000), 107–8.

2. For example, Laura Silber and Allan Little, *Yugoslavia: Death of a Nation*
(New York: Penguin Books, 1996); Misha Glenny, *The Fall of Yugoslavia: The Third
Balkan War* (New York: Penguin Books, 1992); David A. Dyker and Ivan Vejvoda,
Yugoslavia and After: A Study in Fragmentation, Despair and Rebirth (New York:

Longman, 1996); David Rieff, *Slaughterhouse: Bosnia and the Failure of the West* (New York: Simon & Schuster, 1995).

3. Richard Holbrooke, *To End a War* (New York: Random House, 1998).

4. Chris Hedges, "Kosovo's Next Masters?" *Foreign Affairs* 78, no. 3 (May/June 1999).

5. Although our editorial board did not focus on concepts such as "the sacred" and "the sovereign" during our discussions of Kosovo, *Commonweal* did publish essays on such themes during the crisis in Bosnia. See, for example, Drew Christiansen and Gerald Powers, "Send in the Peacekeepers: Sovereignty Is Not Sacred," *Commonweal* 124, no. 4 (28 February 1997): 16–19.

6. *Commonweal* editors weighed in on the possibility of a ground war on several occasions. The following passage, from an editorial titled "Sit Tight," reflected our thoughts on 7 May 1999:

> As we struggle to balance means and ends in this conflict, we need to consider the loss not only of civilian lives in Kosovo, Serbia, Montenegro, and perhaps neighboring Albania and Macedonia, but the lives of NATO troops as well. We also need to reflect on the practices of the Yugoslav army as well as police and paramilitary groups who show no compunction in using civilians as human shields and hostages. Why provide them with any more opportunities than they now have? NATO tank and infantry assaults would have to hold their fire in the face of such tactics. The Serbs pride themselves on their capacity for resistance and their ability to disperse men and materials and to fight a guerrilla war. Why give them the chance to slaughter more Kosovar Albanians along with NATO troops? Let them sit there and wait. It is their war. They started it. Let them decide when they have had enough bombing.

7. UN Secretary-General Kofi Annan took up these themes in a speech opening the 2000 session of the United Nations. For *Commonweal*'s editorial response to these issues, see "Intervention: When and How?" (22 October 1999).

8. William Shawcross, *Deliver Us from Evil: Peacekeepers, Warlords and a World of Endless Conflict* (New York: Simon & Schuster, 2000).

4

Just War, Realism, and Humanitarian Intervention

JEAN BETHKE ELSHTAIN

THE JUST WAR TRADITION IS A THEORY of comparative justice applied to considerations of war and intervention. To grapple better with its complexities and the characteristic form of moral reasoning that enters into the just war tradition, it is important to get a grip on what this centuries-old, continually revised tradition consists of and the ways in which it contests the terrain of war/peace questions with the alternative traditions of *realpolitik*, on one end of a continuum, and pacifism on the other. Approaching humanitarian intervention through a just war lens means that interventions, or their possibility—including, for the tasks this books takes up, interventions into other sovereign nations—must be subjected to intense scrutiny and cannot be played out by appealing to compassion or doing "the right thing." The just war tradition acknowledges the tragedy of situations in which there may be a "right thing" to do on some absolute standard of justice but no prudent or decent way to do it.

This chapter begins with the basics of the just war tradition and the particular burden this tradition places on sovereign states in the conduct of war. This burden derives, in the first instance, from a tradition of specifically Christian theology. This fact speaks to the formation of political bodies in the history of the West and the ways in which politics historically was subject to ethical scrutiny. To be sure, an explicit connection to the sacred now often is only as a trace etched into the scheme of things via the language of justice and human rights, absent any specific, direct theological imperative. Whether the theology is explicit or implicit, I ask whether this complex tradition affords a compelling frame within which to conjure with the issue of humanitarian intervention by drawing on specific instances of such intervention and evaluating these cases against just war stipulations. One matter at stake is whether such intervention is a special category that stands on its own or, instead, falls within a general frame of considerations of justice—in which case all the stipulations of the just war tradition apply to cases of humanitarian intervention. I round things off with a few comments on the politics of humanitarian intervention drawn from the Augustinian tradition. Augustinian realism warns us that no perfect standard of justice or fairness can ever be attained by which to adjudicate questions of war, violence, and intervention. That does not mean, however, that one should exile the language of justice, and the concerns intrinsic to it, from matters of war and peace altogether. That I draw specifically on Augustine displays the ongoing resonance of a specific theological tradition where contemporary matters of war, peace, and international violence or the use of coercive force more generally is concerned.

The Just War Tradition

The just war tradition is a way of thinking that refuses to separate politics from ethics. The tradition of political realism and that of just war embrace contrasting presumptions about the human condition.[1] The great forefathers of *realpolitik* are Machiavelli and Hobbes. Machiavelli holds that men in general are ungrateful, dissembling, backstabbing, and untrustworthy; in Hobbes' account, humans are isolates driven into forward motion, bound to collide violently, and humanity in general is defined by the most horrible equality imaginable—the power each has to kill one another. It takes a lot of coercive force to hold such creatures in check, not in the interest of a positive vision of human possibility but simply to stop them from marauding. It is worth noting that Machiavelli and Hobbes, each in his own way, were determined to free politics from the chastening influence of the sacred in the form of church edicts and strictures and ethical criteria derived from the Christian tradition more generally.

By contrast, just war thinkers begin with a commitment to a view of human beings as creatures who are always conflicted and torn, whose human relationships are characterized by love and kindness as well as selfishness and cruelty, human solidarity and human plurality. This understanding derives from theological accounts of the Fall—specifically, the sin of human self-pride. However dire a theologian considers this fall from the Garden of Eden, all thinkers in the Christian tradition begin from a premise of the temptation of human beings by power—what Augustine calls a lust for domination. These constant features of the human condition are played out in a variety of ways in diverse cultures. Human motives and actions are always mixed: We both affirm and destroy solidaristic possibilities, often simultaneously. For example, we affirm solidarity within the particular communities of which we are a part—every human being is a member of a way of life that embodies itself institutionally as family, tribe, civil society, state.

Plurality is a constant feature of human political and moral life. We may launch ourselves into wider or more universalistic possibilities from a particular site, seeking to affirm our common humanity through organizations, institutions, and ways of being and thinking that draw us into wider streams of existence. Or we may not. And we may not in dreadful and destructive ways—for example, by denying the very humanity of people from plural sites other than our own. This denial of humanity also is a refusal to recognize that all cultures, Western and non-Western, without fail define and refine moral codes and that these moral codes invariably set norms for the taking of human life; all have some notion of what counts as a violation of this norm. Standards of moral conduct pertain in all arenas in which human beings engage one another, from families to polities. The challenging question is which standards and to what ends, not whether moral norms are applicable to the arena of politics (as just one example) or not.

Unlike the competing doctrine of state-centered strategic realism, just war argument insists that one must not open an unbridgeable gulf between "domestic" and "international" politics. The tradition of *realpolitik* insists that the rules that govern domestic moral conduct—here the focus is a body politic internally—are inapplicable to the world of what used to be called "men and states." Just war as politics, by contrast, insists that although it would be utopian to presume that relations between states can be governed by the premises and caretaking that are apposite in our dealings with family and friends, a war of all against all need not kick in once one leaves the hearth or the immediate neighborhood—or even the borders of one's country.

The strategic realist is governed by instrumental calculations and some concept of national interest, the just war thinker by a complex amalgam of normative commitments and pragmatic considerations that overlap in several important respects with those of strategic realism (although the starting points vary). The just war thinker is not nearly so harsh as the *realpolitiker* in his or her evaluation of what usually is called liberal internationalism, with its justifications of intervention in the name of sustaining, supporting, or building a universal culture of Kantian republics. At the same time, the just war thinker would voice considerable skepticism about any such project, not because he or she opposes making more robust an international regime of human rights and greater fairness and equity but because of his or her recognition of the intrinsic value of human cultural plurality.

From the Augustinian side, nothing less than the sin of hubris is implicated in any attempt to weld humanity into a single monoculture: Here the story of the Tower of Babel is instructive.[2] The reason God intervened, scattered humanity, and set us to babbling was to remind humanity of the need for humility and limits. The Babel story is a cautionary tale concerning any and all attempts to forge a uniform humanity under a single scheme of things. (See chapter 9 for a critique of how a particular construal of "humanity" can give way to a universal scheme of justice in international politics that undermines cultural particularity.)

Just war thinkers worry that certain appeals to a more cosmopolitan or internationalist order—whether of a Kantian or a utilitarian sort—and to the alleged possibility of severing military intervention from considerations of strategic or national interest invite radical depoliticizing of national action. Note, for example, that in the multiple cases of resort to bombing in the second Clinton administration, the word "war" dropped away as the phrase "humanitarian intervention" triumphed—as if one could intervene militarily without getting blood on one's hands. If humanitarian intervention involves soldiers, automatic weapons, attack helicopters, bombers, cruise missiles, and the vast arsenal of modern warfare, it *is* a war of one sort or another and must meet the burden of proof required of all cases of resort to force. (I have more to say on this subsequently in this chapter).

As a theory of warfighting and resort to war, just war thinking is best known as a cluster of injunctions: what is permissible; what is not permissible. For example, war must be the last resort; war must be openly and legally declared; war must be a response to a specific instance of unjust aggression: These are the *ad bellum* specifications. The means deployed in fighting a war must be proportionate to the ends (the rule of proportionality); war must be waged in a way that distinguishes combatants from noncombatants (the rule of discrimination): These are the *in bello* norms. Whether evaluating a resort to arms or determining the bases and nature of political order more generally, the just war thinker insists on the need for moral judgments—for figuring out who, in fact, in the situation at hand is behaving in a more or less just or unjust manner; who is more the victimizer and who the victim. Just war insists on the power of moral appeals and arguments of the sort that, for the strategic realist, are mere window dressing, icing on the cake of strategic considerations. For the just war thinker, moral appeals are the heart of the matter—not the only matter, but the place from which one starts.

Just war thinkers do not propound immutable rules—they are not deontologists—so much as clarify the circumstances that justify a state's going to war (*jus ad bellum*) and what is and is not allowable in fighting the wars—or undertaking those "humanitarian interventions" that involve the use of force—to which a polity has committed itself (*jus in bello*). There are thinkers who argue that our moral squeamishness must be laid to rest in times of war—that the image of the violated woman, the starving child, the blown-to-pieces man must be put out of sight and out of mind. This is cruel, they say, but we live in a cruel and dangerous world. We must think in terms of the Big Picture: the system of sovereign states and balance of forces. If we do not think in this way, if we are naïve about the world's ways, many more human beings will suffer over the long run as smaller nations or groups of people within nations are ethnically cleansed, rounded up and murdered, gobbled up by huge empires and tyrants run amok. Just war thinkers acknowledge the importance of this insistence on the ways in which refusing to counter aggression may make things worse, but they insist that we can hold within a single frame a concern with peoples in a collective sense and a commitment to the dignity of each and every human person: The ethical concerns are never simply irrelevant.

This tension between personal conduct and belief, including conduct and beliefs in the realm of the sacred, and the ways in which collectivities act frames many of the discussions in this book. It is a centuries-old frustration that the behavior we might regard as courageous or noble on the part of a person—such as offering himself or herself up for martyrdom on pacifist grounds rather than fighting back against a depredator—would be evaluated in a very different light if a statesman simply offered up his country, without a fight, to a conqueror of known cruelty. What seems heroic and even holy in the one instance would be regarded as cowardly, cruel, inexplicable, despicable in the other. There is no formula to iron this out in any way, simple or complex: The tension is just there.

The Just War Tradition as Frame for Action: *Sic et Non*

The matter in dispute is whether the just war tradition gives us a vantage point from which to assay critically forms of intervention that appeal to humanitarian considerations or, specifically, to the just war tradition itself, often in and through the many conventions and agreements that have solidified and codified that tradition over time. For the just war thinker, military intervention cannot be a knockdown conclusion that follows from the articulation of triggering stipulations, claims, or sentiments.

How, then, would the just war thinker build a case for intervention? Not substantially differently from the ways one would deliberate on other forms of war. I have noted that the just war tradition is demanding and inherently complex, aiming simultaneously to limit resort to arms and to respond to the urgent requirements of justice. There are times when claims of justice may override the reluctance to take up arms; there are grievances and horrors to which we are called to respond—provided we can do so in a manner that avoids, to the extent humanly possible, either deepening the injustice already present or creating new instances of injustice.

The first part of the just war framework is devoted to determining whether a resort to war—including intervention—is justified. For example, war should be fought only for a justifiable cause of substantial importance. The primary just cause in an era of nations and states is a nation's response to direct aggression. Protecting citizens from harm is a fundamental norm, and it scarcely counts as protection if no response is made when one's countrymen and women are being slaughtered, hounded, routed from their homes and the like.

There are other justified occasions for war, however. Aggression need not be directed against one's own citizens to trigger a *jus ad bellum* argument. The offense of aggression may be committed against a nation or a people incapable of defending themselves against a determined adversary. If one can intervene to assist the injured party, one is justified in doing so—provided other considerations are met. From St. Augustine forward, saving "the innocent from certain harm" has been recognized as a justifiable cause: the innocent being those who are in no position to defend themselves.[3] The reference is not to any presumption of moral innocence on the part of victims: Nobody is innocent in the classic just war framework in that sense. This is another way in which the just war tradition, as a theory of comparative justice, guards against moral triumphalism: By insisting that even though the balance of justice may fall more on one side than the other in cases of conflict, there should be no presumption that the aggressor is wholly evil, the aggressed against wholly innocent. Presuppositions of total innocence can and have fueled horrible things. (See chapter 5 for another account of comparative notions of justice as they pertain to the just use of force and terrorism.)

In our time, the saving of the innocent often is referred to as "humanitarian intervention" to avoid the language of war. This does not mean, of course, that any nation or even a group of nations can or should respond to every instance of violation of the innocent, including the most horrific of all violations—genocide and ethnic cleansing. The just war tradition adds a cautionary note about overreach. Before you intervene, even in a just cause, be certain that you have a reasonable chance of success. Don't barge in and make a bad situation worse. Considerations such as these also take us to the heart of the so-called *in bello* rules. These rules are restraints on the means to be deployed even in a just cause. Means must be proportionate to ends: The damage must not be greater than the offenses one aims to halt.

Above all, noncombatant immunity must be protected. Noncombatants historically have been women, children, the aged and infirm, and all unarmed persons going about their daily lives, as well as prisoners of war who have been disarmed by definition. Knowingly placing noncombatants in jeopardy, knowingly putting in place strategies that bring great suffering and harm to noncombatants, is unacceptable on just war grounds. Better by far to risk the lives of one's own combatants than the lives of enemy noncombatants.

Just war thinking also insists that war aims be made clear, that criteria for what is to count as success in achieving those aims be publicly articulated, and that negotiated settlement never be ruled out of court by fiat. The ultimate goal of just war is a peace that achieves a greater measure of justice than that which characterized the antebellum period.

In sum, the *jus in bello* considerations are borne along by two major principles. Discrimination—targeting only legitimate war targets and respecting noncombatant immunity—and proportionality (i.e., avoiding excessive force) are ways of restraining the scope and intensity of warfare to minimize its destructiveness.

How well does the just war tradition bear up when it is specifically evoked as the grounding and framework for recent cases of war and intervention that avoids the provocative word "war"? Two examples of recent vintage afford interesting and ambiguous case studies: the 1991 Persian Gulf War—not, to be sure, a humanitarian intervention per se, although humanitarian grounds, melded to traditional grounds of nonaggression against a sovereign state, were evoked—and the 1999 intervention in Kosovo. The Persian Gulf War was prompted by Iraq's annexation of Kuwait, its brutalization of Kuwaitis, and its gutting of their country and its national resources. These actions were clear violations of basic principles of international order—of sovereignty—that encode respect for the autonomy of states. One need not like the regime in place in a country that is the victim of aggression to acknowledge that an *ad bellum* tripwire has been crossed, a crime (in Michael Walzer's term)[4] committed by one state against another that violates the United Nations charter.[5]

The American response to Iraqi aggression in 1990 evoked just war imperatives from the beginning. Such considerations framed much of the debate about whether to intervene and what means to deploy once one had. The language of "just cause" was repeated endlessly, as was "last resort": The argument was that sanctions were tried and failed. Legitimate authority was articulated explicitly: a twenty-seven-nation coalition acting under the imprimatur of the United Nations and in the name of collective security. So far so good? Yes and no.

Just war principles are ambiguous and complex. Evaluations must be made at each step along the way. Greater and lesser evils (injustices) must be taken into account. Thus, certain questions must be asked, including the following: What would be the cost of resisting Iraqi aggression? Would the postwar Persian Gulf region be more unjust and disordered or less? Might not the human and environmental damage, as well as the assaults to the spirit every war trails in its wake, blight any peace? The ends may be justified—restitutive response to aggression—but the means may be unjust or unjustifiable, even if pains are taken to avoid direct targeting of civilians.

Much of this complexity fell out of the argument as a thinned-out variant on "just war discourse" emanated from the supporters of intervention in the U.S. House of Representatives and Senate, as well as from the elder Bush administration. It was simultaneously heartening and troubling to hear just war discourse being evoked—heartening because concerns of justice were foregrounded and because limits to the use of force, as well as its justification, came into debate; troubling because the rhetoric of justification veered dangerously toward a crusading moral triumphalism, with Saddam Hussein called a Hitler for our time, although the Iraqi people themselves were spared any blanket Nazification, rhetorically speaking.

This rhetorical raising of the ante points to a temptation related to the just war tradition—namely, the way in which it can slide over into the rhetoric of crusades. Must Saddam really be a Hitler to justify going to war against his regime? On the other hand, on the *in bello* front, care was taken in coalition targeting policy in line with just war restraints. If postwar estimates of noncombatant casualties of coalition bombing are at all accurate—5,000 to 15,000 civilians, according to Greenpeace, which scarcely is known for its support of forceful intervention—the total is ghastly because any civilian deaths are terrible. Yet we can be grateful there weren't more casualties. All one need do is compare this discriminatory policy against the indiscriminate terror bombing of civilian targets in World War II to appreciate the restraint the coalition partners placed on themselves in their targeting strategy.

Having said that, one nonetheless should be haunted by the possibility that something as grave as reflecting on "collateral damage"—that is, the harm that comes to nonmilitary targets (e.g., civilian noncombatants or historic sites) from the legitimate targeting of a military site—can too easily become formulaic. This possibility came to light most vividly in the Kosovo intervention. The *New York Times* offered a long reprise on the mistaken bombing of the Chinese embassy in Belgrade. Readers of that piece learned that not only error but also incompetence were involved as what the *Times* called "inexpert" targeters forged forth without higher-level accountability. What most interested me, however, was the visual image that accompanied the *Times* piece. An aerial photograph identifies target 493, "Belgrade Warehouse"—described as a site for "supply and procurement" for the Serbian forces. "Collateral damage" is noted and ranked as "Tier 3 High," with a "casualty estimate" of three to seven civilian workers and an additional calculation of "unintended civilian casualties of 25–50."[6] We've done our moral duty, this image seems to say. Calculating civilian casualties in such a routinized way threatens to violate the spirit if not the letter of just war teaching. All in all, American restraint in targeting is an admirable thing. Yet building in restraints as part of an elaborate code should never remove from the shoulders of those doing the task serious reflection on the precise task they are doing; a single civilian casualty, even if unintended, is a terrible price to pay. Reflection of a particular sort is necessary at each point along the way.

Just war thinking also requires sustained attention even after the shooting has stopped. Let's return to the Persian Gulf War for a moment. Because the media focused nearly all of its inquiries on whether noncombatants were actual targets of coalition bombing strategy during the conflict in the Gulf, the public's attention was deflected from the long-range effects of bombing, including life-threatening assaults on the infrastructure of Iraqi society—energy and water supplies, for example. These matters require explicit attention within a just war framework. The strategic realist can say, "Hit anything that makes them hurt and impairs their ability to fight." The just war thinker must not move so hastily, however. He or she must sift out that which is vital to the opponent's war effort—including "dual-use" power and communication stations—from that which, though it may be drawn into support of military actions, also is essential to sustain civilian life: Water and food supplies are foremost, even paradigmatic, as an example of what noncombatants require.

The First Geneva Protocol (1977) codifies just war thinking on civilian and nonmilitary targeting in language that directs our attention not only to the buildup to war, or the war itself, but to its long-term consequences. Those consequences now include malnutrition and epidemics linked directly to inadequate food and water supplies and medicines.

What this adds up to is the following: If just war is evoked, those evoking it should stay within the framework they have endorsed. This framework was abandoned once the Iraqis had been routed from Kuwait. The war, or the aftermath of the war, continued. The health catastrophes faced by the Iraqi public; the plight of the Kurds; and the disproportionate casualty figures, with estimates of 100,000 Iraqi soldiers killed and 300,000 wounded—raise serious ethical concerns.[7] Was this a fair fight or a turkey shoot? The lopsidedness of casualties is an occasion for debate for the just war thinker as it is not for the strategic realist. Was the rule of proportionality violated? If so, how did this happen? How, for example, did we radically overestimate the enemy's strength and ability to fight back, if this is the background to our overuse of force to get the job done? And so on.

Also worrisome is the fact that just war considerations fell off the rhetorical radar screen once hostilities ceased. Spokespeople for the U.S. government reverted almost immediately to the language of strategic realism and the inviolability of sovereignty, thereby justifying coalition refusal to "intervene" in the internal affairs of Iraq when the plight of the Kurdish people captured our attention. Can we really stand back and say "no intervention in the internal affairs of a sovereign state," whether on principled or prudential grounds, when we have been responsible in part in bringing about those internal affairs in the first place? This attitude creates an ethical schism of the sort that the just war tradition aims to bridge. There is nothing wrong per se with diplomatic and strategic categories—depending on how they are used and to what ends. The problem I am gesturing toward is the taking up of a rhetoric of strategic realism abruptly once the rhetoric of just war seems to have exhausted its utility.

NATO intervention in Kosovo is a paradigmatic instance, for many observers, of humanitarian intervention—calling to mind the Nuremberg precedents and "crimes against humanity." (Hitler and Nazism were evoked repeatedly to characterize Serbian policy.) I emphasize the *in bello* dimensions of just war for the purpose of this chapter, although *ad bellum* issues—including the vexing matter of "right authority"— would come into play in any exhaustive examination of the Kosovo intervention within a just war framework. An editorial in *Commonweal* magazine pointed out that a hawk (or strategic realist) might have refrained from intervention in this situation—James Baker's famous statement, "we've got no dog in this fight," comes to mind—and a pacifist by definition would refrain from intervention unless he or she could squeeze what was going on within the category of a "police action," which pacifism can endorse. Interventionists of various sorts argued forcefully that ethnic cleansing is one of those rare knockdown triggers *ad bellum*.

Interventionists come in several varieties, of course, and *Commonweal* notes one sort, called "genuine interventionists," who hold to a seamless web approach to human-rights violations—namely, that they are all created equal, and justice demands going everywhere to stop certain harms from continuing if you go anywhere (provided, of course, you have the means). "Therefore, international action ought to be taken almost everywhere to stop slaughter and ruin, whether it is born of ethnic and religious rivalries or internal political divisions. The principle of intervention should be universal and uncompromising."[8] That is not the sort of interventionism the just war tradition underwrites so long as it remains tethered to Augustinian realism, which is attuned to the role of contingency—including states' or coalitions' inability to respond evenly and robustly everywhere whenever something terrible is happening, whatever the demands of an absolute standard of justice. (See chapter 3 for a discussion of criteria for humanitarian interventions.)

Humanitarian intervention within an Augustinian frame comes under the category of saving innocents from certain harm. Augustine evokes the requirement of neighbor love. Serving one's neighbor is a form of friendship and stewardship. How did this ideal play out on the ground? As we know all too well, Albanian Kosovars were harassed, tormented, deported, and killed. NATO forces—primarily the United States—did nothing on the ground to stop these actions. Our stated intent, cast within human rights as well as justice language, was to stop ethnic cleansing in the name of humanity itself. The argument was that World War II had taught us that genocide is a crime that must not go unpunished. Other avenues had been exhausted; Mr. Milosevic was immune to diplomatic overtures. NATO, as a legitimately constituted concert of states, therefore had authority to act, if need be, for humanitarian reasons and in the interest of collective self-defense: protecting the whole idea of a European comity of nations. These are grounds for selective humanitarian intervention with considerations that go beyond the crimes themselves. So let's assume the *ad bellum* criteria were adequately met.

From a just war perspective the biggest problem in the Kosovo war was the means deployed to halt and punish ethnic cleansing. In the first instance, our means speeded up the process because the opening sorties in the bombing campaign gave Milosevic the excuse he needed to declare martial law and to move rapidly to complete what he had already begun, entrenching his forces in Kosovo before NATO might change its mind about introducing ground troops into the conflict—which the United States announced from the beginning it would not do. We seem to have blundered into a strategy by not giving due consideration to the likely reaction to our bombs—namely, a deepening of the terror and the expulsions. The optimistic view, based on a refusal to engage in the deep deliberation about likely outcomes the just war tradition requires, was that the Milosevic regime would collapse in less than a week. Hence, there was no preparation for the influx of desperate humanity to neighboring countries and regions, their plight made doubly desperate by lack of food, water, medicine, and shelter at their points of terrified egress. This approach doesn't seem to be a good way to run a humanitarian intervention or conduct a just war, in the name of justice or any other good.[9]

The heart of the matter from a just war framework is this, however: We violated the norm of discrimination consistently by devising a new criterion that I call *combatant immunity*. That is, our combatants ranked higher as a consideration than did noncombatant Serbian—or, for that matter, Albanian Kosovar—civilians. With our determination to keep NATO soldiers (read: American combatants; that was the overriding domestic political consideration, which itself had nothing to do with just war or humanitarian issues) out of harm's way, we embraced combatant immunity for our combatants and indirectly for Serbian soldiers as well. Instead, we did a great deal of damage from the air to Serbian cities, especially Belgrade. This strategy included reducing buildings to rubble, tearing up bridges, and killing civilians in markets and television stations. It is harder by far to face determined combatants on the ground—to interpose one's combatants, in this case, between the Albanian Kosovars and their depredators. This approach wasn't given serious consideration; indeed, we did not even introduce Apache helicopters into the situation for fear of losing just one in combat.[10] If combatant immunity is to become our new organizing principle, the United States surely will face future situations in which we refuse or are unable not only to do what is right but to do what may be necessary, having set zero casualties as a new norm for the way we conduct war.

Obviously, the preceding sentence was written before the horrific events of September 11, 2001, and our response to those events. Under the junior Bush administration, it is clear that we are now prepared, in a justified cause, to place our servicemen and women at risk and to undertake a strategy that combines air and ground forces. From a just war perspective, this is a welcome change because it brings American warfighting strategy into closer alignment with the requirements of the just war perspective.

At the time of the Kosovo intervention, however, our rejection of the rule of noncombatant immunity in favor of combatant immunity for American military personnel constituted a strange turn of events. The Serbian army could operate with impunity without any worry about facing its opponents on the ground, even as civilians sustained collateral damage. Once NATO had exhausted the obvious military targets that could be struck from the air and, as overoptimistically predicted, the Serbian regime had not capitulated, we moved on to degrade the infrastructure on which civilian life depends—despite a disclaimer from President Clinton that we had no quarrel with the Serbian people because they, too, like the Iraqis under Saddam, were victims.[11] Because one cannot entirely and convincingly eliminate atrocities on the ground by dropping bombs from an altitude that keeps troops safely out of range of any possible ground fire (although the Serbians had little ability to fight back), our ends were compromised by our means.

It is a terrible thing for anyone to kill or to be killed. Yet that is the occupational risk, and honor, of men and women in arms. At the time of the Kosovo intervention, there seemed to be a real possibility that the United States was no longer prepared to take any such risk for any cause. If this principle had held, this country would not have been able to fight wars effectively even when a case has been made on comparative justice grounds. Then-president Clinton was looking for a "no casualty" war. One pays a price, however—and not just in monetary terms—for such ventures. Isn't "riskless warfare" an incoherent idea? As Paul W. Kahn argues in a hard-hitting piece on "War and Sacrifice in Kosovo":

> If the decision to intervene is morally compelling, it cannot be conditioned on political considerations that assume an asymmetrical valuing of human life. This contradiction will be felt more and more as we move into an era that is simultaneously characterized by a global legal and moral order, on the one hand, and the continuing presence of nation-states, on the other. What are the conditions under which states will be willing to commit their forces to advance international standards, when their own interests are not threatened? Riskless warfare by the state in pursuit of global values may be a perfect expression of this structural contradiction within which we find ourselves. In part, then, our uneasiness about a policy of riskless intervention in Kosovo arises out of an incompatibility between the morality of the ends, which are universal, and the morality of the means, which seem to privilege a particular community. There was talk during the campaign of a crude moral-military calculus in which the life of one NATO combatant was thought to be equivalent to the lives of 20,000 Kosovars. Such talk meant that even those who supported the intervention could not know the depth of our commitment to overcoming humanitarian disasters. Is it conditioned upon the absence of risk to our own troops? If so, are such interventions merely moral disasters—like that in Somalia—waiting to happen? If the Serbs had discovered a way to inflict real costs, would there have been an abandonment of the Kosovars?[12]

Something called the Clinton doctrine fueled the Kosovo operation, best summarized by Clinton himself: "I want us to live in a world where we get along with each other, with all of our differences, and where we don't have to worry about seeing scenes every night for the next forty years of ethnic cleansing."[13] This doctrine was a muddle: neither strategic realism, nor just war, nor liberal internationalism. It established no clear grounds for humanitarian intervention, offering instead a mélange of ideas and desiderata that were so murky it was nearly impossible to glean from it any clarity for either intervening or refraining from intervening in situations of humanitarian catastrophe. According to Michael Mandelbaum, in a critical piece in *Foreign Affairs*, the doctrine consisted of two parts that involved promulgating "the use of force on behalf of universal values" and "justifying military intervention in the internal affairs of sovereign states."[14]

Mandelbaum argues that this "so-called doctrine" made a hash of things in the Balkans—where spirals of violence continued, where any indication of an American pullout inspired panic, and where the result of the deteriorating mess was de facto partitioning not unlike the outcome in Bosnia, where the Dayton accords ratified the results of ethnic cleansing. In Kosovo, those who were victims became victimizers, with the more brutal members of the Kosovo separatist movement seemingly in ascendancy. These persistent and deteriorated conditions have dropped off our media radar screen, however.[15]

Let's rehearse a few of the problems with this doctrine and policy as it played out in Kosovo as a way of clarifying the difference between this way of justifying "humanitarian intervention" by contrast to a just war politics framework that cavils at risk-free solutions to horrible tragedies and political problems. Consider that our entire purpose in bombing was to save lives. Estimates are that 2,500 people had died before the bombing campaign began and that during the elevent weeks of bombardment,

> an estimated 20,000 people died violently in the province, most of them Albanian civilians murdered by Serbs. . . . By its [the bombing campaign] end, 1.4 million were displaced. . . . The alliance also went to war, by its own account, to protect the precarious political stability of the countries of the Balkans. The result, however, was precisely the opposite. . . .[16]

What Mandelbaum points to is a political failure that emerged, in part, as a result of the means deployed to achieve our stated ends. Evoking strategic realism and national interest as well as state sovereignty as a value, Mandelbaum argues that the Clinton doctrine's squishiness virtually guaranteed that U.S. policy would be driven by media attention and public opinion polls rather than coherence of any sort. To these considerations, the just war perspective invites other concerns.

Starting from a different perspective than Mandelbaum's, I come to similar conclusions. Mandelbaum surely is correct that a quick resort to bombing was the Clinton administration's *modus operandi* in almost every foreign policy jam—whether the administration at any given point was using the rhetoric of national interest, national security, punishing dictators, saving lives, or fighting a global war against terrorism. (The latter was the stated rationale behind the destruction of what turned out to be a pharmaceutical plant—the Shifa Plant—in Khartoum, Sudan. The jury is still out on whether this was an entirely "innocent" plant, but the fact that such a debate is ongoing, even within government circles, suggests a measure of uncertainty that goes far beyond the ambiguity that always attends military action.) Also preferred were embargoes that degraded the civilian infrastructure of targeted societies. Mandelbaum also opposes this way of punishing the innocent to express outrage at the guilty.[17] The clearest rationale available to us to oppose such a strategy lies in the comparative justice considerations that arise from just war imperatives. To be sure, each embargo must be debated and not assumed to be unjust a priori. The point is that embargoes cannot be regarded as ethically pristine by definition within a just war framework.

How would a just war approach help us parse such questions further? Consider President Clinton's comments throughout the Kosovo intervention and as part of the runup to it. Clinton deployed strained domestic analogies in an attempt to put a distinctively American stamp on the Balkans tragedy.[18] The events he selected can be shoehorned within our reigning political preoccupations only via a circuitous logic. The just war tradition, remember, attempts to balance or to hold in fruitful tension the requirements of universal moral commitments with respect for the plurality of polities, cultures, and regimes in and through which humankind realizes itself. We are invited to acknowledge that which is "in common" and to respect and recognize signs of difference as long as they do not violate certain basic norms.[19] Rather than helping us to see suffering humanity in and through the particular plight of the Albanian Kosovars with their quite particular and complex history, Clinton forced domestic analogies: He likened the signing of a federal hate-crime statute to the bombings of Belgrade because each was designed to stop "haters." Thus, the Kosovo intervention got mapped onto the preferred domestic rhetoric of the Clinton administration. The president spun out a vision for a new postwar Kosovo cast in the language of a version of multiculturalist ideology that was unrealistic even for a pluralist democracy—let alone a fractured, destabilized region in the Balkans that will be reeling from the events of the 1990s for the next half-century or more.

Clinton undercut this rhetoric, however, in a May 23, 1999, op-ed in the *New York Times*. On that occasion, he not only proclaimed restoration of the status quo ante his number one priority, he added the caveat that Kosovo would come under a kind of protectorship more or less run by the KLA (the Kosovo Liberation Army)—whose explicit aim for a separatist ethnically "pure" Albanian microstate was no Balkan version of American multiculturalist imperatives. Lost in both presidential rhetorics of justification (which clash with one another) was attention to the somber realities of intervention, including rueful recognition of unintended consequences and limits to what our power can accomplish.[20]

Keeping Just War Augustinian

If just war thinking is to remain honest, it is best placed within a framework of Augustinian realism—by contrast to versions of just war that, in losing a connection to this rich strand of reasoning, become mere variants on liberal institutionalism and quickly degenerate into internationalist sentimentalism. Augustinian realism offers no assurances that one can make the world safe for anything. Estrangement, conflict, and tragedy are constant features of the human condition. Politics is one way human beings deal with this condition. Politics on any level never escapes certain pervasive features of human life in all its complexity and plural modes of cultural expression. Augustinian realism imbeds deep skepticism about the exercise of power, beginning with the aims and claims of sovereignty and any concentration of power. At the same time, this realism recognizes the inescapability of politics and calls on citizens to engage the world of politics faithfully. Politics confronts us with intransigent "otherness," with people who have their own cultures and opinions. Politics requires that we respond in some concrete way to a world of conflicts and oppositions. The realist of this sort worries that we could be overtaken by a sentimentalized notion of compassion and could forget such mordant teachings as Max Weber's definition of politics as the boring of hard boards.[21]

There is little danger of just war turning into either a language of narrow strategic justification or a rhetoric of sentiment within an Augustinian framework. Although there is danger that the just war tradition could be associated with crusades and triumphalism, built into the Augustinian version of the tradition are barriers that keep such impulses in check. Augustinian realists are not crusaders. They insist that we are called to act in a mode of realistic hope with a hardheaded recognition of the limits to action. One can underwrite border crossing with this perspective—because just war thinking doesn't worship at the altar of the state—but one cannot do so with impunity given Augustine's built-in respect for the plurality of cultures in and through which humanity manifests itself.

Augustinianism as a frame for just war stipulations is more likely to emerge as a *via negativa*. There are things that must not be done and that are, by definition, wrong; hence, to the extent possible, these things should be stopped. This list of knockdown violations is not infinite, however: It would include genocide and ethnic cleansing, torture as an instrument of political power, unprovoked aggression against another country or people. The aim of intervening in such cases would be interpositional—not to impose an alternative order but to stop a disorder, an instance of clear injustice.

In sum, Augustinian just war thinking imposes constraints where they might not otherwise exist; generates a debate that might not otherwise occur; and promotes skepticism and uneasiness about the use and abuse of power without opting out of political reality altogether in favor of utopian fantasies and projects. It requires action and judgment in a world of limits, estrangements, and partial justice. It fosters recognition of the provisionality of all political arrangements. It is at once respectful of distinctive and particular peoples and deeply internationalist. It recognizes self-defense against unjust aggression but refuses to legitimate imperialistic crusades and the building of empires in the name of peace. It requires paying close attention to political rhetoric, its use and abuse. It recognizes, in the words of Michael Ignatieff, that

> the language of human rights provides a powerful new rhetoric of abstract justification. Keeping control of war in the modern age means keeping control of this powerful new rhetoric, making sure that the cause of human rights does not lure citizens into wars that end up abusing the very rights they were supposed to defend.[22]

Another warning, from theological ethicist Richard Miller:

> Perhaps because humanitarian intervention can have this prima facie altruistic component, it is tempting to consider it to be different from war, thereby enabling those who would ban war to approve of such action. . . . Insofar as humanitarian interventions might be described (or redescribed) in such terms, they appear to pose little difficulty for pacifists. The paradigm of domestic coercion or police action, allowing for the use of violence in order to stop criminal activity, may enable some pacifists to accept military action (and the prospect of violence) in international affairs.[23]

In other words, humanitarian intervention must bear the heavy burden of justification that just war, in its classical sense, requires of any resort to force. What Miller calls the "intuitively admirable" notions of humanitarian intervention—intuitively admirable "insofar as they spring from selfless or other-regarding motives"—may lull to sleep our critical faculties with regard to deployment of violent means.[24]

The American public seems to be rather inured to the routinization of American bombing in foreign policy situations that it scarcely registers on the radar screen much of the time. This is especially true if our consciences can be kept clear through deployment of a language of justification that speaks to genuine goods. The just war tradition aims to prevent such insouciance without abandoning the language of justice in international relations altogether and leaving it, thereby, to an elastic "humanitarianism" that refuses, much of the time, to conjure with the complexities of the use of force. Admirably, much of this complexity has reentered our vocabulary in the war against terrorism. It is important that it not drop out as we fight terrorists. It is important that the language of evil, even if correctly and rightly used, not segue into a Manichean universe that invites triumphalism.

Taking just war seriously raises serious questions about the use and abuse of humanitarian intervention justifications. What happened in the Kosovo intervention was a collapse of the rhetoric of justification as inapt domestic analogies got mapped onto the Balkans: Bombing Serbia was the same as initiatives against so-called hate crimes. Intervention then becomes a kind of police action—not war, not violence, never a violation of norms of proportionality and discrimination. The rhetoric of noble aim—and stopping ethnic cleansing is a noble aim—may too easily become a cover for troubling and often ineffective means. Augustinian just war thinking would deconstruct masking rhetoric by insisting that those in authority, and citizens of the United States, face up to what is going on and ask themselves the tough questions—not to forestall justifiable intervention but to try to ensure, insofar as anything in the world of politics can be ensured, that the means do not defeat, taint, or undermine the ends.

Although full fleshing out of this position is beyond the purview of this chapter, the foregoing discussion may be enough to indicate that the humanitarian intervention, or appeals to such, should not lull our critical faculties to sleep but should instead engage them deeply because these appeals have a kind of automatic urgency, an ethical imprimatur, of the sort that other sorts of war do not. If the just war tradition cavils at the particular way strategic realists sever international relations from ethical restraints construed as inapplicable to the world of men, war, and states, this tradition also challenges the particular way that appeals to humanitarianism and liberal internationalism collapse, or may collapse, domestic and foreign politics.

Notes

1. Unlike modern epistemology, both traditions—just war and realism—hold that one cannot simply bracket ontological considerations in treating any perspective of social and political life. Whether this is made as an explicit philosophic argument is another matter. Some view of what was once called "human nature" is implied if not unpacked outright.

2. Gen 11.1–9. See Augustine's discussion of the Tower of Babel in *City of God*, trans. Henry Bettenson (New York: Penguin Books, 1972), 16.4–5, pp. 657–59.

3. Augustine, *Against Faustus the Manichaean* XXII.220 in *Augustine: Political Writings* 222, trans. Michael W. Tkacz and Donald Kries, eds., Ernest L. Fortin and Donald Kries (Indianapolis: Hackett, 1994).

4. Michael Walzer, *Just and Unjust Wars*, 2d ed. (New York: Basic Books, 1992), 58–63.

5. United Nations charter, Article 2, paragraph 4.

6. Steven Lee Myers, "Chinese Embassy Bombing: A Wide Net of Blame," *New York Times* (17 April 2000), 10.

7. R. Jeffrey Smith, "U.S Has, but Won't Release Tally of Buried Iraqi Soldiers," *Washington Post* (26 March 1991), A11.

8. "Intervention: When and How?" *Commonweal*, 22 October 1999, 5.

9. There are so many critical questions to ask about this intervention. One concern, voiced by several critics, was whether this ostensibly new "universal dispensation can only apply to Serbia and a mere handful of other states that meet very exacting requirements: they must be sufficiently weak to be easily defeated, yet sufficiently advanced to present worthwhile targets for no-casualty bombardment. . . . Further they must be sufficiently illiberal to perpetrate outright massacres, yet sufficiently semi-democratic to capitulate when the mostly bloodless bombing of electrical supplies and other targets evokes the protests of inconvenienced citizens. . . ." See Edward N. Luttwack, "No-Score War," *Times Literary Supplement* (14 July 2000), 11. Luttwack adds, "What does it mean for the morality of a supposedly moral rule, when it is applied arbitrarily against some, but not others?" The fact that one can draw on Luttwack and other strategic realists to criticize weaknesses in an approach to humanitarian intervention does not mean, of course, that one is reverting to the contours of their approach wholesale.

10. Interservice rivalry was or may have been a relevant factor with regard to the use or nonuse of Apache helicopters, given the rivalry between the Army and the Air Force on the use of planes to attack surface targets. (Thanks to Judge Richard Posner for calling my attention to this issue.) See also Gregg Easterbrook, "Apocryphal Now," *New Republic* (November 11, 2000).

11. See President Clinton's videotaped address to the Serbian people, March 25, 1999, at www.cnn.com/specials/1998/10/kosovo/transcripts/clinton.html (last accessed May 10, 2000).

12. Paul W. Kahn, "War and Sacrifice in Kosovo," *Philosophy and Public Affairs* 1 (spring–summer, l999): 4.

13. See Charles Krauthammer, "The Clinton Doctrine," March 29, 1999, at www.cnn.com/allpolitics/time/1999/03/29/doctrine.html (last accessed May 10, 2000).

14. Michael Mandelbaum, "A Perfect Failure: NATO's War Against Yugoslavia," *Foreign Affairs* 78, no. 5 (September/October 1999): 5.

15. The runup to the Kosovo intervention, of course, was enormously complicated, including savvy use by the Kosovo Liberation Army of the media and international human rights groups to make the case not only for the existence of a humanitarian catastrophe—clearly the case—but for intervention of a sort that would bolster *their* cause and case even though the United States, in 1998, had characterized them as a terrorist organization.

16. Mandelbaum, "A Perfect Failure," 2–3.

17. Ibid., 7.

18. See "Remarks by the President in Media Roundtable," May 6, 1999, at www.usembassy.de/clinton99/prescon.htm (last accessed May 10, 2000). For more on how domestic themes infused the Clinton administration's foreign policy, see Michael Mandelbaum, "Foreign Policy as Social Work," *Foreign Affairs* 75, no.1 (January/February 1996): 16–32.

19. Not all cultural differences are to be respected, clearly. It would take another sort of paper to spell out the norms that every culture should observe. This would not be an impossible list because the most egregious wrongs—those that every political culture agrees are egregious, even if they violate these very norms at the same time—would include genocide or ethnic cleansing, slavery, and torture. There is going to be political controversy on the boundaries. For example, does female circumcision constitute a form of torture? For those who call it "female sexual mutilation" it clearly does; their rhetoric already reflects their commitment. Even if one has agreed that a key norm has been, or is being, violated, it does not perforce dictate what a nation's policy can or should be or what forms of intervention in any given situation can or would be appropriate. There is a routine form of intervention now—one might call it moral intervention—that takes the shape of international human rights protest through a growing list of international agencies and watchdog groups.

20. William Jefferson Clinton, "A Just and Necessary War," *New York Times* (23 May 1999), W17.

21. Max Weber, "Politics as a Vocation," in *From Max Weber: Essays in Sociology,* H. H. Gerth and C. Wright Mills, eds. (New York: Oxford University Press: 1964), 128.

22. Michael Ignatieff, *Virtual War: Kosovo and Beyond* (New York: Metropolitan Books, 2000), 6.

23. Richard B. Miller, "Humanitarian Intervention, Altruism, and the Limits of Casuistry," *Journal of Religious Ethics* 28, no.1 (spring 2000): 5.

24. Ibid., 9.

5

Justice, Political Authority, and Armed Conflict: Challenges to Sovereignty and the Just Conduct of War

JOHN KELSAY

SINCE THE END OF THE COLD WAR, the sovereignty of states has been differently conceived. So we are told, and there is ample evidence to support the statement. In this chapter, I point to three directions from which the sovereignty of states is now challenged: from "above"—that is, in terms of the claims of international organizations; from "alongside"—that is, in terms of states, often operating in loose coalitions with others, who claim the right and/or duty to cross international borders in pursuit of specified interests; and from "below"—that is, in terms of citizens' militias or peoples' armies who present themselves as defenders of a justice to which established state and/or international authorities are indifferent or even actively hostile.[1] In every case, the notion of states as political entities whose borders are sacrosanct appears to be outdated.

Was such a notion ever really in vogue, however? There is much to suggest that the answer is no. The United Nations charter as well as important religious and moral considerations militate against the judgment that the borders of states are inviolable. The idea that borders are sacrosanct did, and does, carry moral weight, largely as a check against imperialism and as a retainer of the international balance of power. Stated in terms of sanctity or inviolability, however, the sovereignty of states is overdrawn. (This is a central theme of Robert Gallucci's argument in chapter 10 of this book.) Post–cold war challenges to sovereignty from above, alongside, and below demonstrate a recovery of the importance of justice in political discourse, specifically in terms of behaviors that legitimate the exercise of political and military authority within a specified geopolitical context. When these challenges are tied to discussions of humanitarian intervention, efforts to limit terrorism, or the pursuit of "peoples' justice," they point to a renewed emphasis on the notion of just cause in the use of armed force. This emphasis on justice helps us to conceive of sovereignty properly as a political framework, albeit not an immovable one.

Such a renewed emphasis has its problems, however. Thus, I close with some reflections on the problematic of comparative justice — of competing notions of justice, as they relate to the justification and especially the conduct of war.

Challenges to State Sovereignty

From "Above"

One sign of a shifting conception of state sovereignty is found in the debate over humanitarian intervention, specifically with respect to the role of the United Nations and other international organizations. In this debate, the contributions of Secretary-General Kofi Annan are most instructive. In his 1998 Ditchley Lecture, and more recently in his report on the state of the UN and his report to the UN Millennium Committee, Secretary-General Annan argues that intervention is a moral and legal necessity in some cases if the UN is to keep its covenant with the peoples of the world. Nonetheless, the secretary-general notes, the UN recognizes state sovereignty as one of its bedrock principles. Its charter regards state boundaries, once established and recognized by the member states, as nearly sacrosanct. Indeed, throughout the charter we read again and again that the UN exists to assist in and regulate international relations between states. States may be penalized or even become the object of armed force for violations of the boundaries of other states. Yet according to Chapter 2, Article 7 of the charter, nothing in the charter should be taken to legitimate interference in the domestic affairs of the members. It is as though the charter builds a wall at the boundaries of each of the member states; respect for these walls is one of the rules of international society codified by the UN. One would need to overcome a considerable burden of proof to justify intervention within the boundaries of states—if indeed it is even proper or possible to speak of overcoming such a burden as a possibility.

The one case in which the charter clearly legitimates intervention in a state's internal affairs might be described in terms of the threat of "spillover." Thus, whenever unrest or strife within the boundaries of a member state poses a threat to international order or other states, the charter indicates that the organization is to take an interest and indeed may be justified in intervening. As the secretary-general puts it, this provision typically has been understood in terms of the type of conflict in which a civil war somehow threatens to spill over into the territory of other states—as, for example, one often heard in the past ten years or so, as European or North American leaders worried about the prospect that the various conflicts within the former Yugoslavia might carry beyond Yugoslav borders into Macedonia, Albania, or beyond. Even here, of course, there is a question of whether such spillover—actual or feared— justified intervention within Yugoslavian borders or more modest attempts to build a firewall to contain the conflict. As the secretary-general has it, however, some form of action by the UN, inclusive of armed force, has been considered justifiable by member states in such cases, and this intervention has been understood as a kind of exception to the general rule against such action.

One may pause here to wonder why the rule against intervention enjoys such privileged status—nearly, if not in fact, the status of an absolute rule. The answer is not hard to find. According to the secretary-general, the UN charter's recognition of the value of sovereignty, and the organization's continued affirmation of it, provides protection against imperialism. The emphasis on sovereignty, and thus against intervention, is tied to the development of international society in a postcolonial world. Small and weak states thereby are protected against domination by the established states, whose will often is identified with the interests of the "international community." In a sense, protection of those smaller states becomes one of the implicit—or perhaps even declared—purposes for which the UN exists.

Nevertheless, the secretary-general asserts, no one should think that the UN was created to protect the sovereignty of states, even small and weak ones, in a way that allows this bedrock principle of international society to be used as a cloak for violators of human rights. The covenant of the UN is with the peoples of the world, not the states, he argues. Thus, in cases in which the interests of peoples conflict with the sovereignty of states, the UN must—in the moral and legal sense of that term—consider intervention, by means proportionate to the problem and calculated to achieve the end of bringing relief. Many problems are the result of poverty or underdevelopment, and therefore are tied to the mandate of the UN to enable the peoples of the world to further their ability to live a decent life. In those cases, economic intervention or economic aid may assist in the provision of relief. In other cases, however, violations of human rights are the result of local elites pitting some portion of a state's population against others; if relief cannot be obtained by other means, armed intervention may be required. If it is, the member states have a duty to support the mission. In his report to the Millennium Committee, Secretary-General Annan stipulates that the UN's covenant with the peoples of the world is to secure freedom from want and freedom from fear. The member states—especially those that are strong—owe a debt of solidarity to peoples who are victims of want or oppression; indeed, says Annan, the UN was created to recognize and pay off this debt.[2]

From "Alongside"

Secretary-General Annan is an advocate for an increased UN role in humanitarian intervention. Others are not so convinced that the UN is well situated to carry out this role. Thus, a variety of just war analysts (including Jean Bethke Elshtain in chapter 4 of this book) argue that if humanitarian intervention is justified at all, it is justified in terms of claims of justice.[3] The question of agency—or, in just war terms, right authority—is less important than the duty to respond to those claims. Consider, for example, the oft-cited essay by Michael Walzer, "The Politics of Rescue."[4] Intervention, Walzer writes, has always been a problem, even for thinkers who favor an "internationalist ethic," by which the suffering of people outside one's own state carries moral weight. This has been so because of fears of imperialism. When the United States was locked in cold war "combat" with the Soviet Union, this attitude made sense. Now, however, "in this post-imperial and post–cold war age," a "small but growing number of people on the left now favor intervening, here or there, driven by an internationalist ethic." Walzer's comment is that these people "are right to feel driven."

> Internationalism has always been understood to require support for, and even participation in, popular struggles. Liberation should always be a local initiative. In the face of human disaster, however, internationalism has a more urgent meaning. It's not possible to wait; anyone who can take the initiative should do so. Active opposition to massacre and massive deportation is morally necessary; its risks must be accepted.[5]

There are important questions about timing and means. Furthermore, there is an important question about who can authorize intervention; Walzer judges that in many cases an international force will be best. Nevertheless, the claims of justice are primary; for the victims of wrongdoing, intervention is necessary: "Anyone who can take the initiative should do so." One cannot rule out intervention by individual states, in cases where such action is a means to prevent massive violations of human rights.

Similarly, consider the 1993 statement by the National Conference of Catholic Bishops, "The Harvest of Justice Is Sown in Peace."[6] "Humanitarian intervention," the bishops say, has to do with "the forceful, direct intervention by one or more states or international organizations in the internal affairs of other states for essentially humanitarian purposes." Such intervention aims at the protection of human rights; in some cases, it is not only permissible but an obligation of the strong, acting out of solidarity with the weak. Here the bishops quote Pope John Paul II's 1987 encyclical *On Social Concern*:

> [When] populations are succumbing to the attacks of an unjust aggressor, states no longer have a "right to indifference." It seems clear that their duty is to disarm the aggressor if all other means have proved ineffective. The principles of sovereignty of states and of noninterference in their internal affairs . . . cannot constitute a screen behind which torture and murder may be carried out.[7]

Thus, the demands of justice are of primary concern. States that violate those demands provide a just cause for intervention. Such intervention may be carried out by international organizations such as the

UN. It also may be carried out by individual states. The point is the defense of justice; agency is a secondary concern.

Discussions of humanitarian intervention therefore suggest that the sovereignty of states is under challenge not only from "above"—that is, from those agencies such as the UN that in some sense constitute humanity's gesture toward world order. These discussions also suggest that sovereignty is under challenge from "alongside"—that is, from states whose governments understand themselves as responding to the duty to defend people who are victims of oppression.

This particular challenge is enhanced by the post–September 11, 2001, campaign against terrorism led by the United States. The campaign against terror announced by President Bush targets not only Usama bin Ladin and the al-Qa`ida organization associated with him but all persons or groups who carry out acts of terror. Moreover, the president's announced program makes no distinctions between those who carry out acts of terror and those who "harbor" or otherwise provide support for them. Thus, a nation that "hosts" groups associated with international terrorism may be subject to attacks. The full implication of the president's program will take years to appreciate fully. In the case of Afghanistan, the "no distinctions" provision led to a direct effort to depose the Taliban in their capacity as governors of Afghanistan.

In other cases, however, one could imagine the president's edict to involve less in the way of direct attacks on an established regime and more in the way of crossing international boundaries to strike at training camps or other facilities related to acts of terror. This strategy could manifest in the form of U.S. military and intelligence cooperation with other nations (as in the Philippines). Suppose, for example, that group X, which has been identified with strikes against American nationals traveling in the Middle East, utilizes bases in Lebanon. The government of Lebanon, though not identifiable as a sponsor of group X and officially desiring to disassociate itself from the actions of the group, is unable to bring the group's members under control. In the strict sense, the Lebanese government is not engaged in state sponsorship of terrorism; its relationship is more one of acquiescence. Yet for a variety of reasons, the government is reluctant to invite a foreign or international organization to intervene. In fact, it resists the idea of intervention, making its objections known in a variety of international forums.

Under the Bush doctrine, would the United States and/or its coalition partners be justified in violating the borders of Lebanon to prevent the members of group X from carrying out acts of terror? It is hard to know in the abstract. In any case, there will be important questions of timing and means. Surely, however, the logic of the president's dictum lends itself to a positive answer. Just as state sovereignty ought not provide a shield behind which governments may oppress their citizens, it also ought not provide a shield behind which terrorist groups may hide, when particular governments prove either unable or unwilling to exercise control. Thus, state sovereignty is under challenge from alongside, as well as from above—from individual states and their coalition partners, as well as from established international organizations.

From "Below"

In our imagined scenario, the government of Lebanon cannot or will not discipline a group based on Lebanese territory, and the United States and its coalition partners intervene to prevent the group from carrying out its program of international terrorism—that is, they intervene in the name of justice. The case can be made more complex, however. If we imagine that group X thinks of itself as engaged in the pursuit of justice (as most such groups do), we have a challenge to Lebanon's sovereignty that proceeds from more than one direction. The challenge is not only from alongside but from "below."

At this point, we do better to turn from imaginary to real-world scenarios. In the case of al-Qa`ida, we have a good example of the phenomenon. Here a group that does not hold the status of a state nevertheless challenges state sovereignty and considers itself justified in doing so. Al-Qa`ida is one of many such groups, and each poses distinctive challenges. Nevertheless, we get a sense of the claims advanced by attending to this singular group.

Consider, for example, the reasoning advanced in the February 23, 1998, *Declaration Concerning Struggle against Jews and Crusaders* signed by Usama bin Ladin and his colleagues.[8] This document argues that the United States and its allies are engaged in a war of annihilation against Muslims. It accuses the United States of occupying the Arabian peninsula, in direct violation of longstanding Islamic tradition. The

Saudi regime, which bases its legitimacy on its role as "guardian" of the integrity of the holy cities of Mecca and Medina, is either too weak to end this occupation or too corrupt to care. In either case, the state cannot be regarded as adequate to the task of defending justice, and Muslims need not wait for orders from the state to defend themselves. In terminology drawn from classical Islamic jurisprudence, the authors of the *Declaration* articulate "the judgment that it is an individual duty for any Muslim who is able to fight the Americans and their allies, civilians and soldiers, in any country where that is possible." By stipulating that the duty is "individual," the authors indicate that this situation is an emergency, which in the Islamic law of war flows from and indicates the existence of a context in which the ordinary lines of authority no longer hold. In classical texts, a woman need not obtain the permission of her husband or father to fight; an underage person need not obtain the permission of his or her parents. By extension, ordinary Muslims need not wait for the order of an existing government. The call, to each and to all, is to fight in defense of Islamic values.

In a 1996 statement—sometimes known as the *Ladenese Epistle*—the call to fight is focused on the Arabian peninsula.[9] Muslims are asked to support efforts, characterized in terms of "lightning-quick strikes" aimed at the removal of U.S. troops from the peninsula—again, without regard for the authority of the Saudi regime. In the 1998 declaration, the scope of the campaign is expanded. One must strike not only at targets close to one's homeland; one also must carry the campaign to an international level. In a sense, this substate group is claiming trans-state authority. Its members or allies are authorized to fight members of the enemy and "plunder their wealth" in any geographic or political location where that is possible. Alongside the claims of justice, the notion of state sovereignty pales.

State Sovereignty: Respect versus Sanctity

Thus, the sovereignty of states is under challenge from a variety of directions. Indeed, some thinkers have argued that the very concept of sovereignty is changing—that international society is moving away from a Westphalian notion, in which the borders of states are inviolable, and toward a liberal or populist notion, in which regard for the borders of states is tempered by considerations of justice — particularly as reflected in international human rights discourse.

On closer examination, however, one wonders if this is so. Were state borders ever really regarded as sacrosanct or inviolable? Or was the integrity of borders more a matter of respect, founded in turn on worries about the ways particular states might turn the notion of justified intervention into an excuse for imperialism? Perhaps the moral value of state borders is better construed as a product of history, a particular way of delimiting conflict between groups of people trying to establish geopolitical identities.[10]

For example, consider again Kofi Annan's comments regarding the UN charter. Chapter 7, Article 42, establishes the duty and rights of members to resort to military force in cases in which international peace and security are threatened. At the same time, Chapter 7 makes clear that nothing in the charter is to be understood as authorizing interference in the domestic affairs of the members. This provision sounds like an absolute limit with respect to intervention. Yet as I have noted, Annan argues that the UN's covenant, as articulated in the preamble to the charter, is with the peoples of the world — not with states or governments. Thus, considerations of justice, particularly as articulated in the Universal Declaration of Human Rights and other international human rights instruments, would seem to override concern for the integrity of borders. Overall, the secretary-general's arguments regarding intervention suggest that state sovereignty is derivative from or complementary to justice — a kind of check against the temptation of strong states toward imperial domination. Thus, the integrity of the borders of members of the UN is not an absolute limit; it is useful insofar as it preserves stability and protects against injustice but not fundamental in the same sense as prohibitions of torture or genocide.

That this is a defensible reading of the status of the particular forms of sovereignty expressed in the UN charter is borne out by consideration of the history of the concept. For example, political scientist Robert H. Jackson argues that international society underwent an enormous change following World War II.[11] The particular change in which Jackson (and I) is interested may be characterized as a shift from positive to negative sovereignty. The regime of positive sovereignty, as Jackson has it, required that states that are recognized as sovereign, and thus as members of international society, have a long track record of the type of behavior members called "civilized." That term summarized a body of norms regulating the behavior of states. It also provided a shorthand for recognizing that civilized behavior in international relations was correlative with domestic institutions that were proven, by and large, to maintain peace within a state's borders. In terms of domestic and foreign affairs, then, the assumption of international society was that member states could be counted on to behave in a manner consistent with the norms of civilization. Or, to turn this foundation around, the prerequisite for recognition of sovereignty was that recognized members of the international club regarded a state as dependable and civilized. From the time of Napoleon to World War I, Europeans—and, to a lesser extent, North Americans—played by the rules of positive sovereignty. At the end of World War I, Woodrow Wilson's proposals regarding self-determination of peoples posed a slight challenge to this regime. This old order of positive sovereignty triumphed, however, until it was finally shattered by the events of World War II.

I want to be clear about Jackson's terms: "Positive" is used in the sense that the enjoyment of sovereignty, and thus full membership in international society, carries with it certain civic, political, and moral requirements. One might make an analogy with certain historic conceptions of citizenship or citizen's rights (for example, voting). In Jackson's terms, a positive (or, perhaps, strong) notion of citizenship might require certain demonstrations of civic virtue or of holding a stake in the long-term survival of a state (for example, ownership of property.) Think of one of the ways a moral value such as autonomy works: One must show the ability to stand on one's own feet to enjoy the rights associated with that value. One might require, for example, that a patient show the ability to comprehend certain medical terminology before going to the trouble of attempting to obtain informed consent. The less the ability is present, the less stringent the requirement for a patient to be regarded as part of the decision-making procedure—and so on.

In this sense, there is nothing inconsistent in the fact that the regime of positive sovereignty allowed—indeed, encouraged—member states to practice imperialism. Intervention in the affairs of peoples "not yet ready for sovereignty" could be considered an act of beneficence. The burden of proof would be on such peoples to demonstrate the presence of leadership and institutions capable of sustaining the type of behavior required by international society.

Post–World War II international society has been irreversibly altered by a shift to what Jackson calls "negative" sovereignty. Here sovereignty becomes the rule rather than the exception. In other words, wherever a group of people can obtain recognition as a state, with borders set by international agreement, sovereignty is a given. Instead of placing the burden of proof on those who would escape the yoke of imperialism and obtain membership in international society, the burden is on those who would deny sovereignty, and thus membership, to a people claiming statehood. If acceptance of the "burdens of empire" provided a certain nobility to the realities of international society from about 1815 to 1945, the charge of imperialism is *prima facie* evidence of wrongdoing in the postwar era. The presumption of negative sovereignty, in other words, is that a "people" deserves recognition as a state whether there is evidence that the state regime can be a stable member of international society or not. And intervention comes to be equivalent to imperialism— a throwback, as it were, to the old order of positive sovereignty.

Jackson's analysis provides the context for the secretary-general's comments. That is, intervention poses a peculiar problem for a postcolonial or postimperial international society in which (to use a domestic analogy) all states are treated as autonomous adults, with full rights of sovereignty and liberty. They clearly are limited in their rights, and therefore may be inhibited, resisted, or punished only with respect to behavior that harms other autonomous adults (viz., member states). The problem is, what does one do about domestic violence? Should adults whose behavior is otherwise unobjectionable be allowed to abuse members of their own household as long as the violence does not spill over into the larger neighborhood? To pose another kind of case, should landlords be permitted to abuse their tenants as long as there is no threat to the holdings of other landlords?

Jackson argues that the move to level the playing field of international society or to expand membership by altering standards of sovereignty could be regarded as insufficient. Self-determination of peoples, though an operative norm of post–World War II international society, was not and has not been applied to every group. Jackson would have us imagine a situation in which elites in a variety of settings have been able to take advantage of the regime of negative sovereignty so that certain borders and states are recognized by the international community. The numbers are striking: There are three times as many sovereign states now as there were before World War II. Yet the recognition of boundaries at the behest—or with respect to the persuasive capacity—of some often is accompanied by a disregard for the claims or potential claims of others. The claims of Bangladesh are recognized; what about those of Kashmir? The claims of Uzbekistan are recognized; what about those of Chechnya? And so on. From Jackson's perspective, although the regime of negative sovereignty responds to real difficulties in its predecessor, it ends up creating numerous weak states. Unable to sustain a viable economy, without strong and established political institutions, susceptible to conflicting claims by the diverse peoples who live within a set of recognized boundaries, such "quasi-states" are made-to-order for conflict. According to the secretary-general, they also are bound to create problems to which international intervention provides one solution.

These considerations demonstrate that respect for the sovereignty of member states of the UN is best viewed as a value constructed in the interests of justice. In other words, justice is prior to or more fundamental than respect for the integrity of borders. The secretary-general's various pronouncements reflect the notion that the justice of states—and thus their legitimacy—is tied to the practice of respect for human rights at home and abroad; the ability to foster economic development to secure a decent standard of living for citizens; and avoidance of aggression against other members of the international community.[12] For much of the period between the development of its charter and the end of the cold war, the UN focused on the third criterion. Thus, the borders of any state should be regarded as worthy of respect as long as it did not pose a threat to other states, either by aggression or by the inability to prevent "spillover" connected with domestic strife.

After the cold war, however, the secretary-general's declarations indicate that respect for human rights and progress in economic development now receive greater weight: Any state sufficiently lacking in these characteristics may be described as in need of help, and at some point such lack becomes sufficient to justify armed intervention. Such reasoning turns political discourse toward classical formulations of religious-moral traditions such as Western just war criteria or the Islamic judgments pertaining to jihad. In both cases, the presupposition of political legitimacy includes, among other things, conformity with standards of justice. Such conformity therefore becomes a critical aspect in the assessment of a political entity's claim of sovereignty. Political entities, we might say, have a claim against intervention as long as their behavior accords with agreed-upon standards of justice (such as those identified above). Insofar as they depart from or fail to conform to such standards, their claim is diminished. Correlatively, insofar as a political entity's claim against intervention is diminished, others may be permitted—or in some cases required—to offer assistance of various kinds, including armed force, in the service of justice.

Consider, for example, the account of just war tradition advanced by James Turner Johnson in *Morality and Contemporary Warfare*.[13] Johnson argues that the post–cold war setting makes increasingly clear the critical contribution of a figure such as Thomas Aquinas to just war reasoning. Thomas' formulation is surprisingly compact. Resort to war, he notes, requires three things: right authority, just cause, and right intent.[14] This list leaves out several criteria that more recent interpreters count as critical; there is no mention, for example, of the idea that war should be undertaken as a last resort or that one must believe that war will maintain or attain a proportionate balance between good and evil. One does not see in Thomas's succinct list a mention of the requirement that there be a reasonable hope of success, though he does tie war to the aim of restoring or securing peace. Rules for just conduct are not specified, though they may be inferred. The focus is on resort to war and in that on the most basic criteria.

Johnson's point is not that the "missing" criteria are unimportant. Indeed, one probably can find most if not all of those criteria at some point in Thomas' opus, if one feels the need.[15] The point is that the three "basic" criteria point to the most fundamental concerns of just war tradition, as it reflects on the relations between political justice and the use of military force. Justice—in the sense of the common good of a people—is the basic value of political life. Establishment of an authority that is understood as "right" or "legitimate" is a requirement in that regard. Indeed, the purpose of such an authority is to administer and protect the common good. In fulfillment of this purpose, a legitimate authority possesses the right and even the duty to make war. When it exercises this right with the intention of protecting the common good, and thus of "securing peace, of punishing evil-doers, and of uplifting the good," a governing authority is fulfilling the purpose for which it was established.[16]

Thus, justice (in the sense of the common good) is primary in thinking about the political life of human beings. Its fulfillment requires the establishment of a legitimate authority to which the right of war is assigned, to be exercised in the pursuit of justice or "the advancement of good and the avoidance of evil."[17] It follows as well that if justice is the reason for the establishment of institutions of governance, service of the common good also is the measure of any particular government's legitimacy.

Why, then, does the just war tradition include the other, "missing" criteria? (Missing, that is, in Thomas' succinct account.) Because, as Johnson puts it, the tradition is realistic about the inability of human beings to discern the meaning of justice in particular contexts. After all, according to Thomas, agreement on first principles is universal, or nearly so, but the more one moves toward the details of practical judgment, the more disagreement and error are likely to appear.[18] Furthermore, the tradition is realistic about the imperfect consonance of human will with standards of justice. After all, we are capable not only of shortsightedness and faulty logic but also of intemperance and weakness of will. That being the case, several secondary or complementary criteria are necessary to fill out the just war tradition's vision of a proper defense of the common good. The requirement of last resort, for example, is best construed as a means of securing deliberation about the various types of injustice one must oppose and about the most fitting means of opposition. Although there is no strong or bright line dividing military and nonmilitary means of pursuing justice, it may be true that a nonmilitary approach will work best for certain cases. Moreover, given the difficulties associated with military force—not least the possibility that persons who are not guilty of injustice will be killed—nonmilitary approaches often are preferred. The requirement that the balance between good and evil be proportionate may be construed as a check on the zeal of those who would pursue justice by means of military force. How much will the pursuit of justice cost, in terms of damage to ordinary life or the resources a community has for sustaining it? After all, to do more harm than good in the pursuit of a just cause would be morally incongruous, to say the least.

Such considerations foster deliberation among those who would oppose injustice. With regard to intervention, such deliberation must address several questions. Questions related to proportionality have been particularly important. Given that intervention suggests a disruption in the affairs of an established political community, will the good to be attained outweigh the uncertainty—even disorder—that is likely to follow? Furthermore, what are the likely costs to the intervening party or parties? Will intervention stem the tide of civil strife in a particular case? Or will it make matters worse—for example, by creating a large refugee population for which no one is likely to take responsibility?

From the just war perspective, the burden of such deliberation falls on those who exercise authority in the administration of political affairs. Such authority belongs to "the sovereign"—which for several centuries has been construed to indicate the head or government of a state recognized as a member of the international community. As I have suggested, however, it is precisely that construal that is under question in the contemporary discussion of intervention. Part of the reason that is so, it must be said, is that justice, understood as promoting and securing the common good, remains primary in thinking about political ethics. Respect for the sovereignty of particular states is an important value, and overriding it requires wise and careful deliberation. Yet the "bare fact" that a government exists does not mean it is ordered toward the common good. If one agrees with Thomas and more generally with just war tradition, the notion that political life is intended to "protect and foster the conditions for human flourishing" presents one way of understanding Kofi Annan's contention that the covenant of the UN (or, more generally, those who exercise authority) is with the peoples of the world—not with states.[19]

This same emphasis on justice as the fount of political legitimacy is found in the Islamic tradition. A. K. S. Lambton observes that there are three primary types of political writing in Islam, each with its own way of articulating the relationships between justice and political life: the treatises of philosophers, the advice given by counselors to rulers as per the "mirror of princes" genre, and the judgments advanced by jurists.[20]

I highlight the last as an example of case-by-case reflection on the relations between the *Shari`a* (or ideal way) and political practice.[21]

If we examine a treatise such as that of al-Shaybani (d. 804 C.E.), a scholar and judge in the Hanafi tradition of *usul al-fiqh* (the attempt to comprehend the *Shari`a* through interpretation of signs provided by God—in particular the Qur`an and the example of the prophet Muhammad), we find that from the start war is conceived as an activity limited by particular values.[22] "When you fight," said the Prophet, "do so in the path of God."[23] In itself, such a saying reflects the Qur`an's most basic statement of the duty of humanity: to "command the good and forbid the evil."[24] It is in the service of this directive that one carries out or exercises *jihad* ("effort") *fi sabil allah* ("in the path of God"). Human beings fight for many reasons; as the historical record shows, lust for fame, fortune, power, and the shedding of blood have all been considered ample cause to engage in fighting. Jurists such as al-Shaybani, however, give approval only for fighting "in the path of God," and thus out of a duty to command good and forbid evil.

Again, as the Qur`an itself indicates, fighting is governed by considerations of justice. At 22:39–40 we read the verses that biographers of Muhammad set forth as the first authorization of justified fighting in Islam:

> Permission for fighting is given to those who are victims of aggression. God is powerful in assisting them. These are people wrongly driven from their land for saying "God is our Lord." If God did not deter one group of people by means of another, then monasteries, churches, synagogues, and mosques where the name of God is abundantly mentioned would be destroyed.[25]

In other places, the notion expressed in these verses is reiterated and expanded. At 2:190*ff.*, we read that Muslims should fight against those who commit aggression—but in doing so should avoid injustice. At 2:154, the Prophet and his community are commanded to fight their enemies even during months set aside as "sacred" because "injustice is worse than fighting." Indeed, even in the famous "verses of the sword" (Qur`an 9: 5, 29)—notoriously cited by various interpreters as authorizing the perpetual waging of war by Muslims against unbelievers—the context makes clear that the justice of war is tied to the provocations given by those who break their treaties and commit aggression. The point—

namely, that war is connected with a vision in which justice is the measure of political behavior—seems clear. Although Muslim authorities typically do not list the criteria for a just war in the succinct manner of Thomas Aquinas or other just war thinkers, their concerns are similar. For example, they wonder whether one may initiate war only in response to an attack by an enemy, or whether the fact that the enemy is unwilling to implement Islamic values as the standard of justice is sufficient to justify war. Some (e.g., the Hanafi jurists with whom al-Shaybani is associated) answer that one knows an enemy only by its aggressive behavior; others (e.g., al-Shafi`i and those who follow his precedent) argue that an unwillingness to implement Islamic values is sufficient. The point that underlies both answers is that political life is to be governed by justice. The sovereignty of states and the integrity of borders are in some sense related to, even dependent upon, adherence to standards of justice.

Nevertheless, one must be concerned about the more prudential aspects of justice identified by the just war tradition in its criteria of last resort, overall proportionality, reasonable hope of success, and aim of peace. From early on, Islamic jurists such as al-Shaybani, al-Shafi`i, and others conceived the right of war—and thus deliberation about such matters—as limited to the head of state, whose legitimacy was partly guaranteed, in turn, by an arrangement securing "consultation" (*al-shura*) with recognized interpreters of the *Shari`a*. In some sense this was a response to the ways that various groups within the Muslim community tended to arrogate the right of war to themselves, with troublesome consequences for ordinary life. The group known as "Kharijites" (more correctly, *al-khawarij*), for example, is presented in Islamic tradition as the prototype of those who, though undoubtedly sincere, nevertheless take the directives provided by the Qur`an and the example of the Prophet to authorize military activity that does more harm than good. Considerations of the "fit" between military action and the injustice it is meant to remedy, or of the overall balance between benefits achieved and harms done, are not a part of Khariji reasoning. At least partly in response to the problem posed by such substate groups, Islamic political thought developed a very strong emphasis on the right of the Caliph, as the embodiment of a centralized authority, to determine the time and occasion of resort to war. When such an emphasis no longer made sense, in terms of shifting patterns of political life, a new generation of scholars declared that the right of war was confined to provincial governors who could claim authorization through the caliphate; when this arrangement passed, the right of war in effect belonged to rulers within Islam who knew no superior except God and God's Shari`a.

In the dispensation we call modernity, Muslim authorities by and large have followed the precedent established at Westphalia. That is, the right of war belongs to the established governments of the geopolitical entities we call states, with important leanings in the direction of the authority of international organizations. Nevertheless, a considerable body of Islamic writing over the past two centuries embodies a debate over the justice of existing state and international regimes—and thus over whether and under what conditions nonstate or substate groups of Muslims might be authorized to carry out military activity in defense of "people's justice." Many Islamic thinkers participating in this debate are concerned primarily with injustice in a particular locale—one thinks, for example, of the authors of the *Charter of Hamas*; the Egyptian *apologia* for the assassins of Sadat known as *The Neglected Duty*;[26] or, in more formal scholarly terms, the treatise on *Islam and the Logic of Power* authored by Shaykh Muhammad Husayn Fadlallah, who was associated during the 1980s with the Lebanese organization known as Hizbullah.[27] Others, such as Usama bin Ladin and his colleagues—though still primarily concerned with the redress of local or at least regional grievances—argue that the root of injustice lies beyond the historic territory of Islam and thus justifies an international campaign against those (such as the United States and its allies) whom they hold responsible.

Problems of Comparative Justice

If conceptions of sovereignty are changing in our time, they are doing so in ways that recover the priority of justice as the primary norm for political life—specifically with respect to the justification of war. As one might ascertain from the foregoing comments, I am not convinced that justice was ever missing from conceptions of sovereignty. Rather, respect for the integrity of modern state formations developed as a particular way of protecting values of justice, in conjunction with particular historical needs. As such, the concept of sovereignty is changing only if one assumes that "respect" meant that the borders of states were "sacrosanct" or "inviolable." I am not sure they ever were, so I am unconvinced that we are seeing a radical shift in the concept itself.

Nevertheless, the post–cold war emphasis on justice does suggest a kind of recovery of an aspect of sovereignty that many thinkers, for prudential reasons, were willing to deemphasize following World War II. In particular, the interest of states in delimiting imperialism was an important feature of the UN charter's strictures against intervention. Since 1988 leaders of the UN as well as important interpreters of just war tradition have argued for the importance of the notion of humanitarian intervention in the name of justice. These arguments can be joined with those advanced by the president of the United States in the name of the post–September 11 campaign against international terrorism, as well as those advanced by groups of irregular fighters who, like those associated with Usama bin Ladin, believe that the governments of states are too weak or too corrupt to defend important values of justice. As the bin Ladin case suggests, many of these fighters appeal to Islamic conceptions of justice and armed struggle as legitimating their behavior.

If we take seriously the arguments of bin Ladin and other activists who claim Islamic warrant, we may be put in mind of historical periods in which the primary authority of appeals to justice had to be joined to prudential concerns to address certain difficulties. Thus, the just war and *jihad* traditions both emphasized the procedural aspects of right authority, in part as a way of dealing with the expansive nature of claims of justice. In effect, both attempted to limit the right of narrowly defined or overzealous groups to use armed force in defense of "people's justice" by imposing a requirement that the right of war be confined to sovereign authorities. The hope was that as a result the secondary, though critical, aspects of justice (delineated in terms of concerns for overall proportionality, last resort, reasonable hope of success, and the like) might be more consistently addressed.

Those who argue that we are seeing a radical shift in conceptions of sovereignty most often consider that we are moving toward a more internationalist notion. In this vein, sovereignty is moving away from particular states and more toward international organizations such as the UN. Certainly, Kofi Annan has been an advocate for an increased role for international organizations with respect to cases of humanitarian intervention.

Humanitarian intervention is not the only kind of case in which military action is justified, however. At least, it is not the only kind of case in which claims of justice involving armed force are being advanced. In the campaign against terrorism, as in the call to armed struggle advanced by al-Qa`ida and analogous groups, claims of justice have been advanced that, in a sense, are made for a head-on collision. Anyone reading seriously the rhetoric of bin Ladin and other "Islamicists" will understand the depth of division between the reading of history advanced there and that advanced by the United States and its allies.

In this context, concerns for justice lead not to an adjudication of values or to possibilities for negotiation but to conflict. In bin Ladin's vision, Muslims are the victims of an international plot that seeks to delimit their ability to carry out the mission assigned by God to the community of those who submit—that is, commanding good and forbidding evil. In this view, the United States and its allies—or, in other formulations, the UN and "the criminal Kofi Annan"—are aligned against Islam in a manner that not only is harmful to Muslims but in the long run is detrimental to the human race.[28]

At stake in this encounter between the United States and its allies on one hand and those who see the world in the manner of bin Ladin on the other are competing visions of justice, which at least as currently formulated are irreconcilable. Not—I repeat, not—that Islamic conceptions of justice are inherently irreconcilable with those advanced by the United States and its allies or those advanced by the UN, in which Muslim delegates have consistently worked to craft and implement the instruments associated with international notions of human rights. My argument is that those who see history in the terms articulated in the 1998 declaration of bin Ladin and his colleagues have a particular way of interpreting Islam and its demand for justice, and that way does not seem to be subject to adjudication with that of the United States and its allies—or, indeed, with other Muslims, for that matter. Like the Khawarij represented in Islamic tradition, contemporary fighters for Islam consider themselves the vanguard of justice in the world, and their zeal for justice does not allow them to hear the warnings—repeated by numerous Muslim authorities—that their actions bring about more harm than good.[29]

If I am right, then the various conceptions of justice currently in conflict are not likely to yield any ground in substantive debate. Nor are they likely to agree on any existing or readily conceivable claim of right authority or sovereignty—even one governed by international organizations and thus claiming to represent the interests of the "international community." In such a conflict, does justice simply become a matter determined by the victors? Or are there procedures or measures by which the competing claims of justice can be compared and perhaps adjudicated? One is reminded of the way the architects of modern international law formulated a conception of "simultaneous ostensible justice." One was to imagine, they suggested, two opposing forces, both appealing to justice as the governing standard for political life and thus as a reason for war. The competing claims could not be easily adjudicated, at least by any human authority. One side must have more justice than the other—but which one? Justice was simultaneous, in the sense that both sides had a legitimate claim or grievance. But the simultaneity also was ostensible, in the sense that one side ultimately must have the preponderance of justice. Which side that was ultimately would be determined in the court of history or time, or by God.

In the meantime, what does one do? One could insist that both sides observe standards of justice in the conduct of war. For the architects of modern international law, schoolmen such as Vitoria and Suarez or lawyers such as Grotius, this approach implied that both sides could be required and expected to adhere to *jus in bello* restraints—that is, to observe the prohibition against direct and intentional targeting of noncombatants, as well as to show due care with respect to the more nebulous but equally important criterion of proportionality in means. In just war terms, one would expect forces engaged in the pursuit of justice to strike directly at targets identified in terms of military necessity alone. One also would expect these forces to show due care with respect to concerns regarding excessive force—understood in terms of the unavoidable yet unintended civilian casualties identified in the cold but important phrase "collateral damage," as well as in terms raised by questions such as "Will the use of a certain weapon or tactic make the resumption of ordinary life, once conflict ceases, easier or more difficult?"

This restriction (analogous to noncombatant immunity) also makes sense in *jihad* terms. One of the points at which the 1998 declaration by bin Ladin and his colleagues involves a clear departure from Islamic precedent has to do precisely with targeting of civilians. As the declaration has it, every Muslim should fight the Americans and their allies, civilians (*madiniyyin*) and soldiers (`askarin`) alike. There is no provision for this strategy in the tradition of Islamic political thought. Even the emergency provision suggested by the declaration's stipulation that the duty to fight is an individual duty for every Muslim deals with the demise of lines of authority—not with broadening the scope of legitimate targets. The *jihad* restraint, like the just war analogue, has to do with a functional delineation of noncombatants. As the late Ayatullah Mutahhari put it, when the Qur`an says (at 2:190*ff.*) that just fighters target those who are aggressors, doers of oppressive acts, it means those who are opposing justice on the field of battle. It does not mean nonfighters or noncombatants, whose "guilt" could be regarded at most as supporting those they love or on whom they are dependent for protection by ordinary human means—sending food, maintaining human contact. These persons can never be legitimate targets of direct military attack.

A full exposition of what might be called the "emergency provision" in Islam and the relationship of bin Ladin's argument to it must await another day.[30] Suffice to say that the need to address this issue is a matter raised not only by bin Ladin but also by the tactics of fighters in Palestine/Israel. For now, however, it will be enough to point to this standard as a hopeful way of adjudicating the competing claims of justice advanced after September 11, 2001. As in another time—when those concerned to maintain the connections between justice, political life, and the use of armed force had resort to an emphasis on *jus in bello* restraints as a minimum criterion for measuring justice—contemporary interpreters of the just war and *jihad* traditions have an interest in the prohibition of direct and intentional targeting of civilians. In other words, all of us have an interest in the words of the Prophet of Islam, who said: "Fight in the path of God. Do not cheat or commit treachery; do not mutilate or kill women, children, or old men."[31]

Notes

1. I note here that Stanley Hoffman uses metaphors that are similarly directional in the discussion of intervention in *World Disorders* (New York: Rowman and Littlefield, 1998), 15–26.

2. The text of Secretary-General Annan's Ditchley Lecture is available in several places, most readily at the official UN website: www.un.org/News/Press/docs/1998/19980626.sgsg6613.r1.html; for the Millennium Report, see www.un.org/millennium/sg/report.

3. Along with Elshtain, see Paul Ramsey's *The Just War: Force and Political Responsibility* (Savage, Md.: Littlefield, Adams, 1983); subsequently in this chapter I discuss the approaches of Michael Walzer, the National Conference of Catholic Bishops, and James Turner Johnson. In this vein, I am grateful to G. Scott Davis for allowing me to read his forthcoming essay on "Humanitarian Intervention and Just War Criteria."

4. Michael Walzer, "The Politics of Rescue," *Social Research* 62, no. 1 (spring 1995): 53–66.

5. Ibid., 61.

6. The text of the bishops' statement appears in Gerard F. Powers, Drew Christiansen, and Robert T. Hennemeyer, eds., *Peacemaking: Moral and Policy Challenges* (Washington, D.C.: U.S. Catholic Conference, 1994).

7. John Paul II, *Sollicitudo Rei Socialis* ("On Social Concern"), 30 December 1987.

8. A translation of the document was published, with my commentary, in "Bin Ladin's Reasons," *Christian Century* 119, no. 5 (27 February–6 March 2002): 26–29. The declaration also is widely available on the Internet—for example at www.fas.org/irp/world/para/docs/980223-fatwa.htm.

9. The epistle, translated from Arabic and posted online by the *Washington Post* in 2001, also has been posted at www.sid-ss.net/911/ref911.htm (last accessed 6 March 2003).

10. For example, see the discussion in Charles W. Kegley and Gregory A. Raymond, *Exorcising the Ghost of Westphalia: Building World Order in the New Millennium* (Englewood Cliffs, N.J.: Prentice Hall, 2001), where the type of sovereignty associated with Westphalia and thus counted as the "root" of modern notions of the inviolability of borders of members of the international community is presented as a response to very specific patterns in international politics. Kegley and Raymond argue that those patterns no longer hold and that the Westphalian model therefore should be replaced by one that is more congruent with contemporary patterns of international relations.

11. Robert H. Jackson, *Quasi-states: Sovereignty, International Relations, and the Third World* (New York: Cambridge, 1990); see also Robert H. Jackson, ed., *Sovereignty at the Millennium* (Oxford: Blackwell, 1999).

12. Kofi Annan, Ditchley Lecture.

13. James Turner Johnson, *Morality and Contemporary Warfare* (New Haven, Conn.: Yale University Press, 1999).

14. Thomas Aquinas, *Summa Theologica* II-II q.40 a.1.

15. For example, see ibid., II-II q.64 a.2 and a.7.

16. Ibid., II-II q. 40.

17. Ibid.

18. Ibid., I-II, q. 94 a. 6

19. For this language, see the statement issued by the Institute of American Values and signed by sixty academics, religious leaders, and activists (including myself) regarding the efforts of the United States and its allies in the post–September 11, 2001, campaign against terror: *What We're Fighting For: A Letter from America* (New York: Institute for American Values, 2002).

20. A. K. S. Lambton, *State and Government in Medieval Islam* (Oxford: Oxford University Press, 1981).

21. See generally my discussion in *Islam and War: A Study in Comparative Ethics* (Louisville, Ky.: Westminster/John Knox Press, 1993), and literature cited therein.

22. Al-Shaybani's great treatise is available in the translation by Majid Khaddurri, *The Islamic Law of Nations: Shaybani's Siyar* (Baltimore: Johns Hopkins University Press, 1966).

23. This saying from the *ahadith* or reports of the Prophet's *sunna* or exemplary practice is cited here as translated by Khadduri; ibid., section 1.

24. Cf. 3:104, among others.

25. My translation.

26. Both are discussed at some length in Kelsay, *Islam and War*, especially 77–110.

27. Ibrahim Abu Rabi' provides one of the more useful overviews of Fadlallah's book in *Intellectual Origins of Islamic Resurgence in the Modern Arabic World* (Albany: State University of New York Press, 1996).

28. Citing the bin Ladin statement, as reported in the *New York Times*, 9 November 2001.

29. See, for example, the various responses to the "creed" of Sadat's assassins collected in Johannes J. G. Jansen, trans., *The Neglected Duty* (New York: Macmillan, 1986).

30. I choose this language deliberately to invoke a comparison with Michael Walzer's famous discussion in *Just and Unjust Wars*, now in its third edition (New York: Basic Books, 2000). I make some gestures toward explicating this dimension of Islamic thinking about war in Kelsay, "Bin Laden's Reasons," and more in an unpublished paper on "War, Peace, and the Imperatives of Justice in Islamic Perspective." I hope to publish a version of the latter in the near future.

31. Saying attributed to the prophet Muhammad, as translated in Khadduri, *The Islamic Law of Nations*, sec. 1.

PART II

Human Rights, Political Authority, and Religious Commitments

6

Religious Concomitants of Transnationalism: From a Universal Church to a Universal Religiosity?

SUSANNE HOEBER RUDOLPH

A PROJECT CALLED "The Sacred and the Sovereign" calls attention to competing visions: the national orientation of the political and the transnational orientation of the sacred. This dichotomy has a venerable history. Churches are among the oldest of the transnationals, having long claimed a role equivalent to or transcending the political—before "nation" or "state" were even articulated concepts. On the other hand, churches were not and are not always transnational, operating above or extending across states. They have a history of being subsumed by states or collaborating with them. There have been times when the acts of popes anointing kings signified the suzerainty of the sacred; there also have been and are times when states have appointed churchmen, licensed churches, and absorbed the sacred into their sovereignty. The questions I address in this chapter are the following: What are the implications for religion of the "fading of the state"?[1] What are the prospects for the universal "ecumene" some religious leaders are attempting to build in the expanding transnational space?[2] Here the term *ecumene* refers to a community of individuals and organizations who believe that diverse religions share sufficient moral and spiritual ground to support cooperation across "civilizational" and political boundaries.

Until the sixteenth century, the unity of the Roman church's ecclesiastical organization transcended political boundaries. Regardless of political jurisdiction, the church controlled the appointment of clergy, collected church taxes from the faithful, controlled monastic lands, and exercised discipline over its priests and the faithful. This universalism came to an end, however, when the state, or the empire, contested the church's claim. From the sixteenth century and the rise of the absolutist state, ecclesiastical appointments, taxation, jurisdiction, administration, and discipline migrated to the hands of secular authorities. By 1523 the Spanish crown had secured the right to nominate every bishopric in Spain. Like the Chinese government today, the French king (on the basis of the Concordat of Bologna) became master of every important ecclesiastical appointment in France.[3] The nationalization or "state-ization" of churches in the fifteenth and sixteenth centuries coincided with the assertion of state sovereignty claims by political kingdoms. When the destructive force of religious competition between Protestants and Catholics was tamed by the principle *cujus regio, ejus religio*, the faith of the rulers of particular polities became the determinant of a country's religious dispensation, breaking the unity of a universal church. *The Church* was superseded by many nationalized churches.[4] These events suggest that there is an intimate tie between forms of polity and forms of religious organization.

Nineteenth-century social thinkers saw an affinity not only between forms of polity and forms of religious organization but also between political forms and how religious phenomena are imagined. Reiterating the verities of much nineteenth-century religious scholarship, Max Weber asserted that "it is a universal phenomenon that the formation of a political association entails subordination to its corresponding god."[5] Weber tells us that Yahweh, having begun his career as the god of a tribe, became the god of a confederation as Israelites expanded to larger areas; "political and military conquest also entailed the victory of a stronger god over the weaker god of the vanquished group."[6] Reorganization of political communities, Weber tells us, tends to entail formation of new cultic communities. He aligns the rise of monotheism with the emergence of empires, assuming a parallelism between the emergence of an imperial figure that subordinates lesser polities with the emergence of a triumphal godhead that subordinates the lesser gods of subordinate units.

I don't want to confirm or dispute the credibility of these assertions. I want to use them to raise fruitful questions for our deliberation: What is the implication for religion of the fading of sovereignty? What are the likely consequences of globalization for the structure of religion? Transnational forms of organization are growing stronger: Economic forces, multinational corporations, and multilateral lending organizations; normative and legal regimes based in transnational communities of discourse around topics such as climate, the environment, human rights, indigenous peoples' rights, and women's issues; and the flow of migrants through permeable and controlled boundaries all collaborate to diminish the monopoly claim of national sovereignty assertions. Such forces encourage the transgressing and thinning of national boundaries. They lead to the creation of a transnational space in which civil society begins to form a transnational politics. This new politics is not an international politics in which bounded states are presumed to be the actors but a politics that transgresses borders, in which substate or cross-state expressions of civil society—such as some churches or transnational nongovernmental organizations (NGOs)—are the actors. It leads to the creation of transnational epistemic communities whose members share common worldviews, purposes, interests, and practices.[7]

What are the implications of these developments for religious communities? Does such a thinning of borders and fading of states approximate the conditions of the world before the Reformation, when Charles V's weakly articulated universal empire coincided with the idea of a universal church ("Christendom")? Does the emergence of transnational civil society provide the environment for a new universal church?

I make a distinction between the possibility for a new or resurrected universal church, which I think is unlikely, and the possibility of a universal religiosity, for which current history provides some support. By *universal church* I mean the worldwide theological and institutional hegemony of a particular religion. *Universal religiosity* refers to an aggregative intellectual and social process of ecumenization, reaching across civilizational and state borders and engaging the full diversity of world religions. Such a process would be at once global and local—composed, on one hand, of intentional, transreligious hermeneutic initiatives by churchmen and churchwomen and, on the other hand, of spontaneous neighborly sharing of informal local practices by adherents of different religions. When universal religiosity is nurtured, it allows for the recognition that there is truth in all religions—a sentiment that is still vigorously challenged by the orthodox in the East and the West alike.

Why is religion in the new transnational space unlikely to take the form of a universal church but likely to take the form of a universal religiosity? The time for the sort of process Weber saw—in which the religion of a political hegemon could assert itself over subordinate or conquered units—is over, disrupted by the experience of colonization and the nationalist and democratic reaction against it. In the age of imperialism, western religions migrated with the flag in ways that seemed to herald the universalization of Christian hegemony in the parts of Africa and Asia that were annexed to empires, just as the march of conquering Muslim peoples—Safavids, Afghans, Ottomans—had seemed to herald a similar hegemony. The pattern of religious diffusion has changed, however. Accelerating population movements in response to shifting labor demand—especially the migration of Middle Eastern and Asian peoples to the West—has broken the earlier coincidence of religion with geographic areas. In the age of migration, despite the best efforts of some Western nation-states to ring themselves with immigration statutes, the bearers of nonwestern religions are migrating to the West, though not with large enough populations or sufficient ideological or material force to herald a counterhegemony.

Redistribution of religions has scattered faiths across the regions of the world in ways never before seen: Islam in Paris, Buddhism in Dusseldorf, Zoroastrianism in Tokyo, Hinduism in Iowa City. To look only at one of the most conspicuous groupings: The Muslim community in the United States, approximately 8 million strong, is growing vigorously; Islam is on the verge of becoming the second-largest religion in America. Europe has 15 million Muslims—2 million in Germany alone.[8] The fall of communism in the Soviet Union and Eastern Europe led to a brisk influx of proselytizers, notably Christian evangelicals but also representatives of minorities already in place (Catholics, Sunni, Shiite), leading to a reaction among the dominant Orthodox community that had been weakened by a century of repression.[9] This modern territorial redistribution layers on top of an older reality, the fruit of medieval migration, conquest, and preaching: Hinduism in Thailand, Islam in Nigeria, Christianity in Korea.

Instead of generating the hegemony of a new universal church, the migratory pattern is likely to spawn multireligious arenas. Such arenas also are not altogether new. Global cities historically have been sites for such multireligiosity. William McNeill notes in his sweeping accounts of world history that ancient cities typically had been constituted of multiple religions and that in the historical record such multiculturalism was more normal than exclusivist regimes. World cities today—Bombay, Frankfurt, New York, Cairo—are nodal points where multiplicity of religious affiliations is incubated and whence it radiates outward.[10]

Multireligious arenas can generate several different kinds of social and ideological outcomes: toleration/compartmentalization, expulsion and/or extermination, or creation of an ecumenical community. *Toleration* is a minimalist noun signifying something less than appreciation— a benign sort of "live and let live" sentiment. *Compartmentalization* is a form of toleration that is based on discrimination: "I'll tolerate your exotic or abominable practices if you confine them to your people," or "I'll tolerate your practices as long as they are privatized and I don't have to see them." Ethnic/religious accommodation in ancient and medieval global cities or empires often rested on social toleration and compartmentalization enjoined by economic and political prudence. The Ottoman millett "system" approximated such an arrangement for a time when it developed self-regulating spheres for minority religious communities—Orthodox Christians, Armenians, Jews—on the assumption that they recognized the primacy and privileges of the Islamic hegemony.[11] The high degree of sectarian and caste difference within Hinduism as well as between Hinduism and other faiths in India was rendered "tolerable" by highly institutionalized compartmentalization, enforced by rules governing interaction. The springing up of immigrant neighborhoods or gated communities in Western cities often accomplishes a similar insulation. Expulsion or extermination as an outcome hardly requires elaboration to any newspaper reader of the 1940s—or the 1980s and 1990s.

Development of an ecumenical mentality—which would characterize what I am calling a universal religiosity, by contrast to a "universal church"—is another possible outcome. I start with the more formal, transnational, ecumene-building aspect of a universal religiosity. Transnational epistemes are communities of outlook: persons and organizations that share common worldviews, purposes, interests, and practices and for whom the relevant arena of communication and action transcends national jurisdictions. *Ecumene* refers to such an epistemic community with religious qualities. There have always been wandering religious virtuosi for whom neither political spaces nor formal religious boundaries mattered, who imagined that they saw common themes in all religions. They were saints, pirs, and sadhus, often mystics in tension with formalized, institutionalized, High Culture religion, vowing to return to the sacred devotional oneness with God. Such were the ("Muslim") Sufis and ("Hindu") Bhakts of the Indian subcontinent, associated with popular religion, whose preachings often were indistinguishable from each other and whose message often emphasized the irrelevance of religious boundaries. What is new in transnational ecumenism is its intentional, rationalized, even bureaucratized form.

The very signs and symbols of transnational flows and arenas have been the epistemes that have sprung up around the eight world summits such as the environment, population, global warming, women, and—immediately relevant to this essay—religion. Summits have been characterized by what Stephen Toulmin called the upstairs/downstairs syndrome—a metaphor that will be understood by readers who followed the British television serial of the same name. In the serial, the rich or noble folks occupied the upstairs floors and the active society of servants—who often ran the upstairs indirectly—occupied the basement. Summits have had an upstairs where state representatives congregated, ostensibly the most important layer of the summit. They also have had a downstairs, where the NGOs congregated with the intent of making their voices heard and to nudge, pummel, and push the upstairs actors into proper conduct. Whereas the upstairs venues of summits demonstrated the persistence of the sovereign nation-state, the downstairs actors showed the increasing significance of transnational civil society, epistemes of nonstate sectors, in the decision process. With the growth of a transnational politics, states no longer are the only actors on the world stage. By the time the phenomenon of "downstairs" organizations moved to Beijing in 1995 for the summit on women, downstairs had become normalized and its significance acknowledged: Even the Beijing hosts, who take a dim view of civil society, had to provide accommodations and facilities, albeit poor ones.

The World Peace Summit of religious and spiritual leaders that met during the wider Millennium Summit of world leaders in 2000 was one version of such a downstairs effort—a nonstate event in which religious congregations of the most diverse kind were represented. It was transnational civil society organizing itself and attempting to create consensus on goals and plans for peace to guide its own actions as well as those of states. The proceedings highlight the fact that ecumenical forces are revisiting the idea of religious universality—not in the form of a universal church but in the formulation of a universal religiosity. Such a project is more likely to address moral than theological objectives: war and poverty rather than the conceptualization of the Godhead. Such reasoning characterized the summit's document, which placed the voice of diverse religions behind the quest for world peace, eradication of poverty, and protection of the environment. The document implied that these goals represented the normative and spiritual common objectives of different faiths.

There have been other initiatives toward formulating some sacred universal principles, such as the ecumenical explorations of the World Council of Churches; the initiatives of the Chicago-based Council for a Parliament of the World's Religions, whose vice chairman served as secretary-general of the Millennium Summit of religions; or the United Religion Initiative, led by Episcopal Bishop William Swing of San Francisco. Older is Pope John XXIII's *Nostra Aetate* (1965), which recognized the possibility of spiritual truth in all religions:

> The church therefore has this exhortation for her sons: Prudently and lovingly, through dialogue and collaboration with the followers of other religions, and in witness of Christian faith and life, acknowledge, preserve and promote the spiritual and moral goods found among these men, as well as the values found in their society and culture.[12]

Nostra Aetate was an important step away from claims of monopoly on religious truth and toward the discovery of common ground. A similar doctrine, which holds that "toleration alone, while desirable, is not sufficient in a world of religious pluralism," has been suggested by an influential Protestant voice, Dr. Joseph C. Hough, Jr., president of Union Theological Seminary:

> I would begin with the recognition that religion is something we human beings put together in an effort to give some cultural form to our faith. . . . [T]herefore we want to be careful about claiming that one religious form is the only one that is authentic or real.[13]

There are challenges to such attempts to formulate a universal ground of religiosity. Some challengers argue that this new religiosity softens the sinews of faith and practice and blots out distinctions that should be observed. One provocative Internet article on the 2000 World Peace Summit observed that its organizers were the sort of morally promiscuous people who thought it made little difference "whether one worships a downed World War II airplane with a cargo cult, is a snake-handling Baptist or a Roman Catholic."[14] In a thirty-six-page declaration released a week after the summit, Cardinal Joseph Ratzinger, prefect of the Vatican's Congregation for the Doctrine of the Faith, rejected what he said were growing attempts to depict all religions as equally true and reasserted that salvation was possible only through Jesus Christ. At about the same time, 10,000 evangelists meeting at Amsterdam under the auspices of the Reverend Billy Graham agreed with Ratzinger.[15] Universal religiosity, though plausible, is not about to command consensus anytime soon. Nevertheless, the increasingly transnational nature of population flows and the increasingly multinational location of all major religions give more and more religious leaders a stake in the transnational and ecumenical dialogues.

Universal religiosity refers on one hand to the product of an intentional intellectual and social process that builds a transnational religious episteme—an ecumene—with common vocabulary, grammar, and worldviews. It also refers to more informal, spontaneous social processes of syncretism, emulation, and exchange among people of different religious affiliations that create the audience and support base for transnational religious epistemes. Ecumenical dialogues by professional church leaders are more visible to newspaper-reading transnational observers than are quotidian, community-level ecumenical practices. Yet without the spontaneous practice of multireligiosity in increasingly multicultural societies—without the normalizing process that ordinary neighborhood-, town-, and district-level exchanges, as well as mutual observation, generate—transnational ecumenic dialogues have no broad constituency.

In accounts of quotidian interactions between religious communities, conflict occupies more space than peaceable regimes. In recent work on South Asian communities of faith, Shail Mayaram has pointed out that social science scholarship has privileged the investigation of conflict and violence in the encounter of faiths. Such scholarship has virtually ignored the wide arena of thought and practice occupied by syncretism and by religious devotees whose identities are difficult to assign to conventional categories. Mayaram would have us explore this other, "normal" world more systematically: "In the South Asian context historically there was a constant movement back and forth across sects and also possibilities of multiple affiliation" as well as liminal identities. Local stories of competition and conversion also are stories of "dialogue, exchange and the self-regulation of difference."[16]

Exchange and syncretism arise out of neighborly observation of one another's practices and the permeability of religious boundaries. The lived dailiness of overlapping moral dispositions creates common ground for moral reasoning, generating experience that may be receptive to elements of a universal religiosity articulated by transnational dialogues.

The question of universal religiosity raises the matter of universal religious freedom—an issue that is becoming increasingly intertwined with the meaning and practice of propagating faith and of conversion. Is preaching with the intent to substitute the preacher's faith for that of the listener freedom of religion or cultural and moral invasion? The notion that there are truths in all religions provides a different platform for thinking about the propagation of faith than does the idea that particular religions have a monopoly on truth. The belief that a religion can claim an ultimate and fundamental truth justifies its believers in the project of bringing the truth to those possessed of false gods—which raises the question of whether it is possible to be a robust Christian or Muslim while exercising tolerance for other religions.[17] The answer depends on what kind of Christian or Muslim one is. Mahatma Gandhi highlighted the tension between toleration and conversion when he questioned the meaningfulness of conversion to people who, like himself, thought there was truth in all religions.[18] Some of the organizers of the World Peace Summit of religious leaders advocated a ban on conversion on the same grounds—namely, that conversion challenged the idea of truth in all religions.[19] According to one prominent Protestant churchman, the difference between an attempt to convert and an attempt to bear witness is great:

> The attempt to bear witness is . . . to state honestly what you have discovered in faith in Jesus Christ. This is to share the things in your life that are of highest value to you, and I think this is an act of friendship. But this is very different from saying, "Now that I've told you this, you've got to believe as I do to experience this." The one is an opening to conversation; the other is closing conversation.[20]

This position obviously has a connection to the possibility of a universal religiosity. Ecumenical conversation is difficult in an environment of competitive conversion. The anticonversion doctrine has some peculiar bedfellows, however—including liberal Christians driven by concern about cultural invasion and Hindu fundamentalists and Russian Orthodox Christians protecting their turf. In India, opposing the propagation of non-Hindu religions has become a favorite policy prescription by Hindu nationalists whose project is to create an exclusivist Hindu religious state. The theoretical ground on which they stand is the reverse of that which motivated Gandhi, who believed that there was truth in all religions. As spokesmen for the dominant faith, they would like to deny entry to others, protecting a single truth and its virtual monopoly in the face of Christian and Muslim alternatives.

Let me tie this question of religious propagation/conversion—and its affinity with questions of religious freedom—to recent U.S. initiatives in this arena. In 1998 the 105th Congress passed the International Religious Freedom Act (IRFA) with the support of the Christian Coalition, B'nai B'rith, and the Southern Baptist Convention. The act, introduced by Senators Don Nickels and Joseph I. Lieberman, requires the United States to respond to countries that persecute religious minorities by issuing anything from a diplomatic reprimand to stiff economic sanctions, while leaving the president substantial discretion. IRFA established elaborate machinery—including an annual State Department report on religious freedom in all countries, an ambassador whose charge is religious freedom everywhere, and a ten-person commission that publishes reports and recommends action to the president to sanction violations of religious freedom.

IRFA raises the question of whether its processes are likely to advance a universal religiosity or threaten it. To what extent will the commission be regarded as constructing a transnational regime of human rights enlarging the arena of mutual respect? To what extent will it be considered an agent of the American nation-state appropriating the issue of transnational religious freedom for its own agendas—using religion as an instrument of national interest or to clear the way for projects of its own majority religion? The fact that at the end of the millennium the United States stood forth as the sole superpower enhances the credibility of the second reading.

The legislation and its apparatus are contradictory, loaded with different projects. One reason for the legislation was the eagerness of conservative Christian forces to protect their Christian coreligionists abroad and provide cover for those called to convert pagans. To that extent, IRFA represented the militant voice of an exclusivist Christianity for whom the charge of cultural invasion posed no problem. On the other hand, the legislation represents a triumph of sorts for ecumenical perspectives. In justifying its work the commission interpreted the act as an ecumenical instrument of human rights:

> The report [of 1999] applies to all religions and beliefs. It targets no particular country or region, and seeks to promote no religion over another. It does, however, recognize the intrinsic value of religion, even as it acknowledges that religious freedom includes the right not to believe or to practice.[21]

The United States, as a multireligious state, cannot legitimately use its resources to protect only messengers of its majority religion. Instead, the legislation had to craft the project so that it promises to protect freedom of worship of all religions—that is, a project that universalizes protection. Most ecumenically oriented Christian groups in the United States, however, regarded IRFA as a tool of intrusive evangelicalism. Some activists on behalf of non-Christian religions—adherents of the Dalai Lama's Buddhism and other Asian denominations—supported it.[22]

IRFA makes religious toleration and protection of religious freedoms the responsibility of sovereign states. It holds them accountable not only for their own antireligious actions, if any (as when China suppresses the unlicensed Catholic Church or Falun Gong), but for the acts of their citizens (as when Hindu governments do not prevent nationalist groups from harassing and killing Christians and Muslims). The Commission for Religious Freedom each year identifies "states of special concern" (SPCs). In 1999 it identified China and Sudan, recommending that action be taken against their conduct. In October 2000, after sporadic attacks on Christians in India, the commission held hearings on India. These hearings were roundly condemned by their potential beneficiaries as intervening in unhelpful ways into their own efforts to mobilize government protection. They also were condemned by the Catholic bishops' conference in India, by the spokesman for liberal Hinduism Swami Agnivesh, and by the widow of murdered Australian Christian missionary Graham Staynes. In 2002 the commission declared India an SPC in light of the terrible death toll in Muslim pogroms in Gujerat.[23]

The case of India, a secular state where religious liberties guaranteed by the constitution normally are enforced, raises some interesting specific problems by comparison with China and Sudan—countries where liberties are restricted. Should the U.S. president intervene in a state that formally proclaims freedom for all religions and whose democratic political institutions provide minorities with significant political and legal protection? Clearly that protection sometimes fails, and not all members of government are equally enthusiastic about religious liberties. How ought we distinguish this case from that of the United States, which formally proclaims religious protections but fails to protect African American churches against arson, or from that of Germany or Great Britain, which sometimes fail to protect Muslims against murder?

I have raised the question of whether the commission on freedom of religion was likely to enhance or threaten the move toward a universal religiosity. IRFA appeared to challenge the sovereignty defense that national governments offer to justify their untroubled violation of civil and religious rights. Where such a challenge on behalf of religious freedom clears the ground for untroubled belief and practice, it comes in on the side of transnationalization of the ecumenical spirit. Where it steps forward as the advance guard of competitive conversion, it "closes the conversation." Furthermore, where initiatives on behalf of religious freedom come from a single nation-state that appoints itself as the enforcer of universal rights, the project is compromised by the suspicion that ultimately a state interest—or, at least, the interest of a powerful religious constituency cloaked by the mantle of the state—is at stake. The legitimacy of the initiative is tainted by the failure to make religious freedom a shared project, an ecumenical project, detached from the interested intentions of a particular nation-state and its cultural and religious preferences.

I began this chapter by exploring the proposition that forms of polity and forms of religiosity are thought to have an effect on each other. If this is so, we should expect the thinning of state boundaries and the expansion of transnational political, social, and economic institutions and epistemes to affect forms of religiosity and the formulation of religious goals. Having excluded the likelihood that the new transnationalism would favor resurrection of a universal church, I have explored the likelihood of a "universal religiosity" grounded in the principle that there is truth in all religions. Moves toward such a transnational ecumenism entail, on one hand, *formal* theological and ethical dialogues, in transnational settings, by religious spokespersons in pursuit of common ground. On the other hand, ecumenical culture is produced by *informal* interactions and exchanges among ordinary devotional persons in multireligious settings. Because conversion challenges the idea that there is truth in all religions, it is not easily compatible with the building of transnational ecumenes.

If ecumenism in an era of fading states and expanding transnational institutions comes to be exploited to project the hegemony of a nation-state (such as the United States) or a civilizational region (such as the traditional arena of Judaeo-Christian religiosity), a universal religiosity cannot flourish. A transnational ecumene must be a shared project that is sensitive to the variations in culture and politics that shape each region's or religion's receptiveness. Universal religiosity must be founded in persuasion and consent, not in the exercise of power and coercion by nation-states.

Notes

1. For a full description of "fading states" and the "thinning" of their monopoly on sovereignty, see Susanne Hoeber Rudolph, "Introduction: Religion, States, and Transnational Civil Society," in Susanne Rudolph and James Piscatori, eds., *Transnational Religion and Fading States* (Boulder, Colo.: Westview Press, 1997), 1–24.

2. The term *ecumene* (or ecumenical) has had different meanings over time. In the sixteenth century, it referred to the universal church or Christendom. Where *ecumenical* today often refers to different religions, the reference generally is to different Christian churches. I am using the term in its Greek sense, where *oikumene* refers to the (inhabited) earth. See *The New Oxford Dictionary of English*.

3. Eugene Rice and Anthony Grafton, *The Foundations of Early Modern Europe, 1460–1559*, 2d ed. (New York: Norton, 1994), 197–99. For the struggle over control of clerical appointments between the Vatican and the Chinese government, see Erik Eckhom, "China Repeats Terms for Ties Pope Seeks," *New York Times*, 26 October 2001.

4. See Jose Casanova, "Globalizing Catholicism and the Return to a 'Universal' Church," in Rudolph and Piscatori, *Transnational Religion and Fading States*, 121–43. Casanova's meaning of *universal* is different from the meaning I attempt here; he argues that the Catholic Church is returning to universalist human rights values after a spell of preoccupation with its own survival.

5. Quoted in Guenther Roth and Claus Wittich, *Economy and Society*, vol. 1 (Berkeley: University of California Press, 1978), 412.

6. Quoted in ibid., 413.

7. Peter Haas, "Introduction: Epistemic Communities and International Policy Coordination," *International Organization* 46, no. 1 (winter 1992): 1–35.

8. Sam Afridi, "Muslims in America: Identity, Diversity and the Challenge of Understanding," working paper, Social Science Research Council, Working Group on Law and Culture, Planning Meeting, 10–13 January 2002, 1; Ian Fisher, "Europe's Muslims Seek a Path amid Competing Cultures," *New York Times*, 8 December 2001.

9. John Witte, Jr., and Michael Bourdeaux, eds., *Proselytism and Orthodoxy in Russia: The New War for Souls* (Maryknoll, N.Y.: Orbis Books, 1999); Jonathan Luxmoore and Jolanta Babiuch-Luxmoore, "New Myths for Old: Proselytism and Transition in Post-Communist Europe," *Journal of Ecumenical Studies* 36, no. 1–2 (winter–spring 1999): 43–65; E. Braker and M. Warburg, eds., *New Religions and New Religiosity* (Aarhus, Denmark: Aarhus University Press, 1998).

10. William McNeill, "Project Report: Fundamentalism and the World of the 1990s," *Bulletin of the American Academy of Arts and Sciences* 47, no. 3 (December 1993): 29–30.

11. Benjamin Braude and Bernard Lewis, eds., *Christians and Jews in the Ottoman Empire: The Functioning of a Plural Society*, 2 vols. (New York: Holmes and Meyer, 1982).

12. Walter M. Abbott, S.J., and Msgr. Joseph Gallagher, eds., *The Documents of Vatican Two* (New York: Guild Press, 1966), 663.

13. "Q&A: Acknowledging That God Is Not Limited to Christians," *New York Times*, 12 January 2002, B9.

14. For this quote and subsequent text see James Harder, "Insight on the News," October 2, 2000, available at web.nexis-lexis.com/universe/ (accessed March 9, 2001).

15. Gustav Niebuhr, "A Bishop Works to Bridge Faith in the Cause of Peace," *New York Times*, 23 September 2000.

16. Shail Mayaram, "Community, Conversion and Coexistence," unpublished paper, 1, 4. For a more extended discussion and exemplars of syncretic formations, see idem, "Rethinking Meo Identity: Cultural Faultline, Syncretism, Hybridity or Liminality," in Mushirul Hasan, ed., *Islam, Communities and the Nation: Muslim Identities in South Asia and Beyond* (New Delhi: Manohar, 1998). For more on the exchanges and overlaps in the local practice of religion, see also Imtiaz Ahmed, ed., *Ritual and Religion among Muslims of the Sub-Continent* (Lahore, Pakistan: Vanguard, 1985). For ordinary syncretism, see, for example, the photographs and captions between pages 64 and 65 in Peter Gottschalk, *Beyond Hindu and Muslim; Multiple Identity in Narratives from Village India* (New Delhi: Oxford University Press, 2001). See also Joyce Burckhalter-Fluckiger, "Religious Identity at the Crossroads of a Muslim Female Healer's Practice," paper presented at South Asia Studies Conference, Madison, Wisc., October 1996.

17. For a discussion of this issue, see T. N. Madan, *Modern Myths, Locked Minds: Secularism and Fundamentalism in India* (New Delhi: Oxford University Press, 1997).

18. Gandhi defined this position in *Young India,* March 21, 1929. See Bhikhu Parekh, *Gandhi's Political Philosophy* (Notre Dame, Ind.: University of Notre Dame Press, 1989), 230. Parekh sees Gandhi as believing that "the religious person should respect, enter into dialogue with and assimilate from other religions whatever he found valuable" (84).

19. A useful introduction to international legal regimes for proselytism is John Witte, Jr., "A Primer on the Rights and Wrongs of Proselytism," *Fides et Libertas: The Journal of the International Religious Liberty Association* (2000): 12–17. Witte encourages proselytizing groups to "negotiate and adopt voluntary codes of conduct of restraint and respect" (16).

20. Joseph C. Hough, Jr., quoted in "Q&A: Acknowledging That God Is Not Limited to Christians," B9.

21 Among the bill's opponents were the National Council of Churches, Human Rights Watch, the U.S. Chamber of Commerce, and the Clinton administration. *Facts on File,* 22 October 1998.

22. *India Today,* 25 September 2000; "Daily News Briefs," *Catholic World News Service,* 14 September 2000; *Telegraph* (Kolkata), 2 October 2002.

23. "Prepared Testimony of Robert A. Seiple, Ambassador at Large for International Religious Freedom, before U.S. House of Representatives International Relations Committee," Federal News Service, 6 October 1999.

7

The Future of Sovereignty:
A Christian Realist Perspective

ROBIN W. LOVIN

CHRISTIAN ETHICS IN NORTH AMERICA spent most of the twenti-eth century acquiring a realistic perspective on political life and so-cial institutions—especially the politics and institutions of the interna-tional order. At the turn of that century, the Social Gospel promised a transformation of life, using ideals taught by Jesus and practices that were based on new scientific knowledge to change the ways that insti-tutions actually work. The result, as Walter Rauschenbusch saw it, would be a world in which church and state share a common aim: "to trans-form humanity into the kingdom of God."[1]

For Rauschenbusch the expanding role of mediation in international conflicts, the movement toward disarmament, and the Hague Agree-ment of 1899 (which established the Hague Tribunal) were signs of the new age that already was dawning: "It is safe to say that the [Hague Tri-bunal] will now perpetuate itself and gradually enlarge its functions. . . . History will do the rest. It will be immeasurably easier to assign addi-tional powers to the Tribunal than to create it in the first place."[2]

Very shortly into this new era, it became apparent that some adjust-ments to the Social Gospel expectations would be required. World War I and the global depression of the 1930s gave rise to a new generation of theologians who connected the Christian message not to the highest hopes of their age but to a clear-sighted assessment of human limitations. This "theological realism" or "Christian realism" gave at least as much attention to the dynamics of historical institutions as to the ideals of the

Kingdom of God.[3] Reinhold Niebuhr and others in the movement did not expect any dramatic changes in the framework of existing institutions and practices, so they sought to find a place for moral action and religious hope within that framework.

Christian realism expected problems to persist, not least because Christians whose faith demanded that injustice be eradicated also profited from its continuation. Under these conditions, history cannot be the struggle of unambiguous good against unadulterated evil. Still less can it be the working out of scientific laws that govern social progress. History is ambiguous—a record of mixed results that can be narrated from many different perspectives. Fulfillment of our aspirations and vindication of our commitments lie beyond history, not within it.[4]

For the Christian realist, then, institutions that are strong because they are supported by power and stable because they serve a wide range of interests are important realities in the moral life, even when they do not conform to our moral ideals. People who seek justice therefore must figure out how to do so in the framework of interest-group politics. Those who want world peace must build on the sturdy platform of nuclear deterrence. And—most relevant for our purposes here—those who are committed to universal human rights must acknowledge the reality of the sovereign state. This realism did not come easily to the generation nurtured in turn-of-the-century Social Gospel idealism, but by the 1950s it had become the accepted starting point for Protestant social ethics.

At the beginning of another century, however, many of those persistent, troubling realities for which Christian realism had demanded theological attention have disappeared. Nuclear deterrence is no longer the cornerstone of international peace. Cold war power alignments no longer divide the world neatly into friends and foes. National borders no longer present impenetrable barriers to commerce and culture—nor to humanitarian interventions on behalf of oppressed minorities. However imperfect and unpredictable the new international order may be, the sovereign state as an entity with exclusive juridical control over economic and political life within its borders today is more an ideal type than an existing reality.

Is Christian realism, then, reduced to a moment in the history of theology? Is it simply a way of understanding what went on when there used to be superpowers, iron curtains, national economies, and autonomous states? If Christian realism is a political discourse that takes these things as unchangeable realities, the answer probably is yes. Part of what gave Christian realism its interpretative power, however, was its attention to the complex origins of things that present themselves as givens in today's experience. The ambiguities of history result from the interaction of long-lasting forces that may not be apparent on the surface of events. Institutions, powers, and systems are not permanent. They are an equilibrium maintained for the present: between the relatively stable elements of human nature and the contingencies of historical diversity, between a reasoned effort to understand and a passionate need to control the forces of nature and society, and between the constraints of self-interest and the limited but real self-transcendence by which human beings make commitments to ideals beyond their immediate interests. All of those things also are real—as real as the powers and institutions that for the moment happen to dominate the landscape.

Unlike the Social Gospel, which projected the future by reference to moral ideals that it confidently expected to realize, Christian realism projects the future by trying to understand the past. Setting the ambiguities of the present in a wider historical framework often helps us understand what is going on, and if it does not provide definitive predictions about the future, at least it helps us identify the forces that are likely still to be at work there, even after their present constellations have changed beyond recognition.

A Brief History of Sovereignty

So understood, Christian realism may help us understand what is going on in the twenty-first century as well as it did in the twentieth, not least in relation to the changing realities of national sovereignty. Christian realism reminds us of the forces in history and human nature that gave rise to sovereignty in the first place. It helps us to recall that there were sovereigns before there was sovereignty. Powerful rulers inspired awe and demanded an allegiance that was both practically political in its requirements and quasi-religious in its intensity. All of this was long before we began to associate such authority with its exclusive exercise within a given territory.

Sovereignty as we understand it in political theory arose as Europe made the transition from feudal to modern forms of social organization. Although the history I review here is distinctly European, similar forms of organization existed in other civilizations, and similar transitions took place in the development of modern states and society. In premodern Europe, obligations were defined primarily by relationships to a variety of superiors—who might, in turn, owe their obedience to another authority at a higher level. Economic, military, religious, and even academic authorities established overlapping jurisdictions, each with the power to extract taxes, control behavior, and impose punishments on persons within its sphere of authority. (University administrators in medieval Europe actually had authority to commit recalcitrant students and faculty members to prison—a prerogative that every dean today occasionally hopes somehow might be restored.) Individuals were answerable to a variety of jurisdictions, and those living in the same territory might be subject to different authorities, depending on their status.[5] Indeed, part of the wise management of one's affairs was to see that one's disputes would be referred to the court system—ecclesiastical, baronial, royal, or municipal—where the rules offered the best chance of success.

At the apex of some of these systems of authority—usually combining military and economic power exercised over a wide region—there arose figures whom we would call sovereigns. Their power distinguished them sufficiently from the ordinary run of overlords in that they inspired a kind of awe, which was reinforced by lavish displays of wealth and, usually, by claims to divine authorization as well as human power. Yet despite this distance from their subjects, sovereigns also provided a focal point for cultural and political identity. To be the people of a sovereign gave them a share in the sovereign's victories and the sovereign's honor. To have a sovereign made them a people. Sovereignty at its origin is this powerful combination of awe and identity that attaches to the person of the sovereign, giving him—or, rarely, her—the position of supreme, albeit not usually exclusive, authority.

Somewhat later, as the medieval order waned, European sovereigns moved to consolidate their power and rationalize the system of competing, overlapping jurisdictions by claiming exclusive control over all systems that wielded power within their territories. They established order within their borders and provided security against external enemies by claiming a monopoly on the use of force. The sovereigns created sovereignty, in our modern sense of that term.

The first Christian realists were intent on demonstrating in various ways that this sovereignty was secular. This project was a resolution to the problem of order, not an independent center of moral or religious authority. The sovereign was not necessarily virtuous or pious—probably not even likely to be so.[6] The sovereign was just the sovereign, and that was exactly what people needed in an era when arguments about virtue and piety were likely to set them at one another with sharp implements.[7] Understanding the ruler's power in its own terms, resting it on the force that the ruler alone had the resources to wield, freed it from confusion with other kinds of moral, spiritual, and intellectual power that might wield their own persuasive influences on the course of events but could no longer compete with the sovereign's powers of coercion.

Thus, the modern theory of sovereignty, developed from these early realist origins, emphasizes the secular nature of sovereign power. Law becomes positive, human law, bereft of the controlling associations with natural and divine law that it had in the medieval account given by Thomas Aquinas. There is no longer a question of the subject conscientiously withholding moral assent from a bad law because law is not about moral assent in the first place. Law is about controlling behavior and the disposition of property—about "life and property and external affairs on earth," as Luther would put it.[8]

This early realism served its purposes, but—as Reinhold Niebuhr would later say about Luther's political pessimism—it was "too consistent."[9] Urgently calling attention to the importance of power for the preservation of social order, the modern account of sovereignty neglected the elements of awe and identity that were still important ingredients in sovereign authority. As long as the modern idea of sovereignty remained intact, the presence of awe and identity in the mix was obscured and could be ignored, for the most part. When the modern idea of sovereignty comes apart, however, it is necessary to pay attention to these characteristics once again, as we shall see in what follows.

First, however, let us try to understand how this breakup of the modern idea of sovereignty occurred. As happens with most comprehensive accounts of political life, the reality that the theory of sovereignty depicted started to erode almost as soon as the theory was articulated. The theoretical order of autonomous states in which the sovereign (whether a person or a legislature) controlled every aspect of public life gave way in practice to a patchwork of constitutional limits, entangling alliances, and federalist compromises of sovereign autonomy.

A sovereignty that sought to end religious wars by the principle of *cujus regio, ejus religio* instead evolved a system of individual rights in which the sovereign remains scrupulously neutral toward the religious preferences of the citizens. Federalist systems theoretically left sovereign power in the hands of their constituent states but limited it practically in ways that created a new, parallel kind of federal sovereignty that usually takes priority over the sovereignty of the states but has its own limitations as well.

More important for the erosion of sovereignty in international relations was the emergence of imperial systems—first colonial and then ideological—that extended sovereign power into other territories, without regard for the systems that might already be in place there. These expansions generally offered economic benefits to the imperial powers, but they also were justified as ways of spreading the benefits of Christian civilization, as necessary protections of freedom, or as extensions of democracy. The cases for expansion may have been rationalizations of national self-interest, but the rationalizations provided several forms of argument that undermined the idea that national sovereignty is inviolable. In the aftermath of World War II, the division of the world into Soviet and American spheres of influence—with a few states nervously clinging to neutrality between them—provided a far more realistic picture of international relations than the system of sovereign states described in international law and political theory. Twentieth-century Christian realists treated this historical snapshot of the world during the cold war era as reality, and they urged policymakers to build their plans to suit it.[10]

Yet even that system of sovereignty attenuated by superpower hegemony was rapidly changing in ways that may be more clear to us now that the superpower system has collapsed. Critics sometimes referred to the growing power of international business during the waning years of the cold war as "economic colonialism," as if the projection of sovereign power by economic means had simply replaced its extension by military conquest. There may have been some point to this formulation, but we are now in a position to see more clearly that the power of multinational companies cannot be simply equated with the imperial aspirations of any single state. The time when what was good for General Motors was good for America is long past, if it ever existed. The interesting point to note is that fifty years ago, the apparently pervasive reality of superpower conflict obscured the growth of independent corporate economic powers to an extent that such a statement seemed plausible. Nobody could say such a thing today. What are we to make of a situation in which the sovereign state of Venezuela tries to hold a Japanese-owned company accountable for the deaths of Venezuelan citizens that result from defects in tires produced in the United States? Whose imperial power is being projected, exactly, if the companies that dominate market forces have interests and purposes that are different from those of any sovereign state?

The erosion of sovereignty continues, and takes new forms, as ideological empires recede. The globalization of commerce, the rise of nationalism, and the fragility of the ecosystem all mean that no state, however firmly it rejects imperial aspirations, can be indifferent to things going on in other states. Wages and working conditions across the border will affect the welfare of its own citizens. Nationalist movements in a neighboring state — or, for that matter, in a state on the other side of the globe — may agitate an immigrant population in one's own country or subject one's own citizens to terrorist threats. Consumers of a nation's exports begin to take a stakeholder interest in the conditions under which their goods are produced, and these pressures will be felt by corporate entities that themselves may be effectively beyond the reach of local sovereign authority.

Observers of this disconcertingly fluid international situation sometimes offer the reassurance that the sovereign state is not about to disappear. It may even become more important in the absence of a dipolar conflict between great powers and the growing presence of nationalist aspirations.[11] Whatever happens to the sovereign state, however, the concept of sovereignty itself is losing its power to explain the behavior of actual states. States are trying to exercise authority in one another's territory for a variety of reasons and at an unprecedented rate, and these developments are unlikely to reverse themselves in the foreseeable future.

Charters of human rights and United Nations resolutions authorizing humanitarian interventions provide philosophical and legal explanations for patterns of interaction between nations that will steadily reduce the range of differences between their various political and economic systems. As has been the case *within* the developed, modern economies of the industrial world, wide disparities in wealth will be tolerated *between* these postmodern, globalized economic centers, but fundamental, systemic differences will not be. Wage scales may differ dramatically between countries, even those that are near neighbors, but no one will be allowed to produce goods for the global market by using slave labor. Disparities of wealth, power, and status may closely track old ethnic divisions, but no one will be allowed to maintain a system that elevates these differences to the status of legal requirements. It has proved impossible to sustain North Korean xenophobia, South African apartheid, and the Soviet command economy in the emerging world economy. It is impossible that anything like them could be created in the future.

A sovereign state may decide how it will be postmodern. It may direct its participation in the global economy in a variety of ways, redistributing its earnings according to somewhat distinctive local standards of justice. It may even provide a protected space for traditional cultures apart from the overarching global reality. One thing a sovereign state cannot do, however, is to decide to be an early modern state with complete internal control over its own destiny. The attempt will end in starvation, be cut short by rebellion, or be terminated by the intervention of other states that find that the experiment in isolation destabilizes key elements in their own internal situations.

After Sovereignty

This brief survey of the history of sovereignty begins to indicate some elements of a Christian realist view of the new situation into which we now are moving. It also provides a broader historical perspective from which to identify some of the elements that will provide the building blocks for the new reality, whatever form it eventually may take.

Although the nation-state continues to be a basic building block of the international order, sovereignty in the strict sense is a thing of the past. Perhaps very few sovereign states ever existed. Certainly sovereign statehood is no longer a realistic aim for a political community. The ambiguities of history predate the sovereign state, however, and history will continue after it. That is the most basic tenet of a Christian realist perspective on the future of sovereignty, and it is a theological claim as well as a historical generalization.

The perspective from which any historical system can be judged lies partly within and partly outside of history.[12] Most of the time we are trying to judge it from within. We are trying to make definitive decisions about what is right and wrong, about what is good policy and what is bad policy. These decisions require both a specific situation coming under judgment and a specific place in which to stand as we make the judgment. They are the sorts of decisions we try to make when, for example, a specific political and military authority applies just war criteria to a specific possibility for military intervention. Such judgments from within history lead to conclusions that are specific enough to guide action, but they tend to obscure the shortcomings of our present system—which is, after all, the perspective from which the judgment is made.

Judgments made wholly from outside history are not really possible for us, except as we acknowledge that we, too, stand under judgment—not only for the obvious wrongs that we can see even as we commit them but also for the flawed versions of righteousness that provide our highest aspirations. The theological task of the Christian realist is to proclaim that that judgment from outside history is always present—even, or especially, when we think we have eliminated injustice and established the basis for justice in the future. The practical, ethical task of Christian realism, then, is to approximate that judgment beyond history as best we can within our present situation. This is less a matter of arriving at sound, discriminating moral judgments within history—important as those are— than of trying to set up systems that will limit our own pretensions to righteousness, when we think we have escaped the limitations of history.

This Christian realist perspective on the future of sovereignty suggests two things, especially. First, whatever system emerges from the present weakening of national autonomy, that new system will have the same tendencies toward injustice that have afflicted the sovereign state. The tendencies may take different forms, but they will still be there. Second, as we look for a replacement of the sovereign state as the key element in international order, we should pay attention to *all* of the factors that made sovereignty work relatively well for several centuries at providing nations with internal peace and external security. That is, in addition to the control of coercive power that our realist predecessors identified as the key ingredient that made sovereignty effective, we also must remember the factors of *awe* and *identity* that helped to create the sovereign's power before there was a theory of sovereignty to explain it.

In the remainder of this chapter, I suggest what it would mean to pay attention first to the temptation to injustice and then to the factors of awe and identity as we try to construct a new way of understanding the relationship between nations after the age of the sovereign state. This project is different from the important attempt that Bryan Hehir makes (chapter 1) to reconstruct the classic Christian just war theory to deal with some of the specific decisions we will have to make about humanitarian interventions that limit national sovereignty. Both projects are important, of course. I simply note in passing that they are not the *same* project.

First, then, the temptation to injustice: It is an axiom of realism that any system that is given exclusive power to adjudicate between important interests held by competing parties will tend to develop interests of its own. Given sufficient power, or lacking adequate checks on its power, it will become an imperial system. That is, it will begin to project its own interests onto the parties under its power, and it will do this precisely in the name of the higher justice that it was established to protect.

This dilemma of justice has been apparent *within* the sovereign state from the beginning of the modern era, and we should not suppose that it will disappear just because we recast the problem in more global terms. The fact that today's international institutions have few interests that we need to worry about, compared to the interests of states, is a function of the fact that they have little real power. Given more power, they would acquire more interests.

This analysis suggests that it would not be wise to project—even as an ideal endpoint for our efforts to limit sovereignty—a single international entity that would have juridical power to adjudicate claims against sovereign states and executive power to enforce its decisions with sufficient force to ensure compliance. Such powers are dangerous enough within a state. Projected on a global scale, the temptation to totalitarianism would be overwhelming. We should not imagine that the solution to the problems posed by the sovereign state is a global sovereign, with a monopoly on the use of force that extends around the world (and probably several thousand miles out into space as well).

Most observers already are realists enough to agree with this assessment, but they do not always understand the corollary—which is that the framework of international institutions that we now have probably is very much like the one we need for the future. We have a code of international law that includes a declaration of human rights. We have international forums that are capable of assessing violations of that code and addressing resolutions to sovereign states requiring them to change their behavior. We can impose sanctions on those that do not change, and in extreme cases—except, perhaps, for those involving very powerful states—we can marshal force to impose the changes we have required. No single institution does this comprehensively; the ball bounces back and forth between the UN, the World Court, global trade agreements, regional human rights courts, and international military alliances.

This separation of powers probably is a good thing, though the system could work a good deal more efficiently than it does. Some new institutions probably need to be developed and inserted into the framework. (Suppose, for example, that there were an Asian Court of Human Rights as effective as its European counterpart or, perhaps more immediately plausible, that there were an African one. An Asian or African court certainly would be different from the European court, but it would be an important addition to the global system for protecting human rights.) We need to make the system more effective and comprehensive, but it is not clear that any other kind of system would serve us more effectively than the present one does.

What seems to be emerging is an international order in which formerly sovereign states retain a high degree of autonomy in managing their internal affairs, but their borders are crisscrossed by a network of international corporations, global markets, regulatory agencies, regional and international courts, international deliberative bodies, and a variety of ad hoc commissions and tribunals. All of these actors have substantial power to intervene in day-to-day operations within nations. In extreme cases, some of them occasionally have the power to impose an international consensus by force. Collectively, they shape the future. We may lament their impotence in the face of some situations that now exist, but there is no way to know the injustices and persecutions that have been averted because they are there.

Curiously, then, we find ourselves at the close of the era of the sovereign state back in a situation somewhat like the one that prevailed in Europe before that era began. We have a system of overlapping jurisdictions that provides multiple channels through which to settle disputes, render justice, and protect individuals from abuse by more powerful parties to which they have obligations. No single institution has all of the authority that we associate with sovereignty, strictly defined, but many of them have a little of it. The system is not very logical, and it is not particularly efficient, but its inefficiency in crisis situations also is what keeps it from being oppressive in ordinary circumstances. Unless and until technology knits us together much more tightly across the globe than we now are bound, or until ecological crisis forces much more draconian resource management upon us, the system that has emerged in the past quarter-century probably will serve us well enough. Realism's counsel would be to postpone utopian planning and devote our attention to understanding more clearly where we now are, keeping in the back of our minds the inescapable fact that we will not remain here forever.

Two things would help this system that seems to be emerging to develop. They would involve the elements of awe and identity that I have already discussed. Because these elements have been missing from our theoretical accounts of the sovereign state, we tend to overlook the need to find a place for them in the system that follows it.

Sovereigns receive obedience because they inspire awe, not just because they command overwhelming force. There is no place in our political theory for the impact of Air Force One sitting on a runway, or the queen delivering her speech from the throne to the assembled Houses of Parliament, or a Kremlin ceremony that for the first time in a thousand years transfers power from one freely chosen leader to another. Our theories overlook these effects, but they are real nonetheless.

Awe, of course, is a dangerous commodity in political life. Protestant leaders at the beginning of the modern era were vigilant to reserve awe for God and to keep it from attaching to the secular ruler. If the ruler is going to have *all* the power, it is best to be clear that what he or she has is *only* power. Today, however, we must risk attaching a little more of this awe to our emerging international institutions, if they are to be as effective as we need them to be. (See chapter 9 for further discussion of awe and international institutions.) Too often, these institutions take on the faceless character of an international civil service. They are regarded with the same attitude we take toward the Social Security Administration or the Department of Motor Vehicles—a familiar presence in our lives, perhaps, but hardly an inspiring one.

International organizations and their leaders must inspire somewhat more awe if they are to compete with the national leaders who hold the trappings of sovereignty.[13] Awe is a part of what secures the power of any public authority to do what we need it to do, and we must invest our international institutions with some of that awe if they are to serve the purposes to which we are putting them in an age when sovereign states no longer have complete control over what goes on within their borders.

The more important missing element, however, is *identity*. Sovereign power is effective not only because it is powerful but because it is *ours*. Along with the awe that may elevate a sovereign inappropriately to a transcendent plane that belongs only to God, there is the identification that raises us to the level of the sovereign, that assures us that this power will be used on our behalf and makes this power an extension of our own power, rather than a negation of it.

In a world that has greatly reduced the risk from confrontations between nuclear superpowers, the people who pose the greatest threat to international stability are those who cannot identify themselves with any of the many centers of power that now occupy the scene. Reasonable prospects for security and prosperity in a system of power that is perceived as alien are no substitute for power that is one's own. It is precisely because people who lack such power understand its historic connection with sovereignty that they demand admission to the system of sovereign states just at the point that those who have lived with it longest are trying to set limits on it.

This analysis suggests that the crucial test for the new framework of international institutions will not be whether they can exert power against the wishes of sovereign states. It will be whether they can effectively persuade those who otherwise lack power that this new center of authority in political affairs is *theirs*. Negatively, this means that these people—ethnic minorities who are rescued from persecution by humanitarian intervention, people who have to depend on international sanctions to secure the victory they have won at the ballot box, or groups that turn to human rights courts to overturn discriminatory practices that are still sanctioned by national legislation—must *not* come away from that experience with the sense that their claims were counters in a power game played by larger sovereign forces, that they were lucky to get what they had a right to receive because it just happened to match the interests of some more important international player. They must be confident that interventions on their behalf will be sustained until results are effectively obtained, not just until the powers that provide the intervening force weary of the cost or encounter domestic political opposition to the effort. More positively, these people must gain confidence over the years that these institutions not only are able to protect them from gross violations of their rights but that they actually will enable them to develop the resources and freedoms that seem foreclosed by the present situation. Finally, they must see in those international institutions a commitment to support them in their own ways of life and culture, not simply to provide them with equal access to rights and opportunities that are important to other people, someplace else.

All of that is a tall order. Realism in a more proximate sense will warn us not to expect it too easily or too soon. Our international institutions have barely begun to meet the negative side of those expectations, let alone to sustain the positive hopes and aspirations. Realism that takes a longer view, however, also will say that this is the direction in which we must move if we are to replace the system of sovereign states with a different kind of international order that will be equally successful in maintaining stability for the future. The aspiration of peoples to join the system of sovereignty from which they have been excluded will express itself in the accumulation of instruments of coercive force that the sovereign states have tried, unsuccessfully, to monopolize. Terrorism avenges exclusion from sovereignty by exploiting weaknesses in security systems that arise when commerce and culture begin to flow more freely across international boundaries. If we do not provide an alternative expression for these aspirations, governments may find themselves required to close their borders and open their jails, reasserting some of the most coercive elements of sovereignty at the expense of the emerging international order.

That is how a Christian realist sees the future, based less on what we might wish for than on where we have been. The international order based on sovereign states is coming to an end, but history will continue. That means that the elements of power, awe, and identity that gave rise to sovereignty will still be with us and will still require our attention. The element of hope in the new situation is not the false hope that these realities might simply go away. The hope is that the new constellations of self-interest and power might constrain us to do justice differently—perhaps even somewhat more effectively—than we have done it in the past.

Notes

1. Walter Rauschenbusch, *Christianity and the Social Crisis* (New York: Macmillan, 1911), 380.

2. Ibid., 379.

3. The term "Christian realism" is associated especially with the work of Reinhold Niebuhr (1892–1971). Others coined the term before him to name a theological movement and to designate the political and social ideas connected with that theology. See Walter Marshall Horton, *Realistic Theology* (New York: Harper and Brothers, 1934); John C. Bennett, *Christian Realism* (New York: Charles Scribner's Sons, 1934).

4. Reinhold Niebuhr, *The Nature and Destiny of Man: A Christian Interpretation*, vol. 1 (New York: Charles Scribner's Sons, 1964), 296.

5. Harold Berman, *Law and Revolution: The Formation of the Western Legal Tradition* (Cambridge, Mass.: Harvard University Press, 1983), 520–36.

6. Martin Luther, "Temporal Authority: To What Extent It Should Be Obeyed," in Timothy F. Lull, ed., *Martin Luther's Basic Theological Writings* (Minneapolis: Fortress Press, 1989), 687.

7. When I refer to "the first Christian realists" in this context, I do not mean Reinhold Niebuhr and John Bennett. I mean Luther, Hobbes, and Locke. Each of these men was shaped by powerful, though very different, versions of Christian faith, and each of them hoped to free divine authority for the supremacy it rightly deserved over the conscience by excluding it from the messy scramble for temporal power. See Joshua Mitchell, *Not by Reason Alone: Religion, History, and Identity in Early Modern Political Thought* (Chicago: University of Chicago Press, 1993).

8. Luther, "Temporal Authority," 679.

9. Reinhold Niebuhr, *The Children of Light and the Children of Darkness* (New York: Charles Scribner's Sons, 1944), 42–47.

10. Reinhold Niebuhr, *The Structure of Nations and Empires* (New York: Charles Scribner's Sons, 1959).

11. Thomas L. Friedman, *The Lexus and the Olive Tree* (New York: Anchor Books, 2000), 157–64.

12. See Reinhold Niebuhr, *Faith and History: A Comparison of Christian and Modern Views of History* (New York: Charles Scribner's Sons, 1949), 120–24.

13. An alternative (to increased awe for international organizations and leaders) might be to continue the process of reducing the aura that surrounds *national* leaders. For example, we could line up 100 heads of state and government for a group photo that looks like a fourth-grade class picture, as the UN actually accomplished at the 2000 Millennium Summit. Or we could continue the practice of having national leaders appear as guests on television talk shows. Maybe we learn something important from that exercise, but watching Charles DeGaulle on the *Oprah Winfrey Show* seems a bit difficult to imagine.

8

Serving Two Masters?
Affirming Religious Belief and
Human Rights in a Pluralistic World

R. SCOTT APPLEBY

Religion Confronted and Challenged

THE MODERN HUMAN RIGHTS ERA, inaugurated in 1948 by the rat-
ification of the Universal Declaration of Human Rights (UDHR),
challenged religious communities around the world to demonstrate their
commitment to the concept and thereby to demonstrate its universality.
An array of international figures, representing numerous religious and
cultural perspectives, endorsed the draft of the UDHR—undermining
the objection that "human rights" is solely a project of the western enlightenment.[1] In recent decades, religions have been called upon anew
to participate vigorously in an effort to build cultures committed to
human rights, nonviolence, and civic tolerance. At this writing, in the
midst of an international "war against terrorism" in which Islamic fundamentalism is implicated, all religions are being scrutinized once again
for evidence of their benevolent intent.

In response to these waves of challenges, religious leaders have initiated internal debates and external dialogues with other religious and
nonreligious traditions on the sources and meanings of universal human
rights. The "grammar" of these various debates and dialogues shifts according to the audience. Within each particular religious tradition,
members share a *first-order* language of commitments and beliefs about

the sacred. Although this primary religious discourse is the ordinary way that believers express their faith, at any given moment it may or may not capture the *internal pluralism* of the historic faith—the striking diversity of interpretations within a tradition regarding the meanings of those beliefs and the obligations that sacred commitments entail.

This internal diversity becomes a potential advantage for believers who wish to reach out beyond the religious community. Thus, their engagement in the international discourse of rights and responsibilities has led some religious communities to develop a *second-order* mode of discourse—or bridging language—that conveys the primary beliefs and commitments, or at least the values underlying them, in language that is accessible to outsiders. Thus, pluralism provides the context within which modern religious communities can bring their first-order traditions of belief and practice into dialogue with, if not full conformity to, the norms, practices, and creeds of the human rights community.

Religious traditions now find themselves moving between these two orders of discourse. Leaders are confronted with demands, often made by members of the religious community itself, to reconcile religious obligations—including the freedom to evangelize or the freedom not to be evangelized—in ways that are consistent with religious freedom and universal human rights norms.

Working with nongovernmental organizations such as the World Conference on Religion and Peace, Catholic Relief Services, and OxFam, religious communities are exploring what it might mean to build local cultures of human rights. At sites of religious and ethnic conflict such as Northern Ireland, the Balkans, and Israel/Palestine, religious leaders have established or supported ecumenical and interreligious dialogues and cooperative ventures that emphasize the connection between peace, reconciliation, and the flourishing of human rights. Each of these tasks depends on the willingness and ability of religious actors to retrieve, articulate, and apply first-order religious concepts and norms that promote human rights and nonviolent conflict transformation.

Though undeniably ambitious, these goals nonetheless are conceivable for religious communities emerging from a remarkable era when nations of Latin America and Eastern Europe, whose political discourse was impoverished of "rights talk" and characterized by "excessively strong and simple duty talk," embraced democracy and moved to strengthen legal protections of the rights of individuals and minorities.[2] Governments in the Middle East, Africa, and Asia that wished to avoid the discourse of self-determination and human rights were brought before the court of international public opinion. In the United States, social critics explored various dimensions of the "American rights dialect." Many intellectuals held the liberal state aloft as a governmental standard to be emulated universally; other self-critical Americans worried that excessive concentration on the autonomous and self-sufficient individual came at the expense of the community and the common good.[3]

In regions experiencing fundamental political transformation, space opened for religious innovation, differentiation, and growth. A new wave of missionaries and proselytizers entered the religious marketplace in eastern Europe and central Asia, transgressing political and spiritual boundaries and undermining traditional religious loyalties already eroded by the fall of the Soviet Union and the end of the cold war. Roman Catholics and evangelical Protestants in Latin America waged "soul wars," as did Christians and Muslims in Africa. Everywhere, it seemed, the explosion of religious faith tested peoples' capacity to tolerate religious diversity and accommodate genuine pluralism under the law.[4]

From within the eyes of such hurricanes, some religions claimed a longstanding witness to "human rights" in ancient scriptures and ethical traditions, appropriated elements of the new rights talk, or hastened to formulate their own parallel discourses in which rights talk was challenged or complemented by the delineation of responsibilities to religion and society. Protestant, Catholic, and Jewish leaders responded to excesses of radical individualism in America by promoting a countervailing discourse of civic responsibility in service to the common good and by reminding their fellow citizens of the longstanding contributions of religious communities to the cultivation of civic virtues and social accountability.[5]

The most visible drama unfolded in the Muslim world, where scholars as well as religious and political leaders became—and remain—immersed in a far-reaching debate over Islam's commitment to freedom, including democracy and human rights. The question posed most feverishly in this context is whether Islam can satisfy Western expectations of "freedom." The Western media's portrayal of the terrorist attacks of

September 11, 2001—as crimes committed by enemies of freedom—and the subsequent war in Afghanistan reinforced the narrative of events and the interpretation of their meaning set forth by President George W. Bush and echoed by prominent members of his administration, not least Secretary of Defense Donald Rumsfeld. That is, the bombing campaign was depicted as the first phase in an "infinitely just" global war against terrorism pitting the virtuous, freedom-loving nations of the West and their allies (including right-minded Muslims) against the Muslim extremist Usama bin Ladin, the "evil one," and his network of minions scattered across the world.

The administration's insistence on this crude dualistic language undermined the president's equally clear distinction between Islam as a world religion of peace, on one hand, and the violence perpetrated by extremist elements claiming to be acting in the name of Islam, on the other. The dualist rhetoric also obscured the painful truth amidst the many lies spoken by bin Ladin: The West, and the United States in particular, was hardly innocent of "evil" acts—acts of aggression and exploitation over the years that had led, whatever their intent, to structural violence against the peoples of the Muslim world and, not infrequently, the destruction of innocent lives.

Nonetheless, Islam—widely perceived as the spiritual home of the world's most aggressive, freedom-hating, and rights-violating religious fundamentalisms—was challenged again to defend its reputation as a responsible member of the human community. In an unusual (if not unprecedented) move that undermined the president's efforts to stave off enmity toward American Muslims, mainstream periodicals and other media published or broadcast editorials equating Islam and religious absolutism. Others in the media resorted to melodramatic language to make their point. "The Osama bin Ladens of the world—like the leaders of the Inquisition and others before and after them—demand that all embrace absolute faith," wrote Andrew Sullivan in an influential essay published in the *New York Times*. "Individual faith and pluralism were the targets on September 11, and it was only the beginning of an epic battle."[6]

In short, the public debate over the legitimacy of Islamism, triggered by the events of September 11, 2001, brought into focus for millions of Americans and Europeans the struggles that have been experienced for decades by believers who seek to serve their God and to act as effective agents and advocates of humanity through support of freedom and universal human rights.

The role of religions in the articulation and reception of universal human rights norms remains ambiguous. Optimistically, one might say that it is "evolving." Religions, as both custodians and critics of culture, are among the primary social agents of cultural change; in many settings around the world, they are uniquely poised to mediate the encounter between the universal and culture-specific elements that must coexist in any viable regime of human rights. If this potential to articulate human rights talk within religious discourse is to be realized, religious as well as secular thinkers must resolve several theoretical questions, each with profound implications for praxis. Who participates in the rights-defining process? Who defines the governing criteria for the interpretation and practice of human rights: nations, international organizations, or some other entities? What should be the role of religion in the process of negotiating cultural identities and human rights norms?

The most intense and conflict-ridden debates—and ultimately, perhaps, the most consequential—are being conducted within and among the religious traditions themselves, as they interact frequently and rapidly with their own diverse and ideologically plural membership, with other religions, and with secular actors and traditions. Religions are implicated most directly and dramatically, of course, in controversies and conflicts that revolve around the delineation, exercise, or violation of religious human rights. What does it mean to endorse a universal regime of individual human rights while also affirming the values of respect for religious integrity and the beliefs of the local community and particular religious tradition? In short, can religious believers serve two masters—man and God?

The world of pluralism in which religious traditions exist offers some promising responses to that question. By pluralism I mean both the internal pluralism of a tradition and the variety of lifestyles and belief systems vying for public space outside the religious enclave. In this chapter, using Islam as a test case, I ask how religions might accommodate pluralism to promote freedom through a culture of human rights while still affirming religious commitments.

I begin with a general survey of the relationship between religion and human rights, including certain challenges and possibilities that this engagement presents for a universal human rights culture, and how religious pluralism is implicated. Then I focus specifically on the plural views within Islam, ranging from the embrace of human rights by more liberal elements to the advocacy of intolerance and violence by fundamentalists. When internal pluralism flourishes, I argue, progressive religious forces are able to do the important work of sustaining and advancing a commitment to human rights as part of their religious mission. I conclude by considering, through an illustration in Islam, how a religious tradition might reconcile its convictions about the sacred with a commitment to freedom and human rights—put simply, how to serve simultaneously both God and man.

Are Human Rights Universal?[7]

The last quarter of the twentieth century witnessed the establishment of more than thirty constitutional democracies and the proliferation of international laws, treaties, covenants, and other instruments devoted to the articulation and protection of human rights. Among these instruments are those devoted specifically to outlawing discrimination against religious belief and practice—most notably, Article 18 of the UDHR, Article 18 of the International Covenant on Civil and Political Rights (ICCPR), and Articles 1 and 6 of the 1981 Declaration on the Elimination of All Forms of Intolerance and Discrimination Based on Religion or Belief.[8]

During the same period, however, it became painfully clear that these international covenants and laws were largely irrelevant to societies lacking a culture in which individual and minority rights are valued. In the dozens of nations crippled by bloody insurrections, civil wars, or genocidal campaigns, advocates of human rights and intercommunal dialogue were overshadowed by religious and ethnonationalist extremists. Nonetheless, solutions to these types of conflicts "must ultimately be grounded in a global regime of law and human rights," contends John Witte, Jr. "The counterintuitive part of the argument is that religion must be seen as a vital dimension of any legal regime of human rights. . . . Religions will not be easy allies to engage, but the struggle for human rights cannot be won without them."[9]

Religion's intimate relationship to culture stands behind this claim because religions invariably provide what Jacques Maritain called "the scale of values governing the exercise and concrete manifestation" of otherwise abstract human rights precepts and laws.[10] The preoccupying question is whether and how "the scale of values" governing local understandings of rights and responsibilities is generalizable across cultures and religions. The language of "universal" human rights, employed since the United Nations promulgated the UDHR, has inspired resistance from various quarters, including religious communities that regard the attempt to build an international regime of human rights law as a new form of Western colonialism.[11] Opponents charge that the UDHR and subsequent conventions impose post-Enlightenment ways of knowing and Western cultural assumptions and ideologies that are no more universally binding than any other culturally determined set of principles. Asian leaders meeting in Bangkok in 1993, for example, voiced strenuous opposition to "the universal human rights regime" because they perceived that such rights talk, formulated primarily by Westerners, reflects what they considered to be an excessive penchant for personal autonomy—a value that is given little priority in Asian cultures. By way of contrast, the Bangkok Governmental Declaration of 1993, issued by a group of Asian nations in advance of the Vienna World Conference on Human Rights, emphasized the principles of national sovereignty, territorial integrity, and noninterference that also frame many of the questions in this book.[12] Cultural relativists doubt the existence or accessibility of universal truth and suspect that universalist claims, including claims regarding human rights, mask imperialist ambitions.

Taking the objections of cultural relativists into account, may we nonetheless speak of overarching moral truths, a universal moral sense, or "core values" held in common by all cultures—for example, prohibitions against the slaughter of innocents, torture, rape, incest, lying, theft, and so on? Does the process of socialization, whatever its range of cultural variations, ensure that humans acquire a universal moral status that ought to be protected? (See chapter 9 for a discussion of how the moral status of the human person is mediated through the universal and the particular in cases involving "crimes against humanity.") Can we agree, with Marcus Singer, that "the nearly universal acceptance of the Golden Rule and its promulgation by persons of considerable intelligence, though otherwise of different outlook, would therefore provide some evidence for the claim that it is a fundamental ethical truth"?[13] Can we speak, further, of "natural law" and fundamental qualities of human nature?[14]

If agreement on the existence of universal moral principles is the minimum requirement for an international legal order, one implication of this agreement seems clear: Certain principles are true apart from their level of enculturation in any given society. Accordingly, a regime of universal human rights necessarily transcends and thus stands in judgment over every particular social embodiment and normative order of rights and responsibilities. In fact, this is what it means to honor a universal standard: All other normative orders of justice and rights must concede to its priorities. A universal standard that is based on justice and rights cannot become "sovereign" or supreme unless and until claims of nations and particular communities give way to and embrace such standards.

Yet even among nation-states, transnational agencies, and moral communities that have reached consensus on universal human rights and responsibilities, specification of practices that violate or uphold them remains an area of controversy. Basic questions are unresolved. Which practices fall within universal norms, and which are left to cultural arbitration? Must a local regime of human rights be predicated on the priority of individual rights, or can the rights of a community take precedence? And what of nations and religious or subnational ethnic communities that are not formally bound by the UDHR and its principles: How and by whom are their interpretations and observances of "human rights" to be evaluated and sanctioned?[15]

Cultural relativists argue, furthermore, that a uniform interpretation of basic human rights provisions is neither possible nor desirable. They point, for example, to Article 5 of the UDHR, which stipulates that "No one shall be subjected to torture, or to cruel, inhuman or degrading treatment or punishment." Because understandings of human dignity tend to be indeterminate and culturally contingent, they contend, the precise meaning of this provision is not self-evident; practices defined as "torture" in one culture may be absolved or approved by another. (Consider, for example, the various viewpoints represented in the ongoing controversy over female "circumcision" or "mutilation.")[16] Conceding the inviolability of "culture," however, runs the risk of naively accepting as normative values that are promoted only by a cultural elite. Frequently, such values are contested by other members of society—or would be contested if marginalized people and groups were allowed to speak and organize politically. Failing to challenge "cultural values" therefore might mean obscuring and thus perpetuating social inequities and injustices. Ultimately, capitulation to the politics of cultural relativism in such cases means abandoning persons who have been silenced and rendered powerless by the culture in question.[17]

There is a middle course, however, between the imposition of a universalist discourse and regime of law, on one hand, and deference to a sort of indigenous cultural imperialism, on the other. Cultures can and should participate in the formulation and interpretation of universal human rights norms binding upon them. I return to this theme subsequently in my discussion of Islam and human rights, but not before briefly taking stock of some of the ways in which religious actors and traditions have been implicated in human rights in recent years.

Religious Defenders of Human Rights

Can the world's religious communities be expected to take a leading and constructive role in efforts to promote human rights? Organized religion in general has a mixed record. Following World War II, Jewish and Christian denominations emerged as vigorous advocates of human rights, issuing bold confessional statements and assigning significant institutional resources to the cause. Jewish nongovernmental organizations (NGOs) such as the World Jewish Congress and the Paris-based Alliance Israeliese Universielle made important contributions to the early development of human rights law; individual religious leaders devoted their careers to advocacy, diplomacy, and the reporting of human rights violations.[18] Religious actors helped to shape the grassroots civil rights movement in the United States and participated in revolutions against oppressive colonial rule in Africa and Latin America.[19] Christian democratic movements contributed to the evolving discourse on human rights in Europe.[20]

In the 1990s, as globalization both displayed and deepened the multicultural and religiously plural character of most developed and developing societies, a greater number and variety of religious actors and religious communities participated at each level of the cultural discourse on human rights. Religious NGOs developed expertise in human rights advocacy and monitoring,[21] human rights education consciousness-raising or "conscientization,"[22] humanitarian assistance to victims and legal representation for victims of human rights abuses,[23] and interreligious and ecumenical relations.[24] Progressive leaders and activists from different religious traditions and communities found similar ways to sacralize human rights. They celebrated the memory of virtuous and holy "progressives" from the religion's past, their lives interpreted and projected as embodiments of the tradition's core human rights values. Hindu human rights advocates, for example, held up for emulation not only Mohandas Gandhi but also Rammohun Roy (1772–1833), the first able spokesperson of modern reformist Hinduism and a crusader against the practice of burning widows alive (*sati*). Roy, the founder of the *Brahmo Samaj*—a theistic, Unitarian religious society open to all—devoted his life to clarifying and promoting the humane ethical values of ancient Indian spirituality.[25]

Progressives also gave much-needed attention to the elaboration of women's rights, freedoms, and responsibilities. A generation of Jewish, Christian, Muslim, Buddhist, and Hindu scholars and advocates—alongside colleagues outside their traditions—reinterpreted what they judged to be outdated teachings and practices and pressed religious leaders to battle male chauvinism in religious communities.[26] In a related initiative, progressives produced an apologetic literature that attempted to account for and delegitimate expressions of extremism within their respective religious communities.[27]

Finally, intellectuals plumbed their traditions' teachings on war and peace, with the intent of strengthening aspects that amplify religion's voice as an advocate of human rights and nonviolent conflict transformation. In the wake of the 1990–91 Persian Gulf War, Christians (and their non-Christian colleagues) reconsidered the viability of the just war theory and gave renewed attention to theologies of nonviolence and pacifism, while Muslims (and their non-Muslim colleagues) revisited the concept of *jihad* with an eye to lifting up and thereby strengthening the scriptural and traditional warrants for nonviolent resistance to oppression and injustice.[28] Jews drew together elements of a theory of conflict resolution from Biblical *mitzvot* and rabbinic rationales.[29] Buddhists formed social movements and NGOs that challenged antidemocratic, corrupt, and oppressive regimes in Burma, Thailand, Vietnam, and Cambodia. Hindus challenged India's traditional caste-based economic and social discrimination—supporting the Mandal Commission's recommendation, in 1990, to reserve a larger number of federal and state jobs and admissions to educational institutions for the so-called backward castes at the expense of the upper castes.[30]

Overall, these religious intellectuals, progressive believers, and faith-based NGOs bear witness to the possibility of serving God as well as man and woman. Whereas believers were among the notable champions of justice during the first fifty years of the human rights era, however, the formal or official religious leadership too often failed to support the religious witness by giving it permanent institutional expression. Because religious officials and institutional leaders are charged with preserving and defending the faith in its concrete social, institutional (and bureaucratic) forms, in general they tend to be more conservative—and more adverse to taking risks—than activists, scholars, and community leaders. Yet the official leadership, more than other actors in the religious sector, commands the material resources and enjoys the public prominence necessary to legitimate and deepen the faith tradition's commitment to human rights, social justice, and the common good. Human rights advocates remember the 1970s, John Witte remarks, as a time when religious officialdom "dropped the ball" by squandering the momentum that had gathered in the 1960s. Most religious groups made only modest contributions to rights activism and the theory and law of human rights. Official religious leaders, with some notable exceptions, did not develop specific precepts or programs to implement the general principles set out in the religious manifestoes of the 1960s, nor did they follow up their general endorsement of human rights instruments with effective lobbying and litigation.

The relatively greater awareness and participation of religious communities in human rights campaigns in the 1990s mainly underscored the fact that the world's major religious bodies possess the conceptual and organizational resources to advance the discourse and observance of human rights in local cultures. Alone, however, they tend to be less effective, or ineffective, in this effort. Part of the reason for the relative inactivity of religious leaders in the 1970s was the withering of support and encouragement from secular human rights activists, who were directing their inadequate resources to the most egregious violations of human rights—physical abuses associated with war crimes, torture, imprisonment, rape, and so on. Religious groups and their rights were assigned a low priority, behind freedom of speech and the press, race and gender issues, and provision of work and welfare. Left to their own devices, many religious communities failed to muster the will or resources to oppose oppression of belief and religious practice or even to document the spiritual and moral abuses accompanying such oppression.

Happily, this situation is changing dramatically today, with the heightened activism of faith-based NGOs (e.g., the Mennonite Central Committee, the World Conference on Religion and Peace, the Society of Engaged Buddhists, World Vision, and Catholic Relief Services). These faith-based organizations have established partnerships with secular NGOs such as OxFam and the International Red Cross, and religious communities collaborate increasingly with intergovernmental organizations to provide good offices, mediation, and social services in nations gripped by civil or regional wars. (One exemplar is the Roman Catholic and ecumenical Community of Sant'Egidio, which has worked with governmental and intergovernmental agencies in conflict transformation in Mozambique, Kosovo, Burundi, and Algeria.) Drawing on these developments, the newly established International Center for Religious Diplomacy, based in Washington, D.C., is working to train faith-based diplomats in the skills of conflict mediation and long-term conflict transformation. The center's director, Douglas Johnston (formerly the director of the Center for Strategic and International Studies), is experienced in the art of bringing together secular and religious actors for peace-building initiatives.

Exclusivist tendencies within religious communities that spurn pluralism also impede progress toward human rights advocacy. Perhaps the most difficult prospect for a religious community to contemplate is its own diminishment or displacement. Religious opponents of dialogue and conciliation with outsiders predict that "diminishment and displacement" would be the likely results of "liberalizing" and tolerance-building measures. Enclave-builders portray their religion's truths, "rights," and responsibilities as inherently superior to those of their rivals.

In their judgment, the strength of a religious community's claim to the loyalty of its adherents rests on the community's ability to present itself as the exclusive bearer of specific moral and/or material benefits. Comparisons to other normative communities are invidious—and therefore useful in sustaining a climate of mistrust and mutual antagonism that reinforces the necessity of membership in the elect community.

Despite the propensity of some embattled religious actors to arouse and exploit collective hostility toward the "other," there are influential religious leaders who believe that commitment to one's own normative system can be compatible with openness to the "other." One can be fully committed to a religion and identify with fellow believers for that purpose, they maintain, while also being fully committed to another normative system for its purposes. "People can and do have multiple or overlapping identities," writes a leading Muslim intellectual, "and can and do cooperate with the 'us' of each of their identities without being hostile to the 'them' of one level of identity. . . ."[31]

It follows that the challenge for religious progressives in the new century is to translate into popular religious idioms their vision of religion as an internally pluralistic, rights-bearing, and rights-affirming sacred trust. The challenge for their supporters is to bring that vision to life in local, national, and regional institutions within those settings where rights are most threatened. In the following section I explore a case study of this dynamic that illustrates Islam's internal pluralism and its commitment to human rights.

Freedom, Violence, and Islam's Internal Pluralism

One unfortunate consequence of the Bush administration's politically charged framing of the tragedies of September 11, 2001, in terms of moral absolutes was propagation of the notion that Islam and its billion-plus adherents are reluctant to embrace personal freedom, human rights, and political self-determination. In Islamic societies today, the precise meanings of these terms are contested, their concrete application and political expression uncertain—as they also have been throughout the history of the United States. "Personal freedom" is a good, certainly, for countless Muslims, but not one to be pursued in isolation from the common good. Similarly, Roman Catholic social teaching, as articulated by the Catholic bishops of the United States, qualifies personal freedom in the same way.

Moreover, recent elections in Muslim countries have resulted in victories for candidates who champion personal freedom. In 1997 Mohammed Khatami, the obscure director of Iran's national library, won 70 percent of the popular vote for that country's presidency. Promising to loosen restrictions on dress, dancing, music, and the press, President Khatami won reelection with 77 percent in 2001. "We believe in the type of Islam that never, ever allows us to interfere with the private lives of individuals," explained the president's brother and political ally, Mohammed Reza Khatami.[32] Turkey's Welfare Party (now renamed the Virtue Party) claimed enough votes in 1995 to lead a coalition government briefly, but only after explicitly rejecting state-sponsored imposition of religious law. In 1999 Abdurrahman Wahid, Indonesia's first democratically elected president in decades (and a religious scholar who headed the world's largest Islamic revivalist organization), repealed Indonesia's longstanding restrictions on the construction of churches and Hindu temples and took other measures to enhance religious freedom as well. "We are not like those Muslims who believe there is a conflict between universal human rights and the Islamic religion," he told the *Bangkok Post*, "we believe in human rights, diversity and religious tolerance."[33]

On the other end of the spectrum are absolutists who claim a monopoly on truth. Within their religious communities, extremists and absolutists attempt to obstruct the processes of pluralism, claiming that revealed or holy truths are monolithic and incommensurable with second-order liberal, humanist values. A staple of the discourse of Islamic extremists is the claim that the traditional religious leaders of the Islamic world, such as the shaykhs of Cairo's al-Azhar seminary and university—the center of the Sunni educational and religious "establishment"—have been coopted by dictatorial accommodationist rulers such as Egyptian president Hosni Mubarak or the monarchy of Saudi Arabia. As a result, these traditional Muslim religious leaders have been marginalized and delegitimated in many circles of the Islamic world, leaving the field open to the religiously unschooled but disgruntled "lay" men, many of whom have educational backgrounds in engineering, applied science, or business.

In the late 1990s, one of these lay men, Usama bin Ladin, began to refer to himself as "Shaykh" Usama Bin-Muhammad Bin-ladin, as he did in the *fatwa* he issued on 23 February 1998 announcing his legal "ruling" that every Muslim now has the individual duty to "kill the Americans and their allies—civilians and military." In attempting to launch a global *jihad* against the West, bin Ladin sought to rally Muslims to his highly tendentious reading of the Qur'an and the *Shari'a*. In so doing he recognized implicitly that Islam—like Christianity, Judaism, Hinduism, and Buddhism—is a living tradition, the meaning of its sacred texts and moral laws ever awaiting a new and compelling *ijtihad* ("personal effort"—that is, "the right of a qualified scholar to go back to the primary sources and work out from them what he thought were the Islamic principles involved").[34]

The self-proclaimed and self-styled expertise of bin Ladin and his comrades such as Ayman al-Zawahiri (formerly the chief of Egypt's Islamic Jihad) has been contested in the Islamic world, however. Religious leaders as well as heads of state within the Sunni Muslim world have denounced the "kill all Americans" *fatwa*, the attacks of September 11, and, indeed, violent approaches to redressing Islamic grievances. Strikingly, Mohammed Khatami, the Shi'ite president of Iran, joined his Sunni colleagues in condemning what he calls "a new form of active nihilism [that] assumes various names, [some of which] bear a semblance of religiosity and some proclaim spirituality." Khatami denigrated religious extremists as "superficial literalists clinging to simplistic ideas," and he called for the development of a cross-religious language that would allow religious communities "to be understood and [provided with] a capacity to listen and understand."[35] President Khatami also proposed an alliance of religiously rooted moderates, from across faith lines, who could offer a vision for their respective societies that uses "neither materialistic secularism nor religious fundamentalism as a starting point."[36] Significantly, his condemnation of terrorism was accompanied by strong advocacy of the notion of religious pluralism and tolerance of religious and ethnic minorities.

On display in this debate about legitimate and illegitimate uses of violence within the domain of Islam was the internal pluralism of the tradition. To various degrees, all of the great religious traditions, in their commentaries on the sacred scriptures and authoritative traditions, contain evolving hermeneutics, or interpretive strategies, designed to identify the sacred—that is, the manifestation of God, or the divine—with a particular school of thought or jurisprudence. Within each of these great traditions, notwithstanding their profound substantive differences, one can trace a moral trajectory challenging adherents to greater acts of compassion, forgiveness, and reconciliation and delegitimating as "demonic" the competing voices of revenge and retaliation that claim the status of authentic religious expression. This internal evolution of the great religious traditions commands our attention because these traditions spawn the most significant religiopolitical movements of our time, from the violent extremist cadres to the organizations of militant peacemakers. Thus, it behooves us to understand how change occurs within these religions, how spinoff movements form to advocate and embody different elements within these internally plural and ambiguous traditions, and how external actors and circumstances influence both processes.

In striving to adhere to traditional beliefs and moral codes in a rapidly changing cultural and technological milieu, religious actors (openly or unwittingly) recognize that tradition is pluriform and cumulative, developed in and for concrete situations. Decisions that are based on religious principles reflect the ways that religious authorities interpret and apply the received tradition in specific circumstances. In this process, the internal pluralism of any religious tradition—the multiplicity of its teachings, images of the divine, moral injunctions, and so on—bestows upon the religious leader the power of choice. It falls inevitably to the evangelist, prophet, rabbi, priest, sage, religious scholar, or guru to select the appropriate doctrine or norm in a given situation and thus to define what is orthodox or heretical, moral or immoral, permitted or forbidden, at a particular moment.

Islamic Commitments to God and Man

The contemporary debate over Islamic polity and the future of Islamic politics demonstrates that shared commitment to the observance of Islamic law does not lead to uniformity or even commensurability of method among Islamists or among Muslims in general. Like any complex legal code, the *Shari`a* admits many interpretations and diverse applications, each of which is unavoidably selective.[37]

The Islamic Republic of Iran provides perhaps the most striking example of the emergence of Islamic "rights talk" under the conditions of cultural modernity. With his brilliantly argued advocacy of human rights and democracy, formulated from the depths of the Shi`ite tradition as well as the larger Islamic jurisprudential tradition, Iranian philosopher and public intellectual Abdolkarim Soroush has sparked a fascinating political debate in the home of the first "fundamentalist" revolution. Popular among Iran's youth and technocratic elite but opposed by the ruling clerical elite, Soroush challenges the latter's political legitimacy and takes issue with the doctrine of *vilayat-i faqih* (guardianship of the Supreme Jurist), which stood at the heart of the Ayatollah Khomeini's religious ideology. For Soroush, religiously imposed ideology is a distortion of religious values. He holds up human rights as *the* criterion for governance of the Islamic state—the criterion that guarantees the state's religious as well as democratic nature.

How does Soroush justify this seemingly radical appreciation for human rights, which is a historical reversal of policy in Iran? Although Islam as a religion is unchanging and eternal, he acknowledges, "religious knowledge" (*ma'rifat-i dini*)—a branch of human knowledge produced by scholars engaged in the study of the sacred Shi`ite texts—is always in flux, conditioned by history and adaptive to the scientific understanding of the time. Shaped in the contemporary era by intense cultural interaction and popular awareness of political options, religious knowledge has found Islam and democracy to be compatible, Soroush believes.[38] In a democratic state, furthermore, human rights cannot be restricted to religiously derived rights alone. Muslims as well as non-Muslims derive their human rights not from their faith but from "their membership within the larger group of humanity," as Valla Vakili—a disciple of Soroush—puts it. Many Muslim opponents of democracy refer to it as *dimukrasi-yi gharbi* (western democracy), thereby identifying it with the threatening "other."[39] By contrast, Soroush considers democracy a form of government that is compatible with multiple political cultures, including Islamic ones. In Muslim societies, governments that derive their legitimacy from the people necessarily will be religious governments, duty-bound to protect both the sanctity of religion and the rights of man. In defending the sanctity of religion, Soroush warns, the government must not privilege a particular conception of religion, lest it sacrifice human rights for ideological purity. The guiding criteria for governance must be human rights themselves rather than any particular religious ideology; indeed, Soroush argues, a society embraces religion in large part because it upholds the society's sense of justice. Today that sense of justice includes a respect for human rights.[40]

This appeal to external (i.e., extrareligious) criteria to evaluate religion's fulfillment of its proper purposes may be the most striking and controversial aspect of Soroush's thought. It constitutes an invitation—an imperative—to cross-cultural and cross-disciplinary dialogue and to an increasingly shared understanding and embrace of norms that are themselves sacred. Politically charged matters such as the relationship between religion and justice, though addressed by the Qur`an and other religious texts, can be defined for the present age, Soroush teaches, only by Muslims entering into a second-order theological debate that includes philosophical, metaphysical, political, secular, and other religious discourses.

Soroush has been a powerfully influential thinker because of the quality of his ideas—as well as because he was an insider in the Iranian revolutionary government. After attending the 'Alavi secondary school in Tehran—one of the first schools to combine the teaching of the modern sciences and religious studies—he studied pharmacology at the university and then attended the University of London for postgraduate work in the history and philosophy of science. A confidant of 'Ali Shariati, the intellectual whose writings on Islamic governance were appropriated by Khomeini, Soroush returned to Iran in the midst of the Islamic revolution and took a high-ranking position on the Committee of the Cultural Revolution, which was charged with Islamicizing Iran's higher educational system. In 1992, five years after resigning from the committee in protest, Soroush established the Research Faculty for the History and Philosophy of Science at the Research Center for the Humanities in Tehran and began to lecture extensively to lay and theological audiences at universities and mosques in Tehran and at seminaries in Qum.

Soroush's academic training, revolutionary credentials, and connections with key figures in the government empowered him to speak with an authority shared by few members of the Iranian religious intelligentsia.[41] In 1997, despite being threatened by hardliners and hounded by young extremists from Ansar-e-Hezbollah, Soroush publicly applauded the election of Mohammed Khatami. He also criticized the new president, however, for indecision in the face of his "fundamentalist" opponents and urged him to stand up for human rights and academic freedom.[42]

Soroush exemplifies a new breed of Muslim intellectuals formed not by the traditional system of religious education but trained in Islamic intellectual traditions and Western schools of thought. This training also illustrates that Islam is capable of making commitments that affirm the sacred claims of the religion and provide robust support for human rights. As religious authority experiences fragmentation throughout the Muslim world, such "postfundamentalist" thinkers are making a substantial impact on religious thought in their respective societies. There is no longer a single voice of the traditional ulama speaking for Islam but many competing voices, the existence of which contributes to the evolution of thought and political culture in Muslim societies. Indeed, Soroush personifies the worldwide multiplicity of Islamic voices arguing that pluralism and popular political participation must become central themes in Islam.[43]

If thinkers such as Soroush continue to win hearts and minds in the Islamic world, significant progress toward building a transcultural regime of human rights seems likely. The idea that human rights belong to humanity itself rather than to a specific religion or the West provides a foundation not only for the necessary intrareligious dialogue on values, rights, and responsibilities; it also establishes the framework for fruitful interreligious dialogue on human rights in an interdependent world.

The relocation of human rights in humanity itself, rather than in a particular cultural or religious identity, was Roman Catholicism's breakthrough in 1965, evident in the documents of Vatican II. Other religious communities also have moved toward consensus around the affirmation that humanity itself is the source of the universality of human rights.[44] That understanding appears to be the *sine qua non* for a rights discourse that is sufficiently nuanced culturally but also capable of winning assent from a broad spectrum of religious, ethnic, and cultural communities.

Conclusion

The variety of attitudes in Islam toward human rights and pluralism has counterparts in Christianity, Judaism, Hinduism, and Buddhism as well. Indeed, Robert Traer writes, support for human rights among religious leaders today is "global, cutting across cultures as well as systems of belief and practice. . . . Clearly, something new is occurring when women and men of different faith traditions join with those of no religious tradition to champion human rights."[45]

No religious tradition speaks unequivocally about human rights; none has earned an exemplary human rights record over the centuries. Religions' sacred texts and canons devote much more attention to commandments and obligations than to rights and freedoms. Paradoxically, their prelates, supreme guides, theologians, and jurists have increasingly cultivated human rights norms even if their application has suffered from inconsistency.[46] Whatever the record reveals, human rights discourse has become the moral language of cultural modernity, in part as a result of its justification and advocacy by members of different religious traditions. In addition, as I have argued, the internal pluralism of Islam (not to mention other major religious traditions) enables religious actors to select and develop theologies and moral precepts that accommodate universal human rights norms and enhance the building of local cultures that sustain them—while maintaining strong commitments to religious faith. Serving man and God in the same moment becomes a viable possibility.

Each religion (and its specific schools or subtraditions) possesses the potential to justify and advocate human rights in its own distinctive way and on its own terms. Each has its own theological and philosophical framework for interpreting human rights, its own constellation of doctrines and precepts modifying the canon of rights, and its own exemplars or champions of human rights. Yet the respective frameworks, doctrines, or models of emulation are not readily reconcilable in every respect; even where different religions proclaim essentially the same luminous core truths, this basic unity is not always transparent to themselves or to others.

The challenge of the next phase of the human rights era will be for religious leaders from these different traditions and subtraditions to identify and enlarge the common ground they share. Human rights discourse forms a bridge linking the particular to the universal. Religious actors engaged in supporting universal human rights possess a powerful tool—a second-order discourse of sophisticated rights talk—for defusing the explosive elements of first-order religious language and lifting expression of faithful commitments beyond the merely sectarian. Recasting particularistic accounts within a broader—indeed, global—second-order discourse to which all competing sides can appeal is a potentially powerful means of redirecting passions from narrowly tribal or extremist expressions.

Second-order rights and obligations language will never replace the primary language of the religious community; and unskilled communicators who render it clumsily cause it to appear leaden, remote, or condescending. To be used effectively, human rights discourse cannot glide over the surfaces of what individuals and communities hold sacred. In the hands of a fluent translator who can comprehend the sensibilities of religious believers while weighing conduct that protects universal norms, however, rights discourse can be a powerful mediator of the sacred.

Notes

1. Mary Ann Glendon, *A World Made New: Eleanor Roosevelt and the Universal Declaration of Human Rights* (New York: Random House, 2001), 225–26.

2. Mary Ann Glendon, *Rights Talk: The Impoverishment of Political Discourse* (New York: Free Press, 1991), 17.

3. Ibid., 14. William A. Galston, *Liberal Purposes: Goods, Virtues and Diversity in the Liberal State* (Cambridge: Cambridge University Press, 1991), and Michael J. Sandel, *Liberalism and the Limits of Justice* (Cambridge: Cambridge University Press, 1982), detail the inadequacies of the procedural liberalism that takes a value-neutral stance on issues. Sandel articulates the need for a morality-based public philosophy as a stay against religious fundamentalism in Michael J. Sandel, *Democracy's Discontent: America in Search of a Public Philosophy* (Cambridge, Mass.: Belknap Press, 1996), 321–23.

4. See W. Cole Durham, Jr., and Lauren B. Homer, "Russia's 1997 Law on Freedom of Conscience and Religious Associations: An Analytical Appraisal," *Emory International Law Review* 12, no. 1 (winter 1998): 101–246; Harold J. Berman, "Freedom of Religion in Russia: An Amicus Brief for the Defendant," *Emory International Law Review* 12, no. 1 (winter 1998): 313–40.

5. For a sampling of the opinions of leading American conservatives on the need for a revitalization of religion in the public sphere, see "The National Prospect," *Commentary* 100, no. 5 (November 1995): 23–116. For a communitarian perspective

that includes but does not privilege religious participation and emphasizes the importance of core religious values that are compatible with secular humanistic values, see Amitai Etzioni, *The New Golden Rule: Community and Morality in a Democratic Society* (New York: Basic Books, 1996), 252–57.

6. Andrew Sullivan, "This Is a Religious War," *New York Times Magazine*, 7 October 2001.

7. Parts of this and the following sections are adapted from R. Scott Appleby, *The Ambivalence of the Sacred: Religion, Violence and Reconciliation* (Lanham, Md.: Rowman and Littlefield, 2000), 247–76.

8. Article 18 of the 1948 Universal Declaration of Human Rights provides that "Everyone has the right to freedom of thought, conscience and religion; this right includes freedom to change his religion or belief, and freedom, either alone or in community with others and in public or private, to manifest his religion or belief in teaching, practice, worship and observance." Article 26 contains a provision calling for education to promote "understanding, tolerance and friendship among all religious groups."

9. John Witte, Jr., "Law, Religion, and Human Rights," *Columbia Human Rights Law Review* 28, no. 1 (fall 1996): 3.

10. Jacques Maritain, quoted in David Hollenbach, S.J., "Human Rights and Religious Faith in the Middle East: Reflections of a Christian Theologian," *Human Rights Quarterly* 4 (1982): 94, 96.

11. Several contemporary social theorists, philosophers, and noted religious thinkers have registered doubts that there are such things as human rights; the influential philosopher Alasdair MacIntyre has gone so far as to call "natural or human rights" "fictions," and neoconservative followers of Leo Strauss, who taught at the University of Chicago for many years, believe that the modern ideology of rights subverts the classical ethical notion of natural rights (*physis*) and the proper exercise of the virtue of "prudence" (*phronesis*). See Max L. Stackhouse and Stephen E. Healey, "Religion and Human Rights: A Theological Apologetic," in Johan D. van der Vyver and John Witte, Jr., eds., *Religious Perspectives*, vol. 1 of *Religious Human Rights in Global Perspective* (The Hague: Martinus Nijhoff Publishers, 1996), 488.

12. See also "Final Declaration of the Regional Meeting for Asia of the World Conference on Human Rights," *Human Rights Law Journal* 14 (1993): 370. Also see Joseph Chan, "The Task for Asians: To Discover Their Own Political Morality for Human Rights," *Human Rights Dialogue* 4 (March 1996): 5; idem, "The Asian Challenge to Universal Human Rights: A Philosophical Appraisal," in James T. H. Tang, ed., *Human Rights and International Relations in the Asia-Pacific Region* (New York: St. Martin's Press, 1995); and Daniel Bell, "The East Asian Challenge to Human Rights," unpublished manuscript, quoted in Etzioni, *The New Golden Rule*, 232.

13. As quoted in James Gaffney, "The Golden Rules: Abuses and Uses," *America*, 20 September 1986, 115.

14. The question is explored in the work of John Finnis, a Roman Catholic legal philosopher. See John Finnis, *Moral Absolutes: Tradition, Revision, and Truth*

(Washington, D.C.: Catholic University of America Press, 1991), and idem, *Natural Law and Natural Rights* (Oxford: Clarendon Press, and New York: Oxford University Press, 1980).

15. Most analysts understand that individual and collective rights are not binary opposites; frequently, the two types of rights converge and reinforce one another. The issue is one of balance and integration. Respect for individual rights entails some degree of respect for the variability and specificity of culture, insofar as the individual's sense of self is a cultural product. For complementary views, see Clifford Geertz, *The Interpretation of Cultures* (New York: Basic Books, 1973), and Lucian W. Pye, *Asian Power and Politics: The Cultural Dimension of Authority* (Cambridge, Mass.: Belknap Press, 1985).

16. For an example in which universalism is strengthened though cultural dialogue, see my discussion of female circumcision in *Ambivalence of the Sacred*, 250–52.

17. "My view," writes Reza Afshari, "is that the search for an indigenous legal foundation for human rights becomes paradoxical in that it has to 'be erected' (Tibi's term) within the confines of the state, whose alien and transplanted, but essentially unalterable, structures have rendered the local tradition impotent as a source of authentically traditional, political assertions." For Afshari, "the neopatriarchal state confines tradition, subjects it to its *modus operandi*, and subverts its authenticity. The question remains whose authenticity we are asked to restore, who would make this judgment, for what political purpose, and at what cost?" Reza Afshari, "An Essay on Islamic Cultural Relativism in the Discourse of Human Rights," *Human Rights Quarterly* 16, no. 2 (1994): 251.

18. Several denominations and ecumenical organizations joined Jewish NGOs in the cultivation of human rights at the international level. See Irwin Cotler, "Jewish NGOs and Religious Human Rights: A Case Study," in van der Vyver and Witte, *Religious Perspectives*, 236.

19. On the religious leadership of the U.S. civil rights movement, see Charles Marsh, *God's Long Summer: Stories of Faith and Civil Rights* (Princeton, N.J.: Princeton University Press, 1997); David Halberstam, *The Children* (New York: Random House, 1998); and John Lewis with Michael D'Orso, *Walking with the Wind: A Memoir of the Movement* (New York: Simon & Schuster, 1998). On Latin America, see Scott Mainwaring and Alexander Wilde, eds., *The Progressive Church in Latin America* (Notre Dame, Ind.: Notre Dame Press, 1989).

20. See the following essays in Johan D. van der Vyver and John Witte, Jr., eds., *Legal Perspectives*, vol. 2 of *Religious Human Rights in Global Perspective* (The Hague: Martinus Nijhoff Publishers, 1996): Peter Cumper, "Religious Liberty in the United Kingdom," 205–42; T. Jeremy Gunn, "Adjudicating the Rights of Conscience Under the European Convention of Human Rights," 305–30; and Martin Heckel, "The Impact of Religious Rules on Public Life in Germany," 191–204.

21. Examples include the World Council of Churches, the Vatican's Commission on Justice and Peace, and the National Conference on Soviet Jewry. See Cotler, "Jewish NGOs and Religious Human Rights." On the contributions of secular

NGOs such as Amnesty International and Asia Watch, see Michael Roan, "The Role of Secular Non-Governmental Organizations in the Cultivation and Understanding of Religious Human Rights," in van der Vyver and Witte, *Legal Perspectives*, 135–59.

22. Examples include the Mennonite Central Committee, Catholic Relief Services, and the Jacob Blaustein Institute for the Advancement of Human Rights (an organization of the American Jewish Committee).

23. In this area, religious NGOs worked closely with secular NGOs; see Roan, "The Role of Secular Non-Governmental Organizations in the Cultivation and Understanding of Religious Human Rights," 154–55.

24. Examples include the World Conference on Religion and Peace and the International Jewish Committee for Inter-religious Consultations.

25. Victor A. van Bijlert, "Raja Rammohun Roy's Thought and Its Relevance for Human Rights," in Abdullahi A. An-Na`im, Jerald D. Gort, Henry Jansen, and Hendrik M. Vroom, eds., *Human Rights and Religious Values: An Uneasy Relationship?* (Grand Rapids, Mich.: Eerdmans Publishing Co., 1995), 93–108. For example, Rammohun translated into English texts of the Upanishads that presented the totality of life as inherently sacred—enveloped by the Divine—and therefore deserving of utmost respect and protection. To advance his exercise in comparative religious ethics, Rammohun authored two major theological works on the ethical teachings of Jesus; he learned Arabic, Latin, Greek, and Hebrew so he could read the Christian, Jewish, and Islamic scriptures in the original. Human rights advocates of the late twentieth century retrieved the example of Rammohun Roy as one of Hinduism's moral exemplars.

Christianity has its own pantheon of human rights heroes, many of whom are central to the churches' narratives of resistance to the totalitarian regimes of the twentieth century. For example, the Austrian priest-martyr Franz Jaegerstadt, the Protestant clergyman Dietrich Bonhoeffer, the Catholic layman Oscar Schindler, and others are celebrated as counterexamples to the churches' generally dismal record of acquiescence to the horrors of Nazism.

26. For a review and sample of this work, see the following essays in van der Vyver and Witte, *Religious Perspectives*: Michael S. Berger and Deborah E. Lipstadt, "Women in Judaism from the Perspective of Human Rights," 295–321; Riffat Hassan, "Rights of Women within Islamic Communities," 361–86; and Jean Bethke Elshtain, "Thinking about Women, Christianity, and Rights," 143–56.

27. With regard to Islam see, for example, Fatima Mernissi, *Beyond the Veil: Male-Female Dynamics in Modern Muslim Society* (Bloomington: Indiana University Press, 1987 [1975]); Shahla Haeri, *Law of Desire: Temporary Marriage in Shi`i Iran* (Syracuse, N.Y.: Syracuse University Press, 1989); and Fazlur Rahman, *Islam and Modernity: Transformation of an Intellectual Tradition* (Chicago: University of Chicago Press, 1982), 130–62. A good example from Christianity is Lloyd J. Averill, *Religious Right, Religious Wrong* (New York: Pilgrim Press, 1989). For responses to Jewish extremism, see David Landau, *Piety and Power: The World of Jewish Fundamentalism* (New York: Hill and Wang, 1993), and, from a different perspective, Yossi Klein Halevi, *Memoirs of a Jewish Extremist* (Boston: Little, Brown and Co., 1995).

28. For an excellent overview of the Christian debate, see Lisa Sowle Cahill, *Love Your Enemies: Discipleship, Pacifism and Just War* (Minneapolis: Fortress Press, 1994). For an excellent overview of the Islamic debate, see Sohail H. Hashmi, "Interpreting the Islamic Ethics of War and Peace," in Terry Nardin, ed., *The Ethics of War and Peace* (Princeton, N.J.: Princeton University Press, 1996), 141–74.

29. Reuven Kimelman, "Nonviolence in the Talmud," *Judaism* 17 (1968): 318–23.

30. For a discussion of the Hindu nationalist backlash against this measure, see Sudhir Kakar, *The Colors of Violence: Cultural Identities, Religion and Conflict* (Chicago: University of Chicago Press, 1996), 158–69.

31. Abdullahi A. An-Na`im, "Toward an Islamic Hermeneutics for Human Rights," in An-Na`im, Gort, Jansen, and Vroom, eds., *Human Rights and Religious Values*, 231.

32. Quoted in Peter Beinart, "New Faith," *New Republic*, 3 December 2001, 8.

33. Quoted in ibid.

34. W. Montgomery Watt, *Islamic Fundamentalism and Modernity* (London: Routledge, 1988), 29.

35. Gustav Niebuhr, "Iranian Contrasts Faith and Nihilism," *New York Times*, 17 November 2001, A10.

36. William F. Vendley, quoted in ibid. After September 11, 2001, however, signs of hope appeared in the denunciation of extremist violence by Muslim leaders such as Dalil Boubakeur, spiritual head of the French Muslim community; Mohammed Sayyed Tantawi, the grand imam of al-Alzhar University of Cairo; and Sheikh Nasr Farid Wassel, Egypt's mufti, who "condemn[s] and deplore[s] what has happened in the United States against innocent civilians, as Islam condemns all forms of terrorism . . . and prohibits aggression against noncombatant civilians of all societies. . . ."

37. See, for example, John Kelsay's discussion of the disagreement involving the statements of representatives of Saudi Arabia and Pakistan at the United Nations with respect to the Universal Declaration of Human Rights. John Kelsay, "Saudi Arabia, Pakistan, and the Universal Declaration of Human Rights," in David Little, John Kelsay, and Abdulaziz Sachedina, eds., *Human Rights and the Conflicts of Culture: Western and Islamic Perspectives on Religious Liberty* (Columbia: University of South Carolina Press, 1988), 33–52. "The discussion of Islam and religious liberty begins, then, with the stipulation that a dialogical approach requires a greater appreciation of the statements of Muslims on matters of human rights," Kelsay writes (p. 34). "Further, it is important to know the extent and nature of disagreement among representatives of Islamic cultures on these matters."

38. Ibid., 22. On Soroush, see Robin Wright, "Islam and Liberal Democracy: Two Visions of Reformation," *Journal of Democracy* 7 (April 1996): 64–75. Wright refers to "a growing group of Islamic reformers" who, "by stimulating some of the most profound debate since Islam's emergence in the seventh century . . . are laying the foundations for an Islamic Reformation." At the end of the twentieth century, "instant mass communications, improved education, and intercontinental movements of both people and ideas mean that tens of millions of Muslims are exposed to the de-

bate. . . . The reformers contend that human understanding of Islam is flexible, and that Islam's tenets can be interpreted to accommodate and even encourage pluralism. They are actively challenging those who argue that Islam has a single, definitive essence that admits of no change in the face of time, space, or experience—and that democracy is therefore incompatible or alien." Wright notes that Iran's Ayatollah Khamenei and other officials often frame their "public remarks as implicit but unmistakable responses to Soroush's articles and speeches" (p. 67). Wright also profiles Sheikh Rachid al-Ghannouchi, a Sunni Muslim from Tunisia and the exiled leader of the Party of Renaissance, which is devoted to establishing an Islamic republic in Tunisia. A popular philosopher and politician, Ghannouchi has been welcomed in Tehran and the Sudan and has condemned Zionism and Westernization. Ghannouchi has become one of Islam's boldest political theorists, Wright notes, embracing a robustly democratic (but culturally specific, not necessarily Western) vision of the Islamic state that includes "majority rule, free elections, a free press, protection of minorities, equality of all secular and religious parties, and full women's rights. . . . Islam's role is to provide the system with moral values" (p. 73). For a more critical view of Ghannouchi, see Mohamed Elhachmi Hamdi, "The Limits of the Western Model," *Journal of Democracy* 7 (April 1996): 81–85.

39. See Hamdi, "The Limits of the Western Model," 84. See also Bernard Lewis, "Islam and Liberal Democracy: A Historical Overview," *Journal of Democracy* 7 (April 1996): 52–63. Soroush does not reject Islam's role in politics; indeed, he argues that democratic government must reflect the society it represents, and a religious society such as Iran must have a government with a religious character. To be avoided, however, is the reduction of religion to ideology—a corruption that only a democratic government can prevent.

40. "We do not draw [our conception of] justice from religion," Soroush writes, "but rather we accept religion because it is just." Abdolkarim Soroush, quoted in Lewis, "Islam and Liberal Democracy," 57.

41. Valla Vakili, *Debating Religion and Politics in Iran: The Political Thought of Abdolkarim Soroush* (New York: Council on Foreign Relations, 1996), 9.

42. Robert Fisk, "Iran's Leader Urged to Stand Up for Human Rights," *The Independent* (London), 8 December 1997, 6.

43. James Piscatori and Riva Richmond, "Foreword," in Vakili, *Debating Religion and Politics in Iran*, 3–5.

44. See, for example, Michael J. Broyde, "Forming Religious Communities and Respecting Dissenter's Rights: A Jewish Tradition for a Modern Society," in van der Vyver and Witte, *Religious Perspectives*, 203–34.

45. Robert Traer, *Faith in Human Rights* (Washington, D.C.: Georgetown University Press, 1991), 1.

46. Witte, "Law, Religion, and Human Rights," 4.

9

Trials, Tribunals, and Tribulations of Sovereignty: Crimes against Humanity and the *imago Dei*

JOHN D. CARLSON

THE FORTRESS WALLS OF SOVEREIGNTY, long enjoyed by states, are crumbling. So claim many "internationalists" who cite the swelling influence of universal human rights, international law, and emerging forms of international justice as evidence of the nation-state's eroding sovereignty—if not its relevance as well. Tectonic shifts in state sovereignty can be charted by developments such as humanitarian military interventions that challenge states' claims to noninterference in their own internal affairs (see part I of this book); international tribunals for individuals accused of "crimes against humanity"; and multilateral efforts resulting in the establishment of a permanent International Criminal Court (ICC). Especially noteworthy for indicting a head of state for genocide and ethnic cleansing, the United Nations–sponsored trial of former Yugoslav president Slobodan Milosevic marks a watershed moment in international law—a case to which I return later in this chapter.

One internationalist argument goes something like this: The defensive bulwark of state sovereignty is rightfully giving way to sacred and universal moral principles such as the inviolability of the individual endowed, *qua* human, with certain inalienable rights. On this accounting, "humanity," not the state, is credited with supreme status, subject to no higher value, authority, or political claim. Nations, it follows, must heel to the demands of a version of justice that knows no borders: States will no longer enjoy immunity if they treat their citizens in ways that decent and rational peoples universally recognize as heinous, pernicious, and evil.

A central internationalist premise in this line of thinking is that states are prone to be self-serving and capricious, eager at times to invoke their sovereignty as a mantle to perpetuate morally dubious activities if not outright atrocities. Hence, impartial international governmental institutions (and perhaps transnational nongovernmental organizations as well) are needed to check the power of states on behalf of humanity. International judicial bodies, seeking to establish minimal ethical standards of conduct, are applying necessary pressure to nations and their leaders: Those who fail to conform to rules of international law can expect to be called to individual accounting before an international trial or tribunal. The picture is framed quite clearly: Sovereignty's heyday of state immunity or absolute "domestic jurisdiction" is over; those who once embraced a cynical *raison d'état*, whereby states do what they will and citizens suffer what they must, must now give way to the enforcement of universal moral laws that, applied globally, sustain respect for the inviolable dignity and rights of all citizens in the human cosmopolis. Such claims herald the march toward what we might recognize as "international justice."

Who could argue with such ethical innovations in political life? The years following the cold war—ironically dubbed the "human rights era"—teemed with atrocities such as those in the former Yugoslavia, Rwanda, Sierra Leone, and Indonesia, to name just a few famous cases. Yet despite plentiful genocidal abuses, the post–cold war era—like no other period—also has been replete with moral impulses (which we should welcome) to make politics more humane, more just, and more protective of the authentic needs of citizens, particularly vulnerable people who suffer under the forces of state politics. We have witnessed, in addition to various forms of military and nonmilitary intervention to alleviate human suffering, increased efforts to punish leaders who perpetrate human rights abuses and, furthermore, steps to seek national reconciliation in the wake of such widespread harm. Some individual nations—such as South Africa, Chile, and Cambodia—have struggled, with varying degrees of success, to come to terms with and bring to justice leaders responsible for earlier eras of repression. More prominently, the United Nations, in appointing tribunals to prosecute war crimes and crimes against humanity in the former Yugoslavia and Rwanda (to be succeeded by the permanent ICC), has sought to codify standards and procedures of justice to which all of humanity (and all nations) must adhere. These developments point to palpable new "internationalist" tendencies, including efforts to universalize how justice is conceived and meted out when crimes against humanity are involved. It is on the point of trials and tribunals that trouble begins to brew.

I want to ask, however: Can this liberal internationalist yarn of progress and justice be spun another way? Can the portrait of eroding state sovereignty be sketched differently? In both cases, salient features are left off or effaced when we succumb too readily to the lure of a new internationalist paradigm. (See chapter 7 for adumbrations of, and cautions about, the forms of sovereignty that are likely to succeed the nation-state system.) Let me be clear at the outset that the individuals who are responsible for the horrendous crimes and atrocities identified by international trials and tribunals must be brought to justice, and organizations such as the UN play pivotal roles when nations are unable or unwilling to prosecute their own crimes against humanity. To avoid any confusion, what follows is not an argument for excusing, overlooking, or failing to prevent gross abuses of human rights.

Many liberal internationalists boldly speak out against oppressive governments, bent on doing great harm to their citizens. One worries, however, that certain voices of liberal internationalism gesture forcefully toward what we might call universal justice—a particularly ambitious version of international justice in which internationalist priorities outflank domestic pursuits of justice. This position is fraught with problematic premises and unintended consequences and is worthy of deeper scrutiny. One such premise is the excessive faith that universal justice places in historical progress. Another is the overly optimistic expectations it holds out for international political institutions in this evolutionary tale. Universal justice often can undermine the moral status, institutional legitimacy, and political mandates of nations and states, despite the fact that—like it or not—nation-states still possess the preponderance of power and resources and continue to serve as the backbone institution of global order and local constancy. When this basic framework of nations falters or is weakened, so too are the intersecting joints of economy, trade, civil society, culture, and travel that depend on global stability for their sustenance. These are all concerns to be reckoned with.

The specific issue I raise in this chapter has to do with the view of human nature—the "moral anthropology," if you will—underlying certain liberal internationalist outlooks. My plaint is directed against these anthropological presuppositions flowing out of the Kantian tradition and into the internationalist discourse of universal justice that animates much human rights thinking and attendant theories of government. This anthropology emerges in a certain rights vernacular that posits the unqualified celebration of "humanity," which is ambiguously maintained by universalizing standards and venues of justice. The by-products of this anthropology present formidable perils that threaten to trample underfoot other authentic possibilities for justice and national reconciliation. A central lesson is that when international institutions step in too quickly to do the bidding of nations, justice eludes the place that is most badly in need of reconciliation.

Given what I take to be an inadequate account of human nature, universal justice also reckons poorly with the sanctity of human dignity that actually undergirds the notions of human rights and "crimes against humanity." An alternative theological rendering of this story—here placed in contexts surrounding international criminal trials and war crimes tribunals—fills in some of the gaps left by more extreme internationalist accounts and offers, for some people at least, a more compelling set of claims about the legitimacy of nations, about the moral standing of humanity, and, hence, about humanity's attendant rights. In the end, I argue, neither the sovereignty of states nor the sacredness of the human person makes much sense absent some theological discussion, however apologetic or unsettling that prospect may sound. In other words, how can two rival claims of supremacy—"sovereignty" and "sacredness"—forswear mention of the source of ultimacy that both share to some degree?

The path of this argument proceeds something like the following. To begin, we might inquire: Just what are "crimes against humanity," and what is missing in the ways we routinely conceptualize them? What moral anthropology—that is, what claims about "humanity"—do such crimes usually presume? Some readers surely will object that achieving clarity about such heinous misdeeds hardly demands a moral or theological anthropology. That may be true, yet it is worth exploring how such presuppositions inescapably pervade politics. What happens when a certain Kantian anthropology is assumed is that a universal justice—as problematic as it appears promising—inevitably seems to follow. Under the canopy of international law, universal justice gives way to a "utopia of punishment" for individual criminals against humanity. The rush to prosecute in this way can readily swallow up other moral goods and political values that are worthy of upholding and necessary to institutional order. Envisioning anew such transgressions, with reference to some transcendent source of value that these crimes besmirch, avoids this problem while reinforcing the dignity of human persons as creatures conceived in the image of God—understood here as the ultimate source of the sacred. The *imago Dei*, as an anthropological claim, evokes the relational character of human sacredness. We might consider too how the image of God is constitutive of, and at work in, political notions of sovereignty. Thus, one section of this essay explores the possibility that one could simultaneously affirm the *imago Dei* and uphold the sovereignty of nations and governments, whose mandate—if we have learned our lessons well from the twentieth century—is to protect human dignity and rights.

Flowing out of this anthropological alternative that I proffer is a political conception of *limited justice* that honors both the sacred status of the human person and the sovereign imprimatur of nations and states, while proceeding cautiously to avoid the overreach that ambitious pursuits of universal justice risk. A more tempered conception of limited justice obliges us in two ways: First, limited justice discerns the necessities of maintaining political order—including the conditions necessary for the protection of ordinary human life and human relations; second, it strives to restore, albeit partially and imperfectly, shattered and discordant relations among persons and their polities. Reconciliation and the reordering of unjust, broken relations to anything resembling preconflict standards will not be remedied easily or fully by human means. In recognizing the limits of human justice, resisting overextension of justice's pursuit or overanticipation of its results, we leave latitude for a fuller realization of justice than may be available in certain international settings. I close this chapter by offering some moral-political guidelines for ways in which limited justice can serve in contemporary international politics and for the roles that international institutions can play in bringing villains of humanity to accounting.

What Are "Crimes against Humanity"?

The term "crimes against humanity" comes to us relatively recently as a label for the magnitude of unprecedented horrors that indelibly stamped the twentieth century. Without overlooking prior episodes in history—of biblical proportions and since biblical times—in which peoples were persecuted or murdered *en masse*, the term usually is traced to the London Agreement of August 8, 1945, which established provisions for trying Nazi leaders for their roles in deporting and exterminating Jews during the Holocaust.[1] Under the agreement, Nazis whose war crimes could not be localized to particular countries were brought to accounting before the Allied war crimes tribunals assembled in Nuremberg, Germany. Ironically, the driving motive behind U.S. Secretary of War Henry Stimson and lead prosecutor (as well as U.S. Supreme Court Justice) Robert Jackson's efforts to prosecute German authorities was not sublime retribution for civilization's most insidious abominations, as people often assume today, but a desire to indict the individuals who were responsible for initiating an illegal war of aggression against the United States. According to historian Gary Jonathan Bass, "The trials are incorrectly recalled as more selfless than they actually were."[2] Yet the moral legacy of the Nuremberg trials would inspire generations of future legalists committed to bringing villains of humanity to justice—not simply "victor's justice" that *realpolitik* always had made available but international justice that guarantees full respect for due process under international law.

The idea of "crimes against humanity" had not fully taken a foothold even sixteen years after Nuremberg, during the trial of Adolf Eichmann—the infamous Nazi henchman who with masterful efficiency managed the European rail system that carried millions of Jews to their deaths. Eichmann eventually was brought to trial in Jerusalem after Israel kidnapped him from Argentina in 1960. While covering the trial, German-Jewish political philosopher Hannah Arendt took strenuous exception to the charges of "crimes committed against the Jewish people" for which Eichmann was ultimately convicted and executed. On Arendt's reckoning, the trial failed to distinguish Eichmann and the Nazis' "new" crimes of genocide from the many other forms of discrimination and expulsion visited upon the Jews for thousands of years.

Arendt insisted that Eichmann's shameful offenses were of a radically different and unprecedented nature: They were "attacks upon human diversity as such, that is, upon a characteristic of the 'human status' without which the very words 'mankind' or 'humanity' would be devoid of meaning."[3]

A new category was needed, therefore, for these inhuman acts and "unheard-of atrocities, the blotting out of whole peoples, . . . crimes that 'no conception of military necessity could sustain' . . . [that] announced a policy of systematic murder to be continued in time of peace."[4] These were no garden-variety crimes or misdemeanors. For Arendt, even expulsion (today known as "ethnic cleansing") was a "crime against humanity" only to the extent that the crime was committed against the "comity of nations." But genocide, with the intent to annihilate an entire race, violates the plurality that is distinctive of the human species, rupturing the diversity of the moral and political order in a way that other crimes do not. These were not "crimes committed against the Jewish people," Arendt prescinded, but "crimes against humanity, perpetrated upon the body of the Jewish people." As such, an international tribunal or court, not an Israeli show trial, was needed to bring justice to "humanity"—that is, to preserve human plurality—in the wake of extensive and unprecedented crimes committed by unprecedented kinds of criminals. Arendt nonetheless found the idea of an international criminal court "inconceivable."[5]

In recent years there have been many examples of misdeeds beyond the moral pale: collectivization under the Khmer Rouge, in which as many as 1.5 million Cambodians are believed to have died; forced "disappearances" that took place under Chilean dictator Augusto Pinochet's regime; genocide in Rwanda and the former Yugoslavia; the systematic rape of women in Bosnia; ethnic cleansing in Kosovo; and the amputation of civilians' limbs (including children's) that took place in Sierra Leone. The category of "crimes against humanity" today usually describes widespread or systematic offenses against civilian populations or groups on the basis of their national, ethnic, racial, or religious identity.[6] This category includes many heinous offenses that Arendt would not have called crimes against humanity, including ethnic cleansing, deportation, murder, rape, torture, enslavement, apartheid, forced disappearance, and a host of other inhumane acts.[7] Many legal settings locate genocide and "crimes against humanity" (such as ethnic cleansing) under separate or overlapping headings, but for lay audiences, "crimes against humanity" usually serves as a catch-all term for crimes that are impermissible everywhere.[8] No one is immune from prosecution, and no one may claim immunity under the plea that he or she was "just following orders." Importantly for purposes of international relations, crimes against humanity sometimes have been covered by statutes of "universal jurisdiction," which entitle any state to hear a case or extradite a suspect for such charges.[9]

Piracy and slavery sometimes are called the first crimes against humanity—or are lumped together with such crimes—because they are crimes that disregard borders and require international jurisdiction to prosecute effectively.[10] Similarly, some people contend that crimes against humanity include acts by nonstate officials (e.g., pirates or terrorists); the September 2001 terrorist attacks on the United States brought forth charges by some observers of crimes against humanity. For reasons that will become clear, I intend to confine the scope of the term to offenses committed by or on behalf of states and governments. For the purposes of this chapter, I use "crimes against humanity" in the colloquial sense that includes genocide, ethnic cleansing, and other charges brought before international tribunals; although I do not adhere to the more limited definition that Arendt offers, the rationale behind her careful description is admirable and worth bearing in mind as we consider how we know a "crime against humanity" when we see it.

Although few people would boast of being proponents of crimes against humanity, those leading the charge against them often are found in liberal internationalist circles of prosecutors, human rights advocates, and legal experts. One leading and distinguished internationalist voice of our day is Richard Goldstone—a justice of the Constitutional Court of South Africa, UN war crimes investigator, the first chief prosecutor of the International War Crimes Tribunals for the former Yugoslavia and Rwanda, and a candidate for president of the ICC. Goldstone also is a powerful voice for universal justice. What bears mention is how he conceives the etymology of these awful misdeeds. In Justice Goldstone's words, crimes against humanity entail "*certain crimes . . . identified as being of such a magnitude that they injured not only the immediate victims and not only the people of the country or on the continent where they were committed but also all of humankind."*[11] Many people today share Goldstone's views. Consequently, such crimes become identified by the magnitude of the offense, the immense numbers of victims involved, and the sheer horror of the acts.

In legal and moral ways, the internationalist position has made crimes against humanity "universal crimes." Legally, this position extends the realm of traditionally domestic law beyond the reach of national borders so that crimes committed anywhere—not just in international waters but in sovereign states—fall under the jurisdiction of international law. By definition, a crime against humanity cannot be circumscribed by geographic borders, so national status and national identity become secondary. Suspects are subject to prosecution outside the nation in which such crimes were committed, regardless of the national identity of victim or perpetrator—an arrangement that made possible the United Kingdom's extradition of Augusto Pinochet to Spain to stand trial for human rights abuses that occurred while he was president of Chile.

Morally speaking, crimes are made universal when the injury extends beyond the immediate victims and is inflicted on all of humanity, as Goldstone's position reflects. This is where things begin to get muddled. Given this understanding of the crime, it is on humanity's behalf that they must be prosecuted; no "decent and rational person," the internationalist position puts forth, can tolerate the idea that such crimes might go unpunished.[12] Criminals may still be prosecuted for the sake of victims and their families, but that is not the ostensible reason for the statute. Some larger statement for humanity's historical record must be made, presumably one that will inscribe such episodes of human malfeasance and evil with history's judgment of moral condemnation—a statement that will bring justice or restitution for all of humanity. We might signal here how difficult it becomes to measure "the injury of humanity" and, hence, what qualifies as a crime against humanity. Whereas Arendt worried about concrete features—such as the measurable loss of human diversity that would be occasioned by the elimination of an entire race—the Goldstone standard, as articulated in his appropriately titled book *For Humanity*, is significantly more amorphous and perhaps prone to sentimentalism and overextension.

The notion of crimes against humanity also marks a departure from pre–World War II processes whereby nations *and* national figureheads were brought to justice for aggression against other *nations*. In the current formulation of these "universal crimes," however, nations bear no collective guilt for the actions of government officials who use the state for their own pursuits.[13] The drive to punish universal crimes for the sake of humanity gives way to a form of "universal justice" that holds accountable only those leaders and agents of the state who orchestrated and executed the crimes—thus shifting the burden away from collective responsibility, including the responsibility of citizens who elect or support their *hostis generis humani*. The willingness to minimize the role of the nation and its citizens in dealing with universal crimes coincides with a move away from political processes—international relations, broadly speaking, among peoples, nations, and governments—toward dispensing universal retribution to individual leaders. This trend is likely to accelerate, not only because the creation of an ICC will facilitate the process but because allowing states to ignore violations committed in their name will marginalize the universal status of crimes against humanity.

My objection to the notion of crimes against humanity as discussed here does not concern the question of whether universal moral norms such as human rights exist. Indeed, I think they do. My concern is that uncritical acceptance of the notion of "crimes against humanity," and the means by which we prosecute them, threatens to deplete politics of much of its moral grit and political efficacy. The following critique is threefold, having to do first with the moral anthropology undergirding common understanding of crimes against humanity; second, with the narrow vision of justice that this anthropology presumes (the "universal" nomenclature of justice notwithstanding); and third, with the institutional structures and political order that universal justice, so conceived, requires.

What Does Anthropology Have to Do with Justice? The Pridefulness of Human Ultimacy

For Goldstone, as for many others, "The essence of justice is its universality, both nationally and internationally. A decent and rational person is offended that criminal laws should apply only to some people and not to others in similar situations."[14] Hence, when nations fail to call to accounting individuals who are responsible for universal crimes, it follows that agents of international law—acting through war crimes tribunals, an international court, or nations exercising "universal jurisdiction"—may step in to assume moral responsibility, on behalf of humanity, for the task of dispensing justice.

Goldstone's outlook seems self-evident and uncontroversial on its face. After all, any "decent and rational person" *should* be offended by the heinous crimes witnessed in recent years. But let's mine deeper the philosophical anthropology underwriting this kind of universalism. My working assumption is that contemporary forces of liberal internationalism and jurisprudence take root in the soil of Kant's moral philosophy, among other sources. There is no room here for a full explication of this connection, but brief attention to a few salient features of Kant's moral anthropology—notably his account of the human person as moral and political agent—demonstrates the intellectual underpinnings of internationalists such as Goldstone. What follows is not a critique of Kant "on his own terms" but a comparative analysis that suggests that certain versions of Kantianism handle the challenges of understanding and prosecuting crimes against humanity less well than other anthropological accounts we might consider. Specifically, the "take-away" from this discussion is that from Kant ushers forth an anthropology that assumes human ultimacy and overemphasizes autonomy—a view that contrasts with a theological alternative I propose, which emphasizes human penultimacy and relationality.

For Kant, the rational, self-legislating, autonomous will is the chief trait of the moral human agent. "Nothing in the world—indeed nothing even beyond the world—can possibly be called good without qualification except a good will," Kant famously pronounced.[15] The human will is our rational capacity to act in accordance with strict moral principles that can be, upon reflection, established with logical certainty. The will is a "faculty of determining itself": The human will is fully free and autonomous to discern the moral law and has no inherent need of external or heteronomous forms of moral instruction such as scripture, natural law, moral tradition, or social convention.[16] Reason alone is sufficient; coupled with a self-legislating capacity, human reason formulates moral laws that are universally and objectively binding for all rational

creatures, including their political institutions. Such laws are imperatives, categorically applied, designed to respect all other rational creatures as ends in themselves; such duty attends "the condition of a will
good in itself, whose worth transcends everything."[17] There is no moral
alternative, in Kant's view, but to uphold the unconditional and ration-
ally ordained obligation to act according to universal moral law. Any
other disposition or action would be immoral, illustrative of a will that
lacks goodness.

This Kantian anthropology lies at the heart of the position of universal justice where crimes against humanity are concerned by maintaining that "every rational being exists as an end in himself . . . [and that]
rational beings are designated 'persons' because their nature indicates
that they are ends in themselves."[18] By extension, universal justice pro-
pounds that political institutions ought to assign, as a chief aim, the
preservation of humans as ends in themselves. For Kant, human autonomy—and the recognition that we are laws unto ourselves—"is the basis
of the dignity of both human nature and every rational nature."[19] An-
thropologically speaking, we are primarily rational and legislating (law-
giving) creatures. Consequently, affirming human dignity entails forming laws that respect human freedom and the autonomy of "humanity,"
not, as we saw, how Arendt conceives "humanity"—as the diversity of
human creation that is given to us—but as "a realm of ends" that we
desire, as a "systematic union of different rational beings through common laws."[20] Arendt's regard for human plurality made her suspicious of
such totalizing ambitions to reconcile conflicting human wills. Today,
this realm of ends coheres in the idea of a human cosmopolis stretching
across national borders, ethnic and racial divides, and other categories
that are understood to be arbitrary from a moral point of view.[21] The second formulation of the categorical imperative is the clearest articulation
for our purposes: "Act so that you treat humanity, whether in your own
person or in that of another, always as an end and never as a means
only."[22] From Kant we inherit an anthropology in which human worth
is sacred and humanity should be respected as such.

The foregoing necessarily short précis makes sufficiently clear, I hope,
the Kantian intimations at work in contemporary understandings of universal justice. I do not seek to indict Kant wholesale, or those with whom
his august philosophy resonates. I do, however, mean to indict a certain

Kantian anthropology that has taken hold in international law surrounding crimes against humanity. It is nigh impossible not to call up the ghost of Kant when Goldstone muses that "a decent and rational person is offended that criminal laws should apply only to some people and not to others in similar situations."[23] On this view, universal justice upholds the principle of the sacredness of humanity by rendering what is due to *all of humanity*—that is, all persons—against whom such crimes have been committed and injury sustained; it does so by indicting and trying "criminals of humanity" consistently in venues that abide by international norms that all (or certainly most) decent and rational people could affirm.

We see vestiges of a Kantian position elsewhere when Goldstone claims that prosecuting war crimes impartially is necessary to uphold the legitimacy of universal justice and its associated international institutions. To achieve universality and consistency, justice must transcend the empirical world of politics. There can be, Goldstone avers, no dealings with politicians or political bodies, lest the mantel of "complete neutrality" and procedural integrity be undercut.[24] Justice must remain pure. Justice also becomes absolute when the preservation of "humanity" (as conceived here) becomes sovereign. Goldstone captures Kantian impulses toward "moral purity"—free from the contingent grounds of experience—when he admits that indicting and trying criminals of humanity may be costly:

> I concede that a prosecutor acting without regard to political reality may well cause problems and might interfere with a peace process. However, this risk is preferable to having politicians dictate to a prosecutor who should or should not be indicted and when indictments should be issued.[25]

Recall that for Kant, intention—meaning a good will—is the essence of moral deliberation, results be damned.[26] Similarly for Goldstone: When universal justice becomes absolute, the intention of defending and vindicating "humanity" outweighs unintended consequences, even if they are known beforehand. All of this seems to point toward the formation of a rarefied realm of disinterested jurists—perhaps a Hegelian pitch for a universal, selfless bureaucracy within the state or a suprastate that operates above politics.

It should give us pause when the Kantian/Goldstone arc toward universal justice is lofted so far above the messy workings of the world in which international politics has no choice but to operate. Many goods and values are lost when universal justice becomes such a sublime, sacral, and sovereign principle. When justice, so construed, is made absolute, nations as well as other political bodies are forced to work within overly restrictive confines to achieve other ends: limiting violence, promoting peace, establishing or preserving order, protecting lives and property, safeguarding the self-determination of nations and their peoples, and so forth. Ironically, ultimate justice can even foster the conditions for appalling forms of *injustice*. Consider a few common objections to international war crimes tribunals, from Bass's comprehensive study of international criminal trials:

> Due process may interfere with substantive justice, through its technical acquittals and delays in punishing people who richly deserve it. The spectacle of foreign-imposed trials may cause a nationalist backlash. Or a moralistic insistence on punishing war crimes may make it impossible to do business with bloodstained leaders who, however repulsive, might end a war.[27]

To take a specific example of injustice, ending human rights abuses may well depend on the cessation of hostilities and warfare—all of which could be forestalled if prosecuting crimes against humanity must be determined independently of "political" considerations such as brokering a peace process.[28] Moral necessities prompt us to ask: Should we really be more concerned with prosecuting human rights abuses than with ending them? This critique is particularly potent given that the West at times has been far more willing to establish international tribunals than to intervene militarily to stop the conditions that precipitate them in the first place.[29]

In addition, a compulsion for consistency—of the kind that universal justice extols—could become an open invitation to absolve some unjust parties because no action was taken in earlier cases involving other injustices.[30] Goldstone, disdainful of political savvy, epitomized such a stance when he sympathized with the Serb minister of justice in 1994 that "the people of the former Yugoslavia could justifiably claim discrimination" if the UN established war crimes tribunals in Yugoslavia but not in other places (e.g., in Iraq, given its use of chemical weapons against its own people).[31] We openly solicit malice (not to mention injustice) if we become, as Goldstone was, "uncomfortable" justifying our positions to aggressor regimes. Such calculating regimes have no authentic concern for justice themselves; as such, they are well postured to exploit the West's own arguments for universal justice. The situation is like apologizing to one murderer for failing to apprehend others. Surely even Goldstone cannot believe that Serbia would have complied more readily with the establishment of a war crimes tribunal if tribunals first had been established for Iraq or Cambodia.

Finally, extradition of war criminals to international courts and tribunals defers justice in the country in which the crimes took place. Universal justice removes from a nation's hands the responsibility for dealing with its own criminals of humanity, which is—or should be—one of the burdens of nations that aspire to self-determination. Alleviating citizens of such moral chores could itself constitute a form of injustice. For example, after Federal Yugoslav President Kostunica defeated Slobodan Milosevic in 2000, the UN and many nations, including the United States, exerted great pressure on the new president to extradite Milosevic to The Hague to face charges for crimes he committed in Bosnia and Kosovo. Trying Milosevic for crimes against humanity, though surely necessary at some point, should not have been the foremost concern in the newly elected president's mind. Kostunica faced numerous challenges, including 40 percent unemployment, 800,000 refugees in Serbia, and rebuilding a nation's infrastructure after the destruction caused by NATO's 1999 air campaign.[32] Establishing credibility with the people of Serbia surely was more urgent, and capitulating to United States and UN demands as a first act in office would not have been prudent. Milosevic, already virtually imprisoned in his own residence, was quickly losing the support of Serbians. Yet the UN and the United States insisted that the floundering nation embrace Western agendas—and requirements—for achieving universal justice. Carla Del Ponte, who replaced Goldstone as chief prosecutor of the UN War Crimes Tribunal, made public her uncompromising goal to bring Milosevic to trial in The Hague. The U.S. government also made clear that it would offer no economic relief to rebuild Yugoslavia until Milosevic was tried for crimes against humanity—regardless of the negative results this could have cost Kostunica's new administration.

An alternative tack that the United States and the UN might have taken was to work confidentially with Kostunica to develop a timetable for bringing Milosevic to trial in the former Republic of Yugoslavia—not just for state crimes of stealing elections and bankrupting the nation, as Yugoslavia seemed prepared to do, but for crimes against humanity. Such a strategy might have taken many years to implement, but it could have begun by bringing discredit to Milosevic by trying him for crimes committed against the state. Once he was safely ensconced in prison, the next phase could begin: a gradually escalating information campaign to release to the people of Yugoslavia evidence of Milosevic's genocidal crimes. If, according to the terms of the timetable, the new administration did not demonstrate a good-faith effort to bring Milosevic to moral accounting for his "universal crimes," the United States and other nations would still be in a position to withhold further aid or to impose sanctions; the UN could always pursue an international trial at a later time.

Because the United States and the UN did not take this approach, however, the people of Yugoslavia were released from bearing any responsibility either for supporting the perpetrator of such awful crimes or for righting the wrongs and reconciling the disordered relations that occurred under Milosevic's tenure. In the words of one British columnist, who lamented the international tribunal:

> Many Serbs longed to try Mr. Milosevic in their own courts, to help them purge their own past and strengthen their shaky political and judicial institutions. The West let this happen in Argentina, South Africa, and more recently Chile. Why not in Yugoslavia which so desperately needs strengthening?[33]

Because the UN insisted on a particular version of procedural justice—justice Hague-style—substantive justice was deferred in the very place where the crimes occurred, the nation that could have benefited the most from retribution and reconciliation. Instead, Yugoslavia and its people in essence were permitted to wash their hands of any responsibility, thus allowing the UN—an institution that Yugoslavia's leader and

people openly resent—to do its ugly bidding. Is this the kind of justice—
"justice our way or no way"—that the international community or the
comity of nations should encourage?

Universal justice is largely a theory of retribution: It seeks to hold individuals responsible for crimes against humanity. The intent of international trials was to disencumber citizens from shouldering "collective
guilt" or responsibility for the crimes of state officials whom they may or
may not have supported. But this process also removes nations and their
citizens from the process of rectifying relations and coming to terms with
the past for which they bear some responsibility. Nations should expect
to be held accountable—by other nations—not for the universal crimes
of a select few but for the process of holding accountable those who perpetrate such crimes. The universal justice sought by the UN left no latitude for the nation of Yugoslavia to come to terms with its own rule of
law, its own obligations as a sovereign and democratic nation, including
its own moral and political duty to determine and seek justice for itself.
Yugoslavia was put on the defensive; even Yugoslavs who were not sympathetic to Milosevic found themselves defending him against a process
that undermined Yugoslavia's national sovereignty. By trying Milosevic
at home and thus issuing a statement for the historical record that dis-
closed the errors of its past, the nation and people of Yugoslavia could
have sought to make amends—to humanity and to the comity of nations—for universal crimes committed on Yugoslavian soil. A national
trial of Milosevic and others' crimes against humanity would have gone
a long way toward beginning to rectify the disharmony and unbalanced
relations for which Yugoslavians must bear some responsibility.

In the end, however, trying Milosevic expeditiously in an international tribunal was easier for the modern mind and more popular in internationalist circles; it was judged to yield greater justice than pressing
the citizens of Yugoslavia to come to terms with the *hostis generis humani* in their midst. With the weight of all "humanity" behind it, liberal
internationalism found it more crucial to score quick retribution against
a defeated war criminal than to engage the patience of a nation in a political process that probably would have taken many years to unfold but
also would have promised greater substantive justice.

I have tried here to narrate a political tale that owes its lineage to a
particular moral anthropology in which "humanity" is conceived with

sacred and ultimate worth. There is no reference point beyond humanity as such. Human justice, then, in this trope becomes ultimate as well
because other values and aspirations of justice do not uphold the sacredness of human dignity as universal justice and retribution is seen to
do.[34] Moreover, the institutions of universal justice and international law
truly do become sovereign over nation, state, and people. There surely
is a certain pridefulness, even an unsettling moral righteousness, that attends a system in which one value—even humanity itself—must be preserved in precisely delineated ways. In making human justice ultimate,
we threaten and stifle other arenas of moral and political life. Knowingly
or inadvertently, we may close off the possibility of achieving other crucial moral-political values—especially pursuits that leave openings to
gesture toward transcendent values and sources of ultimacy beyond humanity itself. An alternative "relational" anthropology that does not es-
pouse human ultimacy but locates and relates to ultimacy in a source
beyond humanity proffers a very different set of claims about justice and
the political order. I now turn my focus to this candidate approach.

What Does Theology Have to Do with Politics?
Penultimate Justice and the *imago Dei*

Within religious circles, no less than in secular ones, discussion of "innate human dignity" is quite familiar. Certainly this is true if we mean
that certain rights are accorded to all people by virtue of their humanity, not by virtue of their ethnicity, national origin, religion, race, sex, or
other "contingent" features of human identity. However, I want to put
forth—in rather stark terms—that, as a religious claim, to speak of *innate* human worth is to suggest that we are self-given—the sources of our
own sacredness, the authors of our own dignity; we are our own idols.[35]
Alternately, let me try out another anthropological story that presupposes
a source of worth and ultimacy beyond humanity. On this telling, our
human dignity is realized as participants in, and bearers of, the *imago
Dei*. With such a vision in place that emphasizes human penultimacy—
through *relational* identity to the ultimate—we are better postured to
understand and pursue limited forms of justice. The position of *limited
justice* avoids the overreach of universal justice and the harm that can

accompany such ambitious pursuits. More modest in scope, yet deeply rooted in ethical conviction, limited justice seeks tempered responses to the necessities of earthly political life in ways that honor our relations to the ultimate by not seeking to become ultimate; in so doing, limited justice honors penultimate relationships among persons and the nations that represent them. This account of justice, no less than the foregoing conception, assumes an embedded anthropology that warrants examination. Here I draw from the tradition about which I am most knowledgeable: strands of Augustinian theology.

Augustine's moral anthropology begins with an understanding of human creation. God is Creator, we are created. We are created *ex nihilo*—that is, *from* nothing *to* God's image. We are not our own makers or definers or inventors of human worth. Commenting in *De Trinitate* on Genesis 1:26, "Let us make man to our image and likeness," Augustine notes that "*Let us make* and *our* are in the plural, and must be understood in terms of relationships."[36] Augustine intends to emphasize the plural relationship of the Trinitarian Creator—Father, Son, and Holy Spirit—as well as the relationship of humans to their author, "so that man might subsist as the image of God . . . [and] that man is the image of the trinity."[37] The relational force of this claim lies in easily overlooked prepositions: that humanity is "*to* the image" entails dignity that resides in a certain likeness to God but that parity with God is never achieved. We are not equal to the trinity but "are approaching it as has been said by a certain likeness, as one can talk of a certain proximity between things distant from each other, not proximity of place but of a sort of imitation." Human sacredness borrows the dignity that belongs, in ultimate terms, only to God: "For man's true honor is God's image and likeness in him, but it can only be preserved when facing him from whom its impression is received."[38]

In ways analogous to Kant, though by no means functionally equivalent, Augustine's anthropology cherishes central capacities of the human mind, such as reason and the will. For Augustine, however, the human mind can never be severed from the image of God, which it bears. It is not "any old part of [our] consciousness" but "the rational mind, which is capable of recognizing God" and of understanding the human relationship that pertains to creatures made *in* and *to* God's image.[39] Reason accrues value through its knowledge of God. Similarly, the will finds its value in the proper object of its love. There is no "innate" value in a good will for Augustine as for Kant; the will is good only because it faces God—it is turned in *caritas* toward its source of value. Another important difference is that, for Augustine, the will is associated with love and desire, which for Kant are matters of self-interest. Love, in a Kantian anthropology, is amoral and apolitical; love's civic manifestations among citizens and within polities are incidental to the moral law or the realm of ethical action.

For Augustine, love itself bears a trinitarian character among the lover, the object of one's love, and love itself: if you see love, you see a trinity.[40] When God is severed from the will's volition to love, then one's relationship to, and participation in, its source of worth also are severed. To love *without God*—whether ourselves, others, ideals of our own invention, or pursuits of our own attribution—is covetous and prideful; it besmirches the image we bear. But to love and delight in ourselves and others *through* God is, for Augustine, true *caritas*: "Just as you ought to enjoy yourself not in yourself but *in* him who made you, so too with the one whom you love as yourself. Let us then enjoy both ourselves and our brothers in the Lord. . . ."[41] The will to re-turn and direct one's love toward its source upholds the relational dignity of the divine image that is impressed upon the human will.

The third component of Augustine's trinitarian anthropology, in addition to reason and will, is memory. Memory includes not just the storing up of experiences, emotions, and images but the very knowledge and awareness of how these dimensions inform the self. Indeed, the way Augustine speaks of memory is the way we speak today of human identity or "the self." Memory or self-knowledge itself comprises the other moral capacities—reason and will—including the desire for and knowledge of God. For Augustine, the self is not complete until it desires for and knows God. A Kantian anthropology assumes that the moral self is self-contained and self-legislating: Human reason inclines toward ultimacy as it ascertains moral truths and authenticates human dignity autonomously, without relation to any transcendent source of being beyond the human mind. Augustine, however, insists that human dignity is always penultimate and relationally inscribed. To reflect God's image is to instantiate God's ultimate, relational, and trinitarian essence through our own penultimate, relational, and trinitarian anthropology.

As penultimate bearers of the divine image, we share God's honor and sacredness by affirming our relations to and through God and by directing our minds and wills accordingly. When we face the illumination of this source of sacredness, we discern the light of human dignity. All humans bear the *imago Dei*. As such, to the extent that humanity is said to be sacred, though not self-sacred, universal human rights remain the most promising way to shore up and protect human dignity.[42]

For our purposes, it is crucial to note that the relational nature of Augustine's theological anthropology carries over to his understanding of political life. Commonwealths and polities are made up of associations of people living together in community, not of individuals autonomously and atomistically conceived. Augustine accepts provisionally the classical notion of the commonwealth put forth by Scipio—an association united by a common sense of right—even as he critiques its application by noting that a "commonwealth" in the Roman Empire never existed because there was no "real justice" in the community.[43] Augustine improves upon Scipio, averring that love has a civic component that is integrally related to substantive forms of justice within the political community. For Augustine, peoples and the character of their polities are known by the common objects of their love: their values, their aspirations, their civic pursuits, their laws and customs, and the political institutions through which these ideals are realized. The redefinition of a commonwealth that Augustine innovates demonstrates that love is not independent of politics or the moral law. As Augustine's portrait of the *imago Dei* makes clear, love of God—and through God, love of fellow man and woman—constitutes even in the *civitas* the proper orientation of one's will and the just ordering of the human soul. Similarly, Augustine makes use of the classical Greek notion of *suum cuique*—justice as the virtue that assigns to everyone his or her due. Again, he theologically reconciles this classical notion of justice by assigning the things that are due to God and due to others *through* God. The same love that is known relationally through the *imago Dei* pertains to citizens and polities, so that justice is known by "the love with which a man loves God as God ought to be loved, and loves his neighbor as himself."[44]

Justice, we see, takes multiple forms for Augustine, all of them social and relational. In the most robust sense of the term, *justice is the proper*

*ordering of right relations of persons and their polities as they reflect —
though never fully achieve — the perfect order of God's divine justice.* Peace
is the frequent analogue to justice that Augustine deploys to describe the
proper ordering and rule of parts among the whole within a society; it
is "the harmony of congruous elements," the "arrangement of things
equal and unequal in a pattern which assigns to each its proper position."
Divine or ultimate justice is the "perfectly ordered and perfectly har-
monious fellowship in the enjoyment of God, and a mutual fellowship
in God" that can only be found in the ultimate realm of the Heavenly
City.[45] Penultimate, earthly justice strives to approximate this heavenly
ideal, chastened by our human limits and ever mindful that ultimate justice awaits a time and place that earthly conditions and politics cannot
bring about.

An Augustinian perspective on limited justice appreciates the problem of sin that justice seeks to correct. (We might note here that sin is a
concept that often is conspicuously absent in Kant and universal justice successors). The "original justice" enjoyed in pre-lapsarian relations
to God is ruptured when the will misdirects its love away from God. As
the story of the fall makes clear, all sin begins with human pridefulness
that leads one to choose human values and pursuits over those that God
enjoins. Sin — the supplanting of the divine — is two-sided, with each side
bearing inscriptions of the common coin of pride. Two kinds of sin cor-
respond to what I understand to be the "lower" and "upper" limits of justice. One form of sin emerges in violent and egregious violations of both
divine and human law (e.g., murder, torture, mutilation, rape). Like genocide or ethnic cleansing, these offenses violate humanity. Theologically
speaking, because these human transgressions violate divine commands
and universal norms, they are crimes against God as well; viewed relationally, these offenses defile the *imago Dei* and shatter humanity's relationships to its rightful end. Regrettably, such wretchedness is and always has been part of the human condition. However, the exigencies and
magnitude of new crimes against humanity such as the genocide and ethnic cleansing we witnessed in the twentieth century place on governments and civil institutions the duty to preserve or restore political order;
halting, deterring, and, where possible, punishing such crimes are morally
necessary. Thus, the limited justice position responds to the "lower lim-

its" of justice by enjoining governments to preserve a modicum of peace, harmony, and well-ordered relations that citizens and their nations require to survive and flourish.

A second form of sin attends when human justice is fueled by aspirations for greatness and ultimacy. Why the theological concern regarding ultimate justice? The proponents of universal justice taken up earlier do not conjure with such concerns. Comparatively benign to heinous crimes, yet equally prideful, ultimate justice seeks to share space with, if not displace altogether, a transcendent realm that, by virtue of human finitude, we cannot occupy. When retribution is meted out for the sake of humanity rather than for the sake of the victims and communities involved; when justice is used for lofty purposes and to satisfy personal animosity—rather than out of the necessity to preserve order and protect citizens in the state—it is a telling sign that the upper limits of justice are being transgressed and the "burning desire for empty glory" may be overtaking the will to reconcile relations among peoples, polities, and the comity of nations.[46]

Limited justice, Augustine-styled, knowing it is frail, seeks modest forms of order and harmony. The necessities of the human condition and the limitations of human nature are such that penultimate justice inevitably is bound to be imperfectly realized. Justice also must be pursued in spite of finite human knowledge that impairs the ability to achieve it. There is a certain irony in being obliged to take up a duty that one is never fully equipped to administer. This irony is made clear in Augustine's story of the wise judge who laments the necessities that his duties demand of him and the human limitations that hinder his ability to carry them out and achieve justice. Yet the judge also realizes that to throw up his hands in desperation would be irresponsible and tragic for the political community.[47] The irony of human justice is further compounded by the outworking of sin's noetic effects in politics. Human conceit and self-importance ceaselessly threaten to obscure the faculties of moral reasoning and political judgment. Yet exigencies such as crimes against humanity cry out for justice. The position of limited justice described here recognizes that the only option available may be to go forth in one's duty, mindful of the limits and burdens that compromise the chores of justice. In the words of one Augustine scholar commenting on what I take to be Augustine's appreciation of limited justice, "The just political community is therefore primarily self-critical; its leaders recognize . . . that they act most justly when they realize just how far off lies the perfection of their justice."[48]

Unlike universal justice, a limited view of justice does not set itself above politics but accepts, albeit reluctantly, the necessity of politics for achieving the lower limits of justice: by ending spates of genocide and human rights abuses, by preserving human life, by restoring order and the minimal conditions necessary for stability, and by safeguarding the goods necessary for sustenance and earthly life. At some time or another, all of these aims may require for their success suspension of the judicial proceedings of universal justice. Limited justice as politics may even call for imperfect means such as the use of coercion and force.

Another important distinction is that limited justice accepts tragedy, albeit regretfully, whereas universal justice may actually engender it. Recall how pursuing justice on Goldstone's terms could entail prolongation of war, which is nothing less than tragic for the victims of such decisions. His emphasis on intention allows ample disregard for unintended consequences that could be quite tragic (even if foreknown). Limited justice, by accepting that tragedy is part of the human condition, draws our attention to the exigencies of political life and the incommensurability of many political goods. It may be that we allow some criminals to escape international trial if that means stopping massacres, ending war's destruction, and ushering in peace. Limited justice recognizes that saving lives and restoring order (again, justice's "lower limits) are, comparatively speaking, more just than fulfilling the hopes of a utopia of punishment that encroaches upon justice's "upper limits."

One might object to the position laid out here, arguing that if crimes against humanity are not tried in consistent international venues, human dignity itself begins to vary from one polity to the next. It is true that universal norms of human dignity must be upheld; the ways in which nations achieve these norms, however, need not be universalized. Equity, as a political and theological concept, contends that diverse means of enforcement can be employed as long as such means strive to uphold a shared and universal end. So John Calvin believed, anyway. His discussion of equity in the *Institutes* also notes that the same crime can be punished in a variety of ways, depending on the particular nation in question and the unique set of political conditions and exigencies it may face in a given age.[49] Calvin cautions against running roughshod over important distinctions among particular polities; "there is not a uniformity of punishment" across the nations, Calvin opines, and to standardize or universalize the forms that justice takes "is neither necessary or expedient." Indeed, it can be quite detrimental, as I have tried to show through discussion of the Milosevic trial. Calvin is no relativist, however: He understood that the moral law is universally binding and furnished to all nations. When the law lapses and ceases to preserve the end for which it was intended, such leniency of justice below its lower limits becomes an "outrage against humanity itself." There is a realistic and prudential need for flexibility—varied circumstances may require varied forms of political response—but at the end of the day, the universality of the principle stands and must be defended.

Similarly, I would append, even the imperfect enforcement of universal moral ideals involving human rights and crimes against humanity—including failure to enforce them altogether—should not be confused with the universality of the principles themselves. *Rights are not abrogated simply because they have not been enforced universally.* An aversion to systems of universal justice should not be associated with resistance to universal moral norms. Our aim, however, should be to try the accused in accordance with principles of equity that work toward a common end that elevates humanity's dignity, safeguards universal rights, promotes justice, and affirms the sovereignty of nations and their peoples.

The limited justice position I articulate here upholds the universality of human rights; it simply cautions that politics and the human condition may be unable to bear the weight when one value—such as human rights or even humanity itself—is made sovereign over all others. Limited human means and the limited capacities of our political institutions oblige us to defer the dream of universal justice and set our sights on more modest and Arendtian ethical pursuits that respect the plurality of interests of international political life. Limited justice proffers an outlook that is at once mindful of universal norms concerning "crimes against humanity" (which must be upheld) yet wary of human schemes of justice to prosecute and issue ultimate judgment upon them.

If justice entails restoring the relational image of God that crimes against humanity defile, simple retribution against individuals who per-

petrated crimes is insufficient; a more vigorous expression of justice involves restoration of civic relations, political reconciliation, and moral
accountability by these nations and their citizens who supported these
crimes. What happens when humanity is made sacred absent God?
When all things are "for humanity," our relational accountability to God
or to the rest of the family of nations withers. If all responsibility for
crimes against humanity is borne solely by individual criminals, none
is borne by the citizens who support them, who may share their distorted
loves and values. Relations within these unjust political communities
are permitted to remain fundamentally disordered, unreconciled to one
another and to the community of other nations. Universal justice does
not address such substantive concerns.

Calling criminals to accounting in one's own land forces a people to
reconcile themselves to one another and to victims. This approach also
can help welcome a people and a nation back into the family of other
nations. To do this, it may be necessary to suspend universal punishment
in which all villains of humanity are brought to final judgment. Because
ultimate justice belongs to God, limited justice may require that we
leave final judgment for another time. In fact, limited or penultimate
justice leaves room for God's justice precisely because we are not obliged
to exact revenge or fulfill all the demands of divine justice. We need
not—and cannot—do all of God's bidding. By not overextending our
finite institutions or the limits of our political arrangements, we allow
room for God's knowledge, judgment, and providence to call to full accounting the many cases we cannot fully assess: cases we are uncertain
about as well as those that completely elude us—which, in the world of
human rights abuses, unfortunately are far too many.

The Religiousness of Sovereignty

In the preceding section, I explore a theological validation for the sacredness of the human person and the preservation of human dignity
that prosecutions of crimes against humanity make possible. I now shift
gears briefly to consider whether there might also be theological warrants
for the mandates of nations and their governments by thinking about
other ways that language of "the sacred" and the image of God is fea-

tured in political thought, particularly in notions of sovereignty that undergird and legitimize political authority. The onus of this section is to consider how one might affirm simultaneously and theologically the sacredness of human dignity and the sovereignty of political rule.

Western political thought is replete with attempts to imbue politics with sacred qualities. Long before the Treaty of Westphalia ushered in modern political sovereignty, medieval notions of authority held that political rule emanated from the hand of God, evidenced by the popes' coronation of political rulers. Yet even as social contract thinkers worked to dispel this "myth" of sacred appointments and top-down rule, seeking instead to legitimate political rule from the bottom up, they retained elements of a religious language that overlaid civil government with a sacred veneer. As Westphalian notions of sovereignty were breaking onto the scene, political philosophers used religious tropes as divine or superadded qualities to reinforce the sovereign authority of political rule. For example, Thomas Hobbes' vision for the commonwealth was nothing less than a mighty Leviathan of Biblical stature, the awe of which was represented by an omnipotent, terrifying ruler charged with the order and preservation of the political community. This "mortal god" would command the reverence of his subjects (who "freely" submitted their liberty and rights in exchange for protection); under the immortal God, the sovereign could expect complete allegiance and obedience for the peace and defense of the commonwealth.[50] Locke, too, was keen to invoke the "religious" character of the sovereign: "the person of the prince by the law is sacred . . . the sacredness of the person exempts him from all inconveniences whereby he is secure, while the government stands, from all violence and harm whatsoever."[51] Even Rousseau could not dispense with the language of "the sacred" to prop up the sovereign supremacy—including the infallibility—of the general will that resides in *le peuple*. When Rousseau professed that "the body politic or the sovereign [derives] its being solely from the sanctity of the social contract," he professed that the social order itself enjoyed supreme and nonpareil status even though it found no basis in a divinely governed or "natural" order, as had been the case for medieval thinkers such as Thomas Aquinas.[52]

Political philosopher Jacques Maritain avers that all of these modern exemplars were clinging to medieval vestiges of sovereignty that saw political rule as the mirror of God's image.[53] It was actually Jean Bodin, working earlier at the cusp of the modern turn, who crystallized the refrain, "The prince is the image of God."[54] Maritain denoted sovereignty, properly speaking, as "independence and power which are *separately* or *transcendentally* supreme and are exercised upon the body politic *from above.*"[55] This means that for the prince to dwell in the image of God, he cannot simply crown the political order, he must rise *above* it, participating through God and serving with accountability only to God.

The moderns would go to innovative lengths to retain medieval assumptions and divine references to sovereignty despite the fact that, by the time of Westphalia, the state had replaced the prince as the seat of authority. The dream of medieval sovereignty—understood as absolute and transcendent authority—was dying on the vine, overtaken by modern theories of political rule. Within the modern social-contract genre that Hobbes, Locke, and Rousseau embodied—in which the legitimacy of the state stems from below, in the people—this medieval notion of sovereignty cannot carry over. Thus does Maritain implore, "The State is not and never has been genuinely sovereign. . . ."[56] Maritain says more: "No earthly power is the image of God and deputy for God. God is the very source of the authority with which *the people* invest those men or agencies, but they are not the vicars of God."[57] If sovereignty so construed only belonged to princes and not to states, then there is less room in Maritain's account to consider theological warrants for state sovereignty, at least with respect to the *imago Dei*. Such magisterial language was relevant only in an earlier epoch in which rulers were accountable to God and hence represented God's image. Now that states are accountable to people, the coating of God's image must be peeled off.

Are there other routes to consider than the one that Maritain takes? Maritain's historical-political analysis of sovereignty adopts a very specific definition of sovereignty that assumes absolute power and no higher earthly authority or human law.[58] Is it possible, though, to explore other theological warrants for government, even those that depend on strong appeals to sovereignty for their accomplishment? When sovereignty or political authority entails a religious or transcendent component, *absolute* sovereignty is chastened. That is, there remains some higher authority or law to which governments are accountable, similar to the medieval sovereign's accountability to the natural law. Without such a framework of celestial reference points and limits, atheistic political rule will collapse the transcendent horizon and move swiftly to replace it and claim complete, absolute, and unsurpassable authority. Indeed, it was this spectre, in the guise of totalitarianism, that most troubled Maritain. Nor is it coincidental that moderns such as Hobbes and Rousseau, in collapsing the transcendent features of political rule, absolutized it as well, which ushered in modern possibilities of authoritarianism and terror.

Where does all of this leave us? We should consider an alternative theological dimension of sovereignty that perceives a rightful source of all authority. This scheme entails the sanction of sovereign mandates— "divinely imposed tasks," as Dietrich Bonhoeffer called them—that require for their fulfillment political institutions that are sovereign. True, institutions such as states may no longer bear the image of God, but they retain power and authority that God instills.

Nor is the power of government absolute. Bonhoeffer sought to assassinate Hitler (a move that would eventually end his own life) without ever making a systematic argument for his actions—a testament equally to his moral support of political authority and his commitment to the goodness of human creation. Bonhoeffer offers instructive clarification for grappling with the relationship between sacred and sovereign. Under the mandate of government, sovereign political institutions become protectors of the sacred—of the human worth and dignity that flow from creation. Only by protecting the created order does government's divine task accrue meaning; government presupposes and fulfills the promise of creation. With characteristic simple elegance, Bonhoeffer discerns:

> Government cannot itself produce life or values. It is not creative. It preserves what has been created, maintaining order which is assigned to it through the task which is imposed by God. It protects it by making law to consist in the acknowledgment of the divine mandates and by securing respect for this law by the force of the sword. . . . Everyone owes obedience to this governing authority—for Christ's sake.[59]

There is in this proposal no stark division between transcendent and secular realms. Ultimate religious allegiance entails penultimate regard for institutions of the political realm; as proprietors of God's mandates, political sovereigns require for their sustenance a certain degree of awe and obedience. National governments, as entities that retain the primary resources of force, that preserve the basic institutions of organized day-to-day living, and whose citizens identify—or should identify—with them, would seem to be the ideal loci of such claims to reverence and respect. (See chapter 7 for more on themes of awe and identity.) As Bonhoeffer's "treason" reveals, however, when states fail to uphold their divine mandates, they undermine their own authority and lose the attendant rights thereof.

A Plea to the Nations (and Their International Sponsors)

I have tried in this chapter to show that gestures toward universal justice may undermine institutional constancies such as national sovereignty that are needed to preserve mandates of government and make possible substantive measures of justice. In our day, such governmental mandates must include, chiefly, prevention but also punishment of crimes against humanity as ways of preserving human creation and human dignity. Restoring sovereignty to nations entails that they uphold the burden of their divine mandates, but it also appeals to the promise of equity that allows nations to use diverse means and venues to seek justice after crimes against humanity are committed. Defending state sovereignty also obliges us to acknowledge when a state has failed, when a nation is no longer willing or capable of upholding its mandate, when it ceases to be a protector of the *imago Dei*. Where there is no state, there can be no sovereignty. (See chapters 3 and 10 and the conclusion to this book for treatments of sovereignty and failed states.)

Establishing baseline conditions for sovereignty and statehood does not erode sovereignty or undermine the idea of "the nation," as some people might think. Instead, we elevate the status of sovereignty by placing it on a footing with the value of human life and dignity that states are mandated to protect. National sovereignty and human rights are fully commensurable. In fact, there is grim irony in the idea of states willfully violating their mandates by perpetrating crimes against humanity, particularly against their own people. The claim that failed states should no longer enjoy the privileges of sovereignty, including the privilege of non-interference in domestic affairs, is the reciprocal of the claim that, for normative and political purposes, they no longer live up to the expectations of what it means to be a state. How can the withdrawal of state recognition by other nations—and the UN as the foremost sponsor of the comity of nations—be anything other than an affirmation that sovereignty is a prized political badge to be coveted, not given away freely? To honor sovereignty and its claims to nonintervention, nations should cease to recognize and extend such privileges to any polity that simply proclaims itself to be a state; instead, nations should recognize only those polities that honor the minimal standards of behavior and accountability and the divine mandates that nations assume on behalf of their citizens. In short, the community of nations must become comfortable with calling to the carpet, and rescinding sovereignty from, failed states.

Nation-states are in unique positions to marshal resources against failed states that threaten to undermine the status and mandates authorizing the existence of all states. Nations that are *unable* to enforce these mandates may require the assistance of other nations. But recalcitrant nations that are *unwilling* to uphold their mandate—nations that pursue or support crimes against humanity—must be made aware that the very existence of their regimes is jeopardized by their conduct. The position of limited justice underscores the necessity of order that mandates seek to preserve. The full panoply of "persuasive" and "coercive" means available to states—ranging from financial incentives, sanctions, and diplomatic censure to military intervention—may be brought to bear to bring into the fold nations who fail to uphold common mandates. Because limited justice also appeals to the relational quality among nations, however, reconciliation follows by restoring fallen nations and welcoming them back into the fold of the community of nations.

As globalization extends the resources and influence that states traditionally have enjoyed, there are new responsibilities for international organizations and transnational actors. International trade and monetary organizations increasingly possess many means of persuasion, full use of which should be made no less than states make full use of their powers. International governmental organizations such as the United Nations have uniquely essential mandates. Perhaps the most indispensable involves leadership in setting the standards for what it means to be a full-fledged member of the family of nations. The relational orientation inherent to limited justice would advise international organizations to foster close and cooperative relationships with nations that resist their mandates or struggle to uphold them.[60] Unfortunately, the UN's prideful cooptation of justice in the Milosevic trial severed possibilities for cooperative relationships between the international sponsor of nations and a state badly in need of reconciliation. In so doing, the Milosevic trial left fundamentally disordered the relations among Yugoslavia's citizens who were relieved of the proceedings of justice—to say nothing of the struggling nation's relationship to its fellow nations.

Assisting nations with their own enterprise of justice remains a potent task of international and perhaps even regional governmental organizations. If these organizations are supported by member nations, they are postured to offer essential provisions such as financial, advisory, staffing, or institutional resources to struggling nations that lack the ability to pursue justice on their own. The UN's International Criminal Tribunal for Rwanda would seem to have been such an example, especially after much of the country's justice system was wiped out by the genocide. Yet the intent should not be to require a common standard of universal justice that would apply to crimes against humanity anywhere and everywhere but to embrace the concept of equity, which allows justice to be meted out in ways appropriate to the national culture in which the crimes against humanity took place. Proponents and sponsors of international trials should consider how their own standards of justice may be insufficient to the task at hand. For example, Rwandans' decision to form local tribunals called *gacaca* (meaning "justice on the grass") surely was related to the fact that, at the time the *gacaca* were formed—eight years after the massacres—the UN war crimes tribunal in Arusha had prosecuted only eight cases, leaving as many as 110,000 other defendants languishing in overcrowded jails while they await trial. Some international observers object to the *gacaca* tribunals for procedural reasons (i.e., defendants will not be able to cross-examine their accusers), but clearly these open hearings, modeled on South Africa's Truth and Reconciliation Commission, aim to offer the offender the opportunity for contrition, to mete out just retribution, to heal the disordered relations between Hutus and Tutsis, and to accelerate the recovery of a wounded nation. [61]

International organizations have different kinds of responsibilities, though, vis-à-vis states that harbor criminals against humanity or refuse to try them for crimes against humanity. International bodies—as organizations that *codify* universal moral norms—should consider issuing coincident statements for the historical record that demonstrate how short of the mark, on their view, a nation has fallen in enforcing commitments to moral norms and political mandates. Alternatively, why not try the defendant in absentia? It would then fall upon other nations—as those who embrace and *enforce* such norms—to evaluate the results and statement of the international judicial body and to weigh various persuasive or coercive options that may be appropriate.

I have argued that the issue before us is not a choice between justice and injustice but a question about what kind of justice is feasible and appropriate to an imperfect world of complex and densely layered relations among persons and polities. Nor is ours a choice between human sacredness and sovereign states. Instead, the choice before us seems to involve what source of ultimacy underwrites our political ideals and institutions and endows human beings with their worth. Are we self-sacred purveyors of our own ultimacy? Are political institutions simply an extension of this prideful belief? Or does humanity's dignity accrue from its penultimate worth, from its relation to and participation in—but not equivalence with—the ultimate? Whatever scheme of justice we adopt to prosecute crimes against humanity, we assume some anthropological narrative, and perhaps a theological design, with embedded responses to these questions.

Notes

The Civitas program, funded by the Pew Charitable Trusts and administered by Keith Pavlischek, provided essential support for the writing of this chapter. Special thanks also are in order to Jean Bethke Elshtain, Robin Lovin, Joshua Mitchell, Daniel Philpott, and the wonderful colleagues in my dissertation group, all of whom read earlier drafts of this paper and offered crucial insights and suggestions.

1. Gary Jonathan Bass notes that the Ottoman court in Constantinople first brought charges, albeit unsuccessfully, of "crimes against humanity and civilisation" against Turks accused in the 1915 genocide of approximately 1 million Armenians. See *Stay the Hand of Vengeance: The Politics of War Crimes Tribunals* (Princeton, N.J.: Princeton University Press, 2001), 106. In this exceptionally thorough and detailed work, Bass offers a revealing account of how war crimes tribunals have evolved to their current state.

2. Ibid., 203–4.

3. Hannah Arendt, *Eichmann in Jerusalem: A Report on the Banality of Evil* (New York: Penguin Books, 1963), 268–69. On Arendt and Eichmann, see also David Novak's essay in the forthcoming volume *A Call for Reckoning: Religion and the Death Penalty*, edited by John D. Carlson, Eric P. Elshtain, and Erik C. Owens (Grand Rapids, Mich.: Eerdmans Press, in press).

4. Arendt, *Eichmann in Jerusalem*, 257.

5. Ibid., 298

6. We might rightly wonder whether the Taliban's sometimes brutal treatment of women warranted extending this category to sex as well.

7. Various definitions can be found on the websites of the International War Crimes Tribunals for Former Yugoslavia (ICTY)—www.un.org/icty/BL/05art5e.htm (last accessed January 15, 2002)—and Rwanda (ICTR): www.ictr.org (last accessed January 15, 2002).

8. The crime of genocide, as defined by the 1948 Genocide Convention, entails the *intent* to destroy civilian groups "in whole or in part." Crimes against humanity need not demonstrate intent, though they may include widespread or systematic human rights violations. See Cherif Bassiouni, "Crimes against Humanity," available at www.crimesofwar.org/thebook/crimes-against-humanity.html (last access January 15, 2002).

9. Universal jurisdiction is (or was) regarded as the choice means of international justice absent establishment of an international criminal court. See Princeton Project on Universal Jurisdiction, *The Princeton Principles on Universal Jurisdiction* (Princeton, N.J.: Program in Law and Public Affairs, Princeton University, 2001).

10. Geoffrey Robertson, *Crimes against Humanity* (New York: New Press, 1999), 234. Robertson goes on to note that because piracy and enslavement are not committed on behalf of governments, the term "crimes against humanity" does not pertain. Not all observers recognize this distinction.

11. Richard Goldstone, *For Humanity: Reflections of a War Crimes Investigator* (New Haven, Conn., London: Yale University Press, 2000), 75.

12. Ibid., 122.

13. Nazi Germany is the most famous precedent; after the failures that flowed from heavily punishing the entire nation of Germany following World War I, the Nuremberg trials adopted a different approach, placing in the dock individual National Socialist leaders.

14. Goldstone, *For Humanity*, 122.

15. Immanuel Kant, *Metaphysics as a Guide to Morals*, trans. Lewis White Beck (New York: Macmillan, 1969), Sec. 1, par. 393, p. 11.

16. Ibid., Sec. 2, par. 427, p. 51.

17. Ibid., Sec. 1, par. 403, p. 23.

18. Ibid., Sec 2, par. 428, pp. 52–53.

19. Ibid., par. 436, p 61. Arendt closes her bleak yet monumental classic *Origins of Totalitarianism* on a hopeful note, citing Augustine and possibilities of birth and new creation: "that a beginning be made man was created."

20. Kant, *Metaphysics as a Guide to Morals*, par. 433, p. 58.

21. Kant, of course, never moved to the level of universals because he knew that there would always be national atavisms that would stand in the way of a truly cosmopolitan world. The end of history will usher in perpetual peace and a league of nations but not world government or a global society. See Kant's "Perpetual Peace" in *Perpetual Peace and Other Essays*, trans. Ted Humphrey (Indianapolis: Hackett Publishing Co., 1983).

22. Ibid., par. 429, p. 54. It is worth noting that Kant often is misunderstood as saying that people should never be used as means; yet he says, quite plainly, that persons are not to be treated *only* as means to an end.

23. Goldstone, *For Humanity*, 22.

24. Ibid., 88, 131.

25. Ibid., 132.

26. The categorical imperative—in this case to prosecute consistently and objectively crimes against humanity—"concerns not the material of the action and its intended result but the form and the principle from which it results. What is essentially good in it consists in the intention, *the result being what it may*" (Kant, *Metaphysics as a Guide to Morals*, p. 38, par. 416; emphasis added).

27. Bass, *Stay the Hand of Vengeance*, 285.

28. Consider the following example of how the pursuit of justice could impede a peace process. Goldstone writes that UN Secretary-General Boutros Boutros-Ghali opposed indicting Radovan Karadzic, president of the Bosnian Serb Republic of Srpska, for war crimes prior to the Bosnian peace talks at Dayton because such an indictment could have threatened the success of the talks. When Goldstone learned of Boutros-Ghali's position, he demurred, saying he would not (in fact, he never did) consult the secretary-general about pending indictments. Goldstone also admitted that he would have, in effect, ignored Boutros-Ghali's advice anyway, which Goldstone felt would have compromised his prosecutorial independence. It turns out, on Goldstone's view, that indicting Karadzic and preventing him from attending the peace talks may have ensured Dayton's success. From where Goldstone sits, however, this happy conclusion is coincidental and completely irrelevant to justice. See Goldstone, *For Humanity*, 102–3.

29. On UN and United States reluctance to intervene in Rwanda, see National Book Critic winner Philip Gourevitch's *We Wish to Inform You That Tomorrow We Will Be Killed with Our Families* (New York: Picador, 1998).

30. Similar hobgoblins raise their heads over questions of consistency involving humanitarian military intervention. Many asked how the United States and other Western powers could justifiably intervene in Kosovo when they had failed to intervene to arrest genocide in Rwanda. Although such inconsistency is a sign of politics' imperfections—a topic worthy of debate—the simple point remains that two wrongs don't make a right.

31. Goldstone, *For Humanity*, 122.

32. See William Pfaff, "Kostunica Has Sound Argument for Trying Milosevic at Home," *New York Times*, February 6, 2001.

33. Simon Jenkins, "New World Order Beset by Old World's Flaws," *The Times* [London], July 4, 2001.

34. Within the scheme of "universal justice," a central justification for retribution is deterrence of future crimes against humanity. Punishment certainly is due for these atrocities, independent of the deterrent value of international law. We should be cautious, however, about how effective an international trial or tribunal may be as a deterrent; the evil and cruelty that criminals against humanity are capable of inflicting is not likely to be swayed by the possibility, even the inevitability, of facing an international jury.

35. My hunch on this matter is that many believers today have adopted, perhaps unwittingly, much of the rights talk that has become a kind of *lingua franca* for human dignity in contemporary conversations, including internationalist discourse. On the idea of locating human dignity or universal human rights in a source of being and worth outside humanity itself, see transcripts of the Pew Forum lecture series "Does Human Rights Need a God?" at www.pewforum.org/humanrights.

36. Augustine, *The Trinity,* trans. Edmund Hill, O.P. (Brooklyn, N.Y.: New City Press, 1991), 7.4, p. 231. Aquinas also cites Augustine in his own discussion of the Image: "The divine nature of the Holy Trinity is the Image to whom man was made" (*Summa Theologica* I, Q. 35, a.1).

37. Augustine, *The Trinity,* 7.4, p. 231.

38. Ibid., 12.15, p. 331.

39. Ibid., 12.12, p. 329.

40. Ibid., 9.2, p. 272; 8.2, p. 253.

41. Ibid., 9.13, p. 278.

42. These are seeds for a theological grounding of human rights—seeds that will have to remain dormant for now.

43. Augustine, *City of God,* trans. Henry Bettenson (New York: Penguin, 1972), 2.21.

44. Ibid., 19.23.

45. Ibid., 19.12–13.

46. Augustine poetically professed, "The more we are cured of the tumor of pride, the fuller we are of love"; see *The Trinity,* 8.12, p. 253.

47. Augustine, *City of God,* 19.6.

48. Robert Dodaro, "Justice," in *Augustine through the Ages: An Encyclopedia* (Grand Rapids, Mich.: Eerdmans Publishing Co., 1999), 483.

49. John Calvin, *Institutes of the Christian Faith* (Philadelphia: Presbyterian Board of Christian Education, 1936), 4.20.15–16.

50. Thomas Hobbes, *The Leviathan* (New York: Macmillan, 1962), 2.17, p. 132.

51. This Locke averred despite limited constitutional provisions when a subject's natural rights were transgressed. These rights also were reinforced by reference to scripture. John Locke, *The Second Treatise of Government* (New York: Macmillan, 1952), chap. 18, p. 115.

52. Jean-Jacques Rousseau, *On the Social Contract,* trans. Judith D. Masters (New York: St. Martin's, 1978) 1.1, p. 47; 1.7, p. 55.

53. Jacques Maritain, *Man and the State* (Chicago: University of Chicago Press, 1951), 28–53.

54. Quoted in Maritain, *Man and the State*, 33.

55. Ibid., 50.

56. Ibid., 43.

57. Ibid., 50 (emphasis added).

58. "But if the State is accountable and subject to supervision, how can it be sovereign? What can possibly be the concept of a *Sovereignty liable to supervision, and accountable?* Clearly, the State is not sovereign"; Ibid., 53.

59. Dietrich Bonhoeffer, *Ethics*, trans. Neville Horton Smith (New York: Macmillan, 1955), 210–11.

60. I am grateful to Mieke Holkeboer for prodding me to think relationally about the place of international organizations within schemes of limited justice.

61. Davan Maharaj, "Genocide Survivors Are Judges, Jury," *Chicago Tribune*, 30 May 2002.

PART III

Sovereignty and Its Critics

10

Weighing Sovereignty in the "Sit Room": Does It Enter or End the Debate?

ROBERT L. GALLUCCI

M Y PURPOSE IN THIS CHAPTER is to help illuminate the decision-making process in some recent cases of American military intervention in which questions of national sovereignty or human rights, or both, were at issue. I selected the cases from my own experience as a State Department official (including my experience with diplomatic crisis management in the "situation room"), and I present them from that perspective. My intent is to use the cases to show how decision makers dealt with or ignored concerns of sovereignty and human rights.

None of the cases deals with a direct confrontation over the competing values of respect for national sovereignty and the moral imperative to act in a situation of gross human rights violations. Taken together, however, they may yield some insight into the weight given those concerns by some individuals in government who were charged with the responsibility for advising about, deciding, and executing decisions concerning humanitarian intervention. In conclusion, I offer some general propositions about the way Americans reconcile the tension between these moral and political concerns in evaluating the wisdom of intervention. Broadly stated, I argue that sovereignty is a secondary concern to policymakers and other citizens when other important moral and political criteria are involved—and even less of a concern when the foreign government in question is unstable or not functioning (as some of these cases exemplify).

The first case is Grenada, where Operation Urgent Fury was conducted in the fall of 1983. The background, in brief, is that four years previously a bloodless coup had resulted in the overthrow of the island's first elected prime minister and the establishment of a Marxist-Leninist government. Then, in October 1983, a power struggle within the government created a situation of general chaos in which the self-proclaimed prime minister and some members of his cabinet were themselves murdered. Although there was a government of sorts in place, its coherence, effectiveness, and respect for human rights—and certainly its legitimacy—were open to question.

Among those on the island whose lives were potentially in jeopardy, and essentially were being held hostage, were several hundred medical students, many of whom were Americans. Added to the United States government's legitimate concerns for the safety of its nationals, as well as broader humanitarian interest in the safety of Grenadian citizens and other nationals who were at risk, were political interests. First among these interests was a concern that the new group, the People's Revolutionary Army, would expand its relationship with Cuba and the Soviet Union, creating a new bridgehead for communism in the Caribbean. There already were Cuban workers with military training on the island, and an airstrip was being constructed that, some observers argued, would have had value to the Soviets for routine reconnaissance purposes or in a confrontation with the United States.

It also is relevant that during the same month, more than 240 U.S. Marines in Lebanon were killed in their sleep when the building they were using for a headquarters was destroyed by a terrorist truck bomber. The Marines were part of the multinational force deployed as peacekeepers to help stabilize the Lebanese political situation. Following the Lebanon tragedy, President Reagan promised retaliation, but there was no target in Lebanon that could be found and struck to punish those responsible. There was, in short, an arguable domestic and international political incentive, or need, to use American military power someplace soon to reestablish its potency. At the very least, it can be said that neither the American government nor the American people were in any mood to stand by while their sons and daughters were again threatened by political radicals or terrorists abroad.

Within the U.S. government, then, the reasons for military intervention in Grenada were complex, involving humanitarian and political concerns—the latter of both the domestic and international kind. When the White House decided to prepare for intervention, it also decided to seek broader regional and international political support, along with some token operational presence. In the Department of State, to preserve operational security two task forces were established in the Operations Center: one quite large and broadly staffed by an interagency team working around the clock to deal with the American families of those on Grenada, the press, diplomatic contacts, and the like, and another that was small and secret, whose purpose was to coordinate a diplomatic and congressional timetable of notification with the military's timetable for invasion.

The presentations that were prepared to explain this use of U.S. military force were designed to create as broad a consensus as possible to establish the legal and political legitimacy of the operation. The participation of the Organization of Eastern Caribbean States was critical, as was at least the sympathy of the Organization of American States (OAS) and the United Nations (UN). Although the United Kingdom's support was vital—both because of our longstanding alliance and because the British government was still in residence on this former possession—participation by the UK was not sought for fear of alienating the OAS, where memories of the Falklands-Malvinas War lingered. Thus, a substantial amount of planning and diplomatic activity was devoted to addressing concerns about sovereignty, even in this case in which an argument could be made that the government was failing the most basic test of sovereignty—namely, competence.

At the same time, the concern for the basic human rights of U.S. citizens on Grenada served as both reason and rationale for intervention. Although the medical students apparently were not in immediate danger, rapid deterioration of the situation could not be ruled out. The political preparation for intervention also created momentum, and once the decision was made to execute the military operation, reversal would have been extremely difficult. Indeed, at the eleventh hour, when it was evident to all observers that the United States was preparing to intervene, a message was received in the Department of State's Operations Center Task Force from Grenadian "authorities," offering to release the medical students; that message was "lost."

A cynical interpretation of that action, or even of the entire U.S. decision-making process, in light of American political interests, might find the government's human rights concerns more pretext than cause for intervention. In fact, however, reversing the decision to intervene once the message was received at the State Department might not have been operationally possible, nor might Washington have been prudent to hold the movement of ships, aircraft, and troops hostage to what could have been the whim of the People's Revolutionary Army. More broadly, it is difficult to impossible to identify the primary reason for intervention among decision makers from the president down.

For the sake of this discussion, however, there are at least two questions to consider. First, how important were humanitarian concerns, and did those concerns turn entirely on the American nationality of the people at risk? Second, would the invasion have proceeded regardless of whether all those efforts at creating political and legal legitimacy had succeeded? I believe that concern for American lives on Grenada was a genuine and primary concern, and, together with political concerns, probably would have led to invasion no matter what level of legitimacy was ultimately achieved—that is, notwithstanding concerns over Grenadian sovereignty.

In other words, it seems to me that the United States took several steps to enhance the legitimacy of military intervention, even though it was arguably intervening where no legitimate or effective authority prevailed—and thus where no breach of sovereignty could result. At the same time, had the Grenadian authorities demonstrated greater legitimacy by maintaining public order, and had the United States failed to gain support for intervention from regional and international organizations, but the lives of American citizens on Grenada appeared nevertheless to have been at risk, I believe that the American government and the public would have found intervention the proper and ethical course. Concern for human rights would have prevailed over respect for the sovereignty of the state.

The second, briefly noted case involves discussion of a proposed intervention in a small country that will have to remain unnamed. I include this case only because it would have involved the use of covert action, unlike the others discussed here and elsewhere in this book. The discussion involved representatives from the intelligence community, the Department of Defense, the National Security Council staff, and the relevant regional and functional bureaus within the Department of State.

One of the key meetings in the decision-making process began with a presentation that described the current situation in the country, focusing on the potential for political unrest and violence. The regime was characterized as unsavory, and the potential for damage to American private, corporate interests in the country was underlined, as was the possibility of civilian casualties in the event of the collapse of the government. The discussion then turned to the scenario of a covert intervention that would have been aimed at assisting a favored faction to gain control of the government, reducing the threat of widespread violence and protecting American private interests on the ground. In assessing the virtue of the operation, the debate circled around how likely it was that a dramatic deterioration of the political situation would actually occur; how damaging it would be to American interests if the worst happened; how likely it was that a covert operation would succeed in producing the outcome sought; and how plausible it was to expect that the intervention would remain covert—that is, that the United States would not be identified as having intervened.

There was no direct discussion, at least in this relatively senior interagency meeting, of the legal or ethical concerns raised by armed intervention in the internal affairs of another country. Obviously, the concern that the operation remain covert reflected an appreciation for the potential political consequences of allowing the revelation of an illegitimate American intervention. Because the discussion did not sharply distinguish between American concerns for loss of life, on one hand, and damage to corporate interests on the other, the value placed on the threat to human rights in this case is hard to assess. The meeting ended with serious doubts remaining about the magnitude of the threat and the likelihood that a successful covert operation could be mounted to address it. Ultimately, the decision was made not to intervene.

The third case is the intervention in Somalia in December 1992. The situation there had been steadily deteriorating over a three-year period marked by a catastrophic drought and constant warfare between several Somali clans that were competing for power. By the summer of 1992, several hundred thousand Somalis had already died of starvation, and several thousand more were dying each day—more than a thousand of whom were children. At the same time, international relief efforts were thwarted by intimidation, theft, and murder committed by armed clan members. Food deliveries authorized by the UN were turned away or stolen, and Pakistani peacekeepers sent to stabilize the situation failed to do so. Food was not reaching the victims of famine in the interior of the country, and nongovernmental relief organizations were departing in frustration. Although the U.S. military was involved in airlifting food, it was clear to the American government that the introduction of a significant increment in external military presence would be necessary if effective relief operations were to be conducted.

By the fall of 1992, morale in those quarters of the Department of State that were responsible for coordinating the U.S. military airlift of supplies to Somalia and Bosnia was at low ebb. The military and foreign service officers at the working level in the Bureau of Political-Military Affairs wanted the United States to intervene with force in both countries to end the humanitarian disasters. As assistant secretary in charge of the bureau, I worked with staff members to prepare "blind" memoranda—addressed to no one and coming from no one—that I would deliver "outside the system" directly to Secretary of State Lawrence Eagleburger. In a private meeting in November 1992, the secretary heard my oral argument for intervention in both Bosnia and Somalia. I presented a brief concept of operations for both cases, along with a rationale that emphasized the relatively low cost and risks and the high payoff in the saving of lives in Somalia. I also noted the relatively higher costs and risks, and lower stakes, in the Bosnian case. The secretary indicated no real enthusiasm for either argument but substantially greater disdain for our lack of appreciation of the complexities of the Yugoslavian situation. He also wondered out loud if we had noticed that President (George H. W.) Bush had lost the election.

I left the meeting discouraged, but I was called back for another private session a few days later to be told that the president had decided to commit U.S. forces to Somalia. I understood that the secretary had argued the case for Somalia but not Bosnia. The plan would be to form a multinational force under a UN mandate limited to stabilizing the security situation and protecting humanitarian activities. The United States would lead the coalition, committing two divisions. I also was soon told that I would join the deputy chairman of the Joint Chiefs of Staff, Admiral David Jeremiah, and travel to Little Rock, Arkansas, to brief President-elect Clinton and his national security team-in-waiting on the plans for Somalia—on why he would find U.S. forces committed to Africa when he came into office in January.

During the Little Rock meeting, Admiral Jeremiah explained the concept of operations and the limited mission and responded to questions about the rules of engagement and other military aspects of the operation. I explained the rationale, the formation of the coalition, the relationship with the United Nations, and the plan for transition to UN control and exit. The first question came from Governor Clinton, who wanted to know how soon after our troops landed we could expect the awful daily death toll of thousands of innocents to end. It was the right question.

For the purposes of this chapter, the salient point is that no one in the Bush administration or the incoming Clinton administration thought that there was any vital national security interest at stake in Somalia: Not only was the United States committing significant military force to bring peace to a country where armed hostilities were under way between internal factions, but it was doing so where there clearly were no national security or economic interests at all at risk, never mind vital ones. Indeed, one had to stretch pretty far to find any motivating political interests, internal or external, to explain the decision by the outgoing Bush administration. Certainly nobody cared or even noticed that Somalia was in the Horn of Africa—a locale that had geostrategic importance to some people when there was a Soviet Union. This intervention was a humanitarian action. It is notable, however, that it was not launched into a state controlled by an effective government; the warring warlords did not add up to a legitimate regime. Somali sovereignty therefore was not a major concern for American policymakers. Nevertheless, to achieve international legitimacy and to increase domestic political support, the intervention was carried out in coalition and under UN authority.

The intervention succeeded in stabilizing the security situation, so aid workers returned and the starvation ended. As everyone knows, however, America's military presence in Somalia came to an end under the worst of circumstances sixteen months after it began. After the UN took control of operations in Somalia in May 1993, the mission was substantially broadened. Soon casualties among Somalis and UN peacekeepers increased, and in October 1993 eighteen U.S. soldiers were killed and their mutilated bodies dragged through the streets of Mogadishu. The announcement by the president that the United States was withdrawing from Somalia followed almost immediately.

The fourth case is North Korea, officially known as the Democratic People's Republic of Korea (DPRK). Although this case clearly contemplates the compromise of sovereignty, by an airstrike or the use of special operations forces, it is less clear that concern for human rights would have been the cause for such action. The argument would have to be—and some people have made it—that when a rogue, irrational regime is about to acquire weapons of mass destruction, perhaps in violation of international undertakings, other governments have a right to act preemptively to protect their own citizens and the rest of the international community from the potentially catastrophic consequences of possession as well as use. In fact, this is the argument in the National Security Strategy of the United States of America—a document issued in September 2002. One year after the attacks of September 11, 2001, by international terrorists and identification of Iraq, Iran, and North Korea as an "axis of evil," the Bush administration created a doctrine on which to base preventive war. Preemption was always justifiable in self-defense; in these times, however, when we cannot be certain when or where we will be attacked, we have to adapt the concept to allow us to strike an enemy that seeks weapons of mass destruction, even when we have no evidence that we are about to be struck first. Iraq seemed an ideal case, North Korea and Iran far less so.

The background here would begin with a recounting of the violence and disregard for human life exhibited by North Korea over a forty-year period, beginning with the Korean War. There is no question about North Korea's responsibility for the war, nor for its outrageous acts of international terrorism, including the bombing of a civilian aircraft, a suicide attack on the South Korean Blue House, an unprovoked attack on American servicemen in the Demilitarized Zone, and the kidnappings of South Korean and Japanese civilians. By the time international concerns about North Korea's nuclear weapons program began to emerge, there was a good case for labeling the DPRK a rogue regime. Then, in

1985, under pressure from the Soviet Union, North Korea joined the Nuclear Non-Proliferation Treaty (NPT). Soon after it did so, however, the North's nuclear program began to look more clearly like one aimed at nuclear weapons production than a legitimate nuclear power program.

The international community did not formally respond until 1993, when the International Atomic Energy Agency (IAEA) found the DPRK in violation of its safeguards agreement undertakings as provided by its NPT obligations. The IAEA reported the matter to the UN Security Council, which expressed its concern and implicitly threatened sanctions if the matter was not resolved through negotiations. The United States undertook such negotiations on a bilateral basis but came to an impasse in the spring of 1994 when the DPRK began to discharge fuel from its nuclear reactor, moving one step closer to separating the plutonium contained in the fuel and thus to nuclear weapons manufacture. At this point, the U.S. government began to prepare for a UN Security Council sanctions resolution, as well as the possible use of military force to stop the North Korean nuclear weapons program. As it turned out, preparation for diplomatic action also required military preparations because the North had indicated that it would regard imposition of sanctions by the UN—a belligerent in the Korean War—as an act of war. The crisis was defused and the ground prepared for resumption of negotiations when former president Jimmy Carter persuaded the North Koreans to freeze their nuclear activities.

When the outcome was still in doubt, there was discussion of a range of military steps that might be taken, including a strike on North Korea's nuclear facilities to prevent that country from acquiring nuclear weapons. If that option were chosen, it was clear that South Korean and Japanese support would be sought and that UN Security Council and IAEA actions would be cited as a basis for legitimacy. The threat posed by the North was immediate for South Koreans; for Americans deployed in South Korea; and for Japan, which was within range of the North's ballistic missiles. There also was concern that the North might spread its nuclear weapons capability around the world—particularly to the Middle East, where it had already sold military equipment. In retrospect, it seems clear that most decision makers were deeply concerned about the potential havoc that might follow from the North's acquisition of nuclear weapons and that intervention in light of both the threat and the North's violation of its treaty undertakings was thought to be justified. The inhibition to action would just as clearly have come from concern about the North's reaction, the possibility of a full-scale war on the Korean peninsula, the Chinese reaction, and the willingness of the South Koreans and Japanese to support the move. Given the high stakes for the world community in this case, concerns over North Korean sovereignty simply would not have played a major role in the deliberations of U.S. policymakers.

I conclude by suggesting some criteria for politically supportable humanitarian intervention that seem to emerge from these cases and appear to be consistent with experience in other such cases. Unlike several contributors to this volume, I am not a moral philosopher, and this is not a strictly ethical argument. I am suggesting, however, that ethical concerns are interwoven into the foreign policymaking process, not least because American citizens bring moral considerations to bear when they assess U.S. military intervention for humanitarian rather than purely political reasons. The implicit proposition is that respect for a nation's sovereignty in the face of gross human rights violations would not relieve the United States of its moral obligation, but it also would not relieve the United States of its political obligation to intervene. In fact, it seems to me that the political criteria for intervention outlined below also serve as adequate moral criteria.

First, an intervention must have limited costs and risks associated with it. The cost is the price you expect to pay if things go well, and the risk is a measure of the losses you may sustain if things go badly. The price is measured in lives and dollars as well as intangibles, such as the respect of other nations. When the national security or some vital interest of the United States is claimed to be at risk, such a constraint would not apply. The best case to illustrate this point is Somalia, where there was no national security interest at stake, but the humanitarian concerns were compelling and the costs and risks seemed to be not too great.

The second condition is that the United States act in concert with other nations or international organizations. This is important to Americans not because it dilutes the image of the lone superpower imposing its will for its own political goals, as some observers have argued, but because it avoids the message that the United States is acting as the world's policeman. Americans are not afraid of dominance; they are worried about excessive altruism, about being duped into taking on more of the burden for protecting the world's victims than is in our interest. For some observers, acting in coalition under international mandate provides the legitimacy necessary to overcome the barrier of sovereignty. For Americans, however, it validates a judgment that the cause is worthy enough to incur the costs and take the risks of intervening. Again, Somalia is the best case. The issue does not arise the same way in the cases of Grenada and Korea, where intervention would have been politically defensible to Americans in terms of self-interest.

The third condition is that those whom the United States would presume to help must appear to want the help. There is no virtue in helping someone across the street who does not wish to go. In the Somalia case, the decision to withdraw did not follow the events of October 3–4, 1993, so quickly simply because of the loss of American lives. The widespread call for withdrawal among the public and in the Congress came as much because the killing of Americans appeared to have been so popular on the streets of the Somalian capitol. The peacekeepers had been cast as occupiers; the victims no longer wished to be rescued. The case of Grenada was similar because there was early serious concern in the Reagan administration that the medical students would resist repatriation, making the rescue operation appear foolish. Indeed, there was great relief in the administration when the returning students kissed the tarmac as they deplaned in the United States; that image made the losses sustained in the operation appear justified.

Finally, a humanitarian intervention must have a good prospect of succeeding or of ending fairly promptly. This is not exactly the same point as insisting on an exit strategy. If an intervention fails, the public will expect the government to have planned for an exit. But not all deployments must be short-lived, particularly if the force remaining can be reduced to a relatively small size. As it turns out, some interventions may have to be sustained for a long time, and it may well be possible to sustain popular support for them notwithstanding their duration, provided that the costs and risks remain bounded and the operation generally is regarded as efficient and effective. The Cyprus and Sinai deployments may be reasonable examples; Bosnia and Kosovo will be even better—if they are sustained.

In closing, I should note that respect for territorial sovereignty is not among the criteria I have outlined—for good reason. As the four aforementioned cases indicate, U.S. policymakers do not consider sovereignty a major impediment to military intervention in foreign lands. This view is consistent with that of the majority of American citizens, for whom other moral and political criteria outweigh respect for sovereignty as legitimate reasons to support humanitarian intervention.

11

Religious Allegiance and Political Sovereignty: An Irreconcilable Tension?

PAUL J. GRIFFITHS

"RELIGIOUS ALLEGIANCE" AND "POLITICAL SOVEREIGNTY" are phrases with a wide range of significance—so wide, in fact, that their users are forced to treat them as terms of art and to paint a definitional picture that will fix their use in accord with particular argumentative interests. My definitional picture highlights a fundamental sense in which these phrases identify concepts that cannot coherently be held together. I do this in the service of a deep concern that currently widespread understandings of the claims of the ideal-typical late-modern Westphalian state to sovereignty are destructive of religious identity. There are important senses in which the American experiment with religious liberty within the framework of a constitutional democracy is more destructive of religion than, for example, the Chinese attempts to eradicate Buddhism in Tibet since the 1960s or the Soviet empire's restrictions on the practice of Christianity in the regions under its sway from the 1920s to the 1980s. Gaining some understanding of the ways in which religious allegiance and political sovereignty are in fact at odds will be helpful in understanding how this can be. Out of necessity I paint the picture with a broad and schematic brush. Also, and without apology, I am extreme in both tone and stance. Occupying an extreme position often provokes more—and more useful—thought than sweetly irenic reasonability.

States lay claim to sovereignty; indeed, they are in large part to be understood precisely as entities whose defining characteristic is that they make such a claim. The claim they make has two key elements. The first is to the unsurpassable allegiance of its citizens with respect to the state's core interests—a claim that is evident in the state's monopoly on the use of police power within its boundaries to enforce this allegiance. The second is the state's claim to freedom from external interference in its control of its core interests, whether this interference comes from other states or multinational entities such as McDonalds, the International Monetary Fund, or the Catholic Church. The state ideal typically does not recognize any trump within its boundaries as far as its core interests are concerned. (Of course, this unrestricted claim on the part of states is increasingly under siege by a variety of transnational agencies, principally those concerned with the enforcement of international trade agreements. Nevertheless, the claim remains in place as an ideal.)

The extent to which the state is willing to recognize the sovereignty (and indeed the right to exist) of alien states usually will be indexed to the extent to which the commitments evident in the aliens' political arrangements are like those evident in its own. The greater the likeness, the greater the willingness to acknowledge the sovereignty of the other within its bounds; the less the likeness, the less the willingness. Thus, late-capitalist democratic nation-states have little difficulty in recognizing the sovereignty of other states of that sort and often actively cooperate with them by formal alliance or otherwise (think, for instance, of the special relationship between the United States and the United Kingdom). States of this sort have considerably greater difficulty, however, in acknowledging the sovereignty of (for example) religion-based totalitarianisms: Consider the United States' relation with Afghanistan during the Taliban's rule or its longstanding difficulties with Hussein's Iraq.

So much for state sovereignty. Religious allegiance, by contrast, is an unsurpassable allegiance of a comprehensive sort. If your allegiance is unsurpassable, its claims cannot be trumped. If it is comprehensive, nothing falls outside its embrace: All other allegiances are subsidiary to it, embraced by it rather than existing alongside or in competition with it; when subsidiary allegiances conflict with it, they must be rejected in some fashion, usually by being ignored or actively opposed. Religious allegiance recognizes no trump of any kind. This is why it is such a problem for post-Westphalian nation-states: They were founded principally to tame and domesticate religious allegiance—a more difficult task than it seemed to be at first.

In Christian terms, as in Islamic and Jewish ones, God typically is identified as the only proper recipient of allegiance—from which it follows, first, that all other claimants to allegiance are idols to the extent that they do not recognize their subsidiarity to God, and, second, that people are idolaters with respect to the state to the extent that they treat it as the kind of thing that can make unsurpassable claims. A classical Augustinian form of these claims would be that only God can be enjoyed, and everything that is not God can only be used.[1] For the sake of shorthand in what follows I use the term "God" to identify the proper object of religious allegiance. This is a shorthand, of course, because there are forms of religious allegiance without interest in what Jews, Christians, and Muslims call God. Attention to the appropriate corrections and qualifications would delay the argument for too long, however, were they fully to be entered into here.

These construals of religious allegiance and political sovereignty create an obvious tension of a strictly logical sort. If the state's claims to unsurpassable sovereignty with respect to its core interests within its boundaries are proper, then religious allegiance, as I have defined it, is ruled out of court from the beginning. This is because religious allegiance, so defined, can recognize no form of sovereignty to which its claims are subsidiary in any sphere, and the monopolistic sovereignty of the state is, ideally-typically, just such a form. From the other side of the equation, if religious allegiance really is unsurpassable and comprehensive in the way I have suggested, then the claims of state sovereignty to unsurpassability within the boundaries of the state are improper because those claims are, *ex definitio*, subsidiary to the claims of religious allegiance if they have any force at all. This is the strong form of the tension, a form that generally is conceptually irreconcilable (as I mean to suggest by my title). There are some familiar strategies for dealing with it, however, among which three stand out.

The first is to develop an understanding of the state such that it can itself be understood as the object of a properly religious allegiance. A relatively pure form of this move was evident in Hitler's Germany. More subtle forms were evident in the Holy Roman Empire and perhaps also in Stalin's Russia and Pol Pot's Cambodia. Those who make this move transmute the state into God and make of it a proper object of unsurpassable and comprehensive allegiance.

A second strategy is to develop an understanding of the state such that its claims to sovereignty are properly religious, even though it is not it-self God and its claims are not (or may not be) exhaustive of the de-mands of religious allegiance. This typically means that allegiance to the core interests of the state, however exactly these interests are construed, is understood as a proper part of the demands of religious sovereignty but not as co-extensive with it. Some readers might argue that the forms and procedures of a democratic state (perhaps of the kind that citizens of the United States inhabit) are just what God wants for us in the spheres of social and communal life and that, for precisely that reason, our alle-giance to them in those spheres ought to be unsurpassable for us. Such moves make allegiance to the state's sovereignty an aspect or element of properly religious allegiance.

In a constitutional democracy such as that of the United States, a sign or mark of this move having been made is treatment of the claims of the Constitution as having sacred significance. Exegesis and application of these claims then becomes an aspect of or moment in exegesis and ap-plication of the claims of the religion of which they are now understood to form a part. An example is the tendency among some intellectuals in the United States today, Catholic and Protestant, to argue that be-cause a constitutional justification can be found for a right to legal abor-tion it therefore follows that the existence of such a right commands un-restricted allegiance from American citizens, their other convictions and allegiances notwithstanding. This command follows, according to this second strategy, because a constitutional demand has now become a properly religious claim.

There are nondemocratic forms of this move as well: Perhaps the Tali-ban's efforts to establish a fully Islamic state in Afghanistan provide an example. For them, perhaps, the state had to be transformed into the hand of God, and insofar as this transformation is successfully achieved, its demands are properly treated religiously because they have become a proper part of a broader religious allegiance. To suggest another ex-ample, some elements of the Bharatiya Janata Party (BJP) in India may think of the state in something like this way.

If the first strategy transmutes the nation-state into God, this second strategy transmutes the state's claims into sentences spoken by God and the state into God's political presence here below. A third strategy, deeply different from the first two, is to recognize the irreconcilable tension I have identified and to respond to it by attempting to remove one of the elements in which its irreconcilability consists.

A religious version of this third strategy typically entails radical reduction of the state's claims to sovereignty. These claims are reduced from claims to unsurpassable allegiance within the boundaries of the state to claims of incidental, local, and conventional interest. For instance, if your traffic laws tell you to drive on the left and to stop when the light is red, your religious allegiance may permit you to identify these laws as a matter of local convention and to obey without further ado. Whenever the claims of the state impinge upon the claims of religious allegiance, however, the religious person who follows this third strategy will dismiss them with very little thought. The point of central importance about this strategy is that it makes the state's claims to allegiance largely uninteresting and insignificant.

If the first strategy transmutes the nation-state into God and the second transmutes the state's claims into sentences spoken by God, the religious version of the third strategy understands the state's claims as the trivial or pernicious mutterings of idolaters and the state's sovereignty as a matter of no deep interest or abiding concern.

There are active and passive forms of this third strategy. A passive form, like that of the Old Order Amish in the United States, will retreat from the demands of the state, showing little interest in them, obeying them insofar as they do not conflict with the demands of their religious allegiance, but simply ignoring them when they do. An active form will oppose all claims of the state that are perceived to conflict with those of the religious allegiance and attempt to make the claims of the state coextensive with the claims of the religion. Again, the Taliban might serve as an example.

The third strategy embraces the irreconcilable tension I have identified by recognizing its very irreconcilability and attempting to remove one of the elements that constitute that irreconcilability. I have discussed the religious version of this strategy, according to which the legitimacy of the state's demands as the state understands them is simply denied or ignored. Unsurpassable allegiance for those who follow this strategy is restricted to God. But there is also, of course, a statist version of this strategy. Those who follow this line—and their number is legion in the contemporary United States—deny the legitimacy of religious allegiance as religious men and women ideally-typically understand it (which is as I've sketched it here). They privatize religion, restrict its claims to the preferences of the individual, and use the force of the state's police power whenever religious allegiance produces actions that conflict with the state's demands. The sophisticated conceptual version of this strategy is found in the recent work of the philosopher Richard Rorty, according to which claims produced by religious allegiance are simply incomprehensible in a late-modern democracy, and those who make them seriously and insistently are simply insane.[2]

Rorty's line of thought is the apotheosis of John Locke's. Locke advocated toleration by the state of individuals with religious commitments.[3] But toleration, as John Courtney Murray so elegantly and precisely indicates, is a concept of the moral order that indicates the error of those at whom it is directed.[4] For Locke, as for all contemporary democratic nation-states, permission to act in accord with your religious convictions extends only as far as the persons identifying the core interests of the state say it may; when it goes further, it will be punished by violence. And for Locke, those worthy of such punishment included Catholics ("Papists," as he preferred to call them) and radical dissenters (whom he occasionally labeled "fanatics"). This understanding of toleration is the one on which modern constitutional attempts to define and settle the question of religious liberty are founded. It is interesting to observe this point because it shows that such settlements are shot through with the assumption that the fabric of a fully religious conviction about human life and its setting is woven of error and confusion.

This secular-statist form of the third strategy understands the claims of properly religious allegiance as the insane ravings of the clinically certifiable. And although the pacific and civilized tones of a Rorty on this matter are rhetorically different from those of his Stalinist counterparts in the middle days of the Soviet empire, the conclusion is the same: Religious people ought to be either killed or committed when they step out of line. I would add here, had I space—in support of what might appear to be extreme claims—an application of Michel Foucault's genealogies of clinical ideas about insanity, an exegesis of Aleksandr Solzhenitsyn's impassioned protest against both the Soviet Union and the American empire, and a discussion of Pope John Paul II's increasingly deep criticisms of the social and economic forms fostered by—and probably indissolubly connected with—late-modern democracies. They all make essentially the same point, though in very different keys and registers.[5]

In the United States today, the lively options for thinking about the relations between religious allegiance and political sovereignty are the second strategy and the statist version of the third. According to the second strategy, a construal of religion is found that makes the demands of the state in their sphere worthy of properly religious allegiance. This understanding leads, almost inevitably and certainly in practice in the United States, to the transmutation of God into a servant of the democratic state and of God's word into the constitution of that state. The appropriate icon for this move is Thomas Jefferson's gospel book: a cut-and-paste object, in which he kept the parts he liked and incinerated the parts he didn't. The church rejected Marcion as a dangerous heretic long ago, but Jeffersonian democracy is more dangerous than Marcion, and it's time the church rejected it, too, as an insidious danger. Persons with genuinely religious allegiances should have no more time for extolling the delights of democracy than they have for extolling the delights of totalitarianism. The principle of equivalence here is in part a theological one (avoidance of idolatry) and in part an epistemological one (avoidance of undue epistemic optimism).

According to the third strategy, religious allegiance is a matter of insanity, and religious individuals are to be consigned to the clinic. This position is clear, at least. It ought to be resisted by religious people; if, as is likely, such resistance creates martyrs, from a religious point of view that is nothing but good. The martyr is the ideal type—indeed, the icon of the religious person. That this is the case and so difficult for contemporary Americans to understand may serve as an icon of the central thesis of these brief and inadequate remarks: Religious allegiance and political sovereignty are indeed irreconcilably in tension.

Finally, politics is largely a matter of the imagination. In this it is like sex. The bonds of citizenship have no sacramental reality, which differentiates them from the bonds of marriage or those produced by incorporation by baptism into the body of Christ. The bonds of citizenship also have no biological or physical reality, and this differentiates them from the bonds of biological family. Their reality is of the imagination only. This observation doesn't mean that they are unreal: The imagination has great power. It does mean, however, that if the imagination's gaze is turned away from them for long enough, they will wither. For religious people, I suggest, the time is ripe simply to cease imagining the post-Westphalian nation-state, to cease dreaming that dream. Imaginations of the bonds of democratic citizenship that attempt melioration of the defects of democratic nation-states—well-intentioned imaginations of a civil society ordered around the principle of subsidiarity, for example—will always be coopted (usually in about five minutes) by the market, with its stiflingly unnuanced individualism and its grim identification of freedom with choice. This cooptation has already occurred in the imaginations of civil society that informed some of the Eastern European revolutions of the late 1980s and early 1990s. It would be better for religious people to stop wasting their imaginative energies and instead to dream the dream of martyrdom and to occupy the stance of prophetic critique. That, at least, is a coherent position that is adequate to the fundamental irreconcilability of the claims of religious allegiance and political sovereignty.

On September 11, 2001, many people were killed and much property damaged in New York City and Washington, D.C., by commercial airliners hijacked by persons intent on destructive martyrdom. Those events may illustrate the thesis I argue here. It may be that the people who planned and executed these terrible events did so from an understanding of the full depth of the irreconcilability between the claims to allegiance made by Islam and those to sovereignty—increasingly to world sovereignty—made by American-style polities. If so, I endorse this understanding as accurate, without endorsing the particulars of the action. From the viewpoint of a Catholic Christian (which is the viewpoint from which I make these remarks), what was done was beyond moral defense and can call forth only lamentation and despair. Yet that judgment neither assumes nor implies the reconcilability of the claims to unrestricted sovereignty made by the United States with those comprehensively unrestricted claims to allegiance made by Catholic Christianity (or by Islam). The dreadful events of September 11, 2001, dramatize—and in part may be explicable by—the irreconcilable tension of my title.

Notes

1. For a standard statement of the use/enjoyment distinction in Augustine, see the first book of his *De doctrina christiana*. A translation appears in R. P. H. Green, *Saint Augustine: On Christian Teaching* (Oxford: Oxford University Press, 1999), 8–29. The older Augustine largely abandoned this way of talking, but the distinction remains operative in his thought, even if the language does not.

2. For a representative sample of Rorty's extreme views, see "Religion as Conversation-Stopper," *Common Knowledge* 3 (1994): 1–6.

3. For Locke's views on toleration, see *Essay Concerning Toleration* (1667) and *Epistola de tolerantia* (1685). There is change in his thought on the topic between these two texts, but not of a sort that need detain us here.

4. For John Courtney Murray on toleration as a concept of the moral order, see *Religious Liberty: Catholic Struggles with Pluralism*, ed. J. Leon Hooper (Louisville, Ky.: Westminster/John Knox Press, 1993), 150.

5. For a recent lively analysis of the legal aspects of this irreconcilability, see Stanley Fish, "Mission Impossible: Settling the Just Bounds between Church and State," *Columbia Law Review* 97, no. 8 (1997): 2255–333.

12

Sacred Nonsovereignty

FRED DALLMAYR

IN RECENT TIMES, THEOLOGY HAS TURNED its attention to narrative. In the view of leading practitioners, sacred scripture offers not so much a doctrine or system of ideas as a treasure chest of stories capable of transforming lives. Here is one such story—an instructive one as we consider the relation of the sacred and the sovereign.

After having been captured or apprehended, Jesus was first taken to the high priest and then to Pontius Pilate, who, in line with Roman custom, began to interrogate him—albeit in a half-hearted manner. One question that seemed to intrigue Pilate was the alleged authority or power of Jesus. He asked bluntly, "Are you the king of the Jews?"—to which Jesus answered with a counter-question (according to John 18:34): "Do you say this of your own accord, or did others say this about me?" In the three synoptic gospels the answer is more concise and perhaps more telling (Matthew 27:11, Mark 15:2, Luke 23:3): "You have said so"— which might be rendered as, "These are your words, not mine" or "This is your way of speaking, not mine." Unsurprisingly, Pilate was not satisfied with this response and kept pressuring Jesus on the issue. At this point, Jesus was willing to elaborate a bit more and said (again according to John 18:36), "My 'kingship' is not of this world. If my 'kingship' were of this world, my servants would fight that I might not be handed over to the Jews; but my 'kingship' is not from the world." Taking this answer as a kind of admission, Pilate shot back, "So then you are a king?" To which Jesus gave this memorable reply (John 18:37): "You say that I am a king [or this king-talk is your kind of talking]. But I was born for

one thing, and for this I have come into the world: namely, to bear witness to the truth."

As we know, the biblical story continues and leads the reader ultimately and ineluctably to a somber ending. It will be necessary at a later
point to return to the ending of the story. At this juncture, however, it
seems advisable to stop and reflect briefly on the meaning of the story
recounted so far. First we may wish to glance at the questioner and his
possible motives. It seems reasonable to assume that Pilate, as a provincial governor appointed by imperial Rome, was primarily preoccupied
with political power and governance; from this perspective, Jesus' religious faith or status was for Pilate likely to be a matter of sublime indif-
ference (Pilate's interrogation at no point showed any interest in the
topic). If Jesus was indeed a king—as some people apparently asserted—
then this claim clearly was a cause of apprehension: Politically understood, kingship constituted a challenge to the power or *potestas* of the
governor and ultimately a challenge to the supreme power or *suprema
potestas* of the emperor in Rome—something that later came to be articulated as "sovereignty." No matter how puzzled or irritated Pilate may
have been by the answers he received, these political points were quite
clear in his mind. In modern or contemporary terminology, we might
describe him as a devotee of *realpolitik*—and from the perspective of
realpolitik, only power, especially supreme power, counts.

As the story shows, Pilate—to reduce his confusion—was tempted to
interpret Jesus' replies precisely in terms of his own familiar political
framework. In this respect, Pilate is not alone. As it happens, his interpretation has been a perennial temptation hovering like a shadow over
the history of Christianity (or what some theologians now call "Christendom"). When Jesus stated, "My 'kingdom' is not of this world" or
"from this world," Pilate immediately jumped to the conclusion, "So you
are a king"—perhaps not here and now at this place, but somewhere
else, at another place. It is unlikely that Pilate's mind was able to move
beyond a realist, geopolitical perspective: If Jesus' "kingdom" was not
right here in Judaea, it was probably next door, in some other province—
and as such still a potential danger to Rome's *suprema potestas*. Without
departing entirely from Pilate's geopolitics of place, more metaphysically
inclined readers have interpreted Jesus' statement as postulating

"another world" behind this world, another spiritual kingdom behind the worldly kingdom. According to this metaphysical reading—which reverberates powerfully throughout the ensuing "Christian" centuries—there are basically "two worlds": a spiritual or immaterial world and a worldly or material world; as a corollary, there are two kinds of supreme power: the supreme power or sovereign kingship of God and the *suprema potestas* or sovereignty of worldly rulers. In the view of metaphysical theologians, the two worlds and types of power exist side by side but ultimately are—or should be—related in the mode of subordination: The worldly power responds or is subordinated to divine power—just as a provincial governor (say, Pontius Pilate) was subordinated to imperial Rome.

It was the fault not of Pilate but of his metaphysical successors that Christian religion became embroiled in power plays, in the endless competition for supreme power or sovereignty. Throughout the Christian Middle Ages, Europe was in the grip of intense and nearly interminable struggles between worldly (or temporal) and spiritual (or ecclesiastic) power-holders, with each side claiming to hold the ultimate trump card: the ability to depose and humiliate the other. Whatever damage this contest may have inflicted on "worldly" politics, the price exacted from religious faith was higher. By being sucked into power plays, the metaphysical distinction between "this world" and the "other world," between temporal and spiritual realms, was leveled into a Pilate-style geopolitics—with the result that the presumed omnipotence of God became nearly indistinguishable from the might of a Genghis Khan. In the memorable words of Merleau-Ponty, God was assigned the position of an "absurd emperor of the world."[1] Even after the collapse of the medieval empire, the geopolitical streamlining of religion persisted. Following the horrendous experiences of the religious wars, Europe in the Peace of Westphalia settled on a formula that joined temporal and spiritual power in the hands of a territorial ruler (*cujus regio ejus religio*)—a formula that approximated, at least in part, the caesaro-papist arrangement that was prevalent for a long time in Eastern Christianity. From this time forward, the main energies of churches and religious believers in the West were invested in the struggle to loosen again the juncture of spiritual and temporal realms—a struggle carried on chiefly under the banner of religious freedom or freedom of religious belief. Aided and abetted by the

Enlightenment and other progressive modern tendencies, this struggle for religious freedom was largely successful—but it again exacted a price. In its effort to extricate itself from public-worldly affairs, religious faith increasingly retreated into inwardness or allowed itself to be "privatized." Yet as a purely private affair, the encounter between Jesus and Pilate, as recounted above, becomes pointless or a matter of taste. Under secular-liberal auspices, faith basically becomes an individual pastime—perhaps nobler and "higher" than other pastimes but not substantially different from playing golf or watching video games.

No doubt Western Christianity through the centuries has seen resolute attempts to counteract the cooptation and domestication of religious faith by "worldly" rulers or potentates. In fact, both worldly cooptation and private complacency have been the repeated target of religious resistance or countermovements—sometimes fueled by revolutionary and even millenarian zeal. Students of history will recall the intermittent upsurge of radical antiauthoritarian sects during the Middle Ages, as well as the more effective uprisings of Puritans, Levellers, Diggers, and "*Schwärmer*" during the early part of modernity. In terms of their intrinsic logic, movements of this kind are basically *anti*movements predicated on radical negation: antipolitical, antigovernmental, antichurch, and even antiworld. In lieu of worldly *potestas*, they postulate the annihilation of *potestas*, in lieu of hierarchy some form of anarchy. If one pushes their logic to the extreme, one ultimately arrives at a radical dualism, not far removed from a gnostic Manichaeism: a dualism opposing a purely spiritual realm inhabited by God and his saints to the corrupt "this-worldly" realm ultimately governed by an evil demiurge and his potentates. In the eyes of gnostic millenarians, this dualistic scheme vindicates the project of a radical eschatology or global conflagration: the utter destruction of "this" world with all its evil ways (including politics) leading to the apocalyptic triumph of God and his millenarian (though antipolitical) militants.[2] Even when not carried to this extreme, the spirit of gnostic Manichaeism still hovers behind metaphysical construals of "two worlds" seemingly exiting from geopolitics.

As the example of millenarianism shows, radical antipolitics still is a form of politics, though operating in the mode of denial; like every radical negation or antithesis, antipolitics remains linked to what it denies or rejects. From the perspective of power or *potestas*, one might say that radical antisovereignty still pays tribute to the idea of sovereignty (now construed as negative power or power of destruction). Glancing back at the encounter of Jesus and Pilate, one can readily see that Jesus was not antipolitical in any millenarian sense. At no point during the interrogation does Jesus threaten the destruction of imperial Rome, its provincial governance in Judaea, or political life per se. According to many historians of the period, Jesus probably was quite familiar with the sect of Essenes and their gnostic-dualistic beliefs; nowhere in his ministry or during his trial, however, does he resort to their millenarian rhetoric. He does suggest to Pilate the possibility that armies of "servants" could come to his rescue—yet he immediately adds that this was not going to happen simply because his "kingdom" (if the term was at all applicable) was not a kingdom of that kind, his rulership not the rule of a worldly potentate.

When Jesus was brought before Pilate, one of the specific charges leveled against him by his accusers was that he was "perverting" the people, forbidding them "to give tribute to Caesar" in light of his own, alternative kingship (Luke 23:2). Yet the falsity of this charge must have been evident to Pilate and other Roman authorities—who, no doubt, had kept watch of his public teachings precisely on this issue. They probably were familiar with one particular episode in which Jesus' enemies had tried to lure him into a trap, in the presence of the "Herodians" (who were sycophants of Rome). "Tell us then," his enemies asked him, "is it lawful to pay taxes to Caesar, or not?" Aware of their scheming design, Jesus urged them to produce a piece of money, and when they had done so, he pointed to the coin's surface, asking, "Whose likeness and inscription is this?" When they responded "Caesar's," he told them plainly and without equivocation, "Render therefore to Caesar the things that are Caesar's, and to God the things that are God's" (Matthew 15:17–21).

What this episode reveals is that Jesus at no point aimed to establish a counter-regime to the prevailing political regime, nor an alternative *suprema potestas* to the *potestas* of the provincial governor or imperial Rome. This does not mean that Jesus' life and ministry did not represent a genuine alternative to prevailing politics, but the alternative was predicated neither on competition nor on negation or destruction but on transformation. In other words, his ministry was designed not to trump the world (by establishing a worldly superpower) or to destroy or eradicate this world (along millenarian lines) but to salvage and redeem the world through truth and divine grace. In political terms, Jesus' ministry inaugurated neither a superpolitics nor an antipolitics but an "other" kind of politics—what might be called a politics of sacred or redemptive nonsovereignty. The notion of an "other" kind of politics seems to collide with a widespread (liberal) view that faith is entirely a private matter.

This view, however, is contestable. That religion for Jesus was more than a private idiosyncrasy is evident from the public character of his life and ministry. As he said to the high priest, "I have spoken openly to the world . . . (and) have said nothing in secret" (John 18:20). One of the things Jesus had spoken about publicly was his conception of worldly rulership and community life. As reported in Mark's gospel, two of Jesus' disciples once came to him, asking him to be able to share in God's sovereignty or supreme power (namely, by sitting "one at your right hand and one at your left, in your glory"). Rebuking them, Jesus taught them about nonsovereignty (Mark 10:37–44):

> You know that those who are supposed to rule over the gentiles lord it over them, and their great men exercise power over them. But it shall not be so among you; but whoever would be great among you must be your servant, and whoever would be first among you must be slave of all.

One of the tragedies of Christianity is that Jesus' teachings about nonsovereignty have fallen for so many centuries mostly on deaf ears. Even today, the hankering for sovereignty has not subsided—even among otherwise religious people. One of the standard accusations leveled by religious "fundamentalists" against democratic rule is that democracy challenges or undermines the absolute power or "sovereignty of God."[3] Fortunately, the situation is no longer devoid of encouraging initiatives. Among theologians (Christian and non-Christian), the upsurge of "liberation theology" has put a dent into traditional preoccupations with *suprema potestas* (in both temporal and spiritual domains). Among contemporary political theorists, major strides toward a deconstruction of "sovereignty" have been undertaken especially by Hannah Arendt and Jean Bethke Elshtain. As Hannah Arendt has written pointedly, human freedom and responsibility are incompatible with *suprema potestas*; hence, to salvage these goods, "it is precisely sovereignty that they [people] must renounce"—a view that has been further developed and fleshed out by Elshtain, especially in *New Wine and Old Bottles*.[4] Similar initiatives can be found in the works of recent and contemporary philosophers (sometimes under "postmodern" auspices). Thus, when Claude Lefort writes that in modern democracy the locus of ultimate power becomes "an empty place," he does not simply refer to a vacuum or a negative antisovereignty but to another kind of politics or another way of conceiving political rule—a conception that is not too far removed from the "other" mode of politics often invoked by Jacques Derrida. One of the most significant interventions in this debate has been made by Martin Heidegger, a philosopher who is not often credited with political insight. In several treatises dating from the 1930s, Heidegger formulated the idea of a "power-free" realm (*das Machtlose*)—a realm equally far removed from *suprema potestas* and from the negation of *potestas* or impotence.[5]

Let us put philosophy aside here, however, and return to our initial story. We have left Jesus standing before a puzzled and increasingly bewildered Pilate. As far as this prisoner was concerned, Pilate must have felt completely out of his depth: He did not comprehend the main charges brought against Jesus, and those he did understand were patently false or unsubstantiated. Repeatedly Pilate made an effort to get the charges dropped and to wash his hands of the entire affair, to no avail. Under growing pressure from the accusers, Pilate finally relented and grudgingly pronounced his sentence. From this moment on, the story quickly gathered momentum and hurried to its bitter conclusion. What particularly must have annoyed or irritated Pilate was the fact that, at the moment when he sentenced Jesus, he also was induced or compelled to set another prisoner free. That prisoner's name was Barrabas—and he was "a murderer and an insurrectionist" (Mark 15:7, Luke 23:19). Setting this man free must have greatly irked Pilate because the insurrection was against his own rule and the *suprema potestas* of Rome. Whereas he did not comprehend the crime committed by Jesus, the situation in the case of Barrabas was crystal-clear. As a Roman governor involved all his life in *realpolitik*, he felt comfortably on familiar ground with Barrabas. Together with his fellow insurrectionists, Barrabas operated on the customary ground of *realpolitik* and geopolitical conflict. His aim was basically to replace one power by another power, to substitute the power of the insurrectionists for the *potestas* of Rome. And there was a clear and well-known punishment for insurrection.

By that time, however, things had taken their course and were basically out of Pilate's hands. What followed was the beating and flagellation of Jesus and then the road to Calvary. In the end, however, Pilate managed to take revenge—a peculiar revenge that was unexpected by the accusers. When Jesus was nailed to and hoisted up on the cross, Pilate had an inscription placed over his head that read: "Jesus of Nazareth, king of the Jews." To make sure that passers-by could read the message, Pilate had the sentence written in three languages: Hebrew, Latin, and Greek (John 19:19–20). At this point the accusers had second thoughts about their accusations—a key charge being Jesus' counter-kingship against Rome—and urged Pilate to change the inscription so that it would read not "king of the Jews" but "this man claimed to be king of the Jews." At this juncture, however, Pilate proved to be stubborn; a hard-boiled Roman politician, he had no taste for esoteric double-talk. Having given in too much earlier, he now stood his ground firmly, saying, "What I have written I have written (*Quod scripsi scripsi*)" (John 19:21–22).

At this moment, Pilate—unwittingly and probably against his intentions—became a participant and a witness in a much larger salvation history. The words he had written (perhaps out of spite) reflected a wisdom that great philosophers might envy. So, at the very end, Jesus was proclaimed a "king" after all. But what kind of a king? Surely not a sovereign potentate—not the kind of mighty overlord that one finds among the gentiles whose rulers "lord it over them." A king nailed to a cross and seemingly devoid of all power or *potestas*—except for the power of sacredness or holiness. But then, this is what Jesus had stated at the very beginning of his interrogation when he said that he was born and came into the world for one purpose alone: "to bear witness to the truth"—which is a truth not of empire but of grace and redemption.

Notes

1. Maurice Merleau-Ponty, *In Praise of Philosophy*, trans. John Wilde and James M. Edie (Evanston, Ill.: Northwestern University Press, 1963), 47.

2. On millenarianism see especially Michael Walzer, *The Revolution of the Saints: A Study in the Origin of Radical Politics* (Cambridge, Mass.: Harvard University Press, 1965); see also Howard Hotson, *Christian Millenarianisms: From the Early Church to Waco* (London: Hurst and Co., 2000).

3. For a discussion of this charge, especially in the context of Islamic fundamentalism, see Roxanne L. Euben, *Enemy in the Mirror: Islamic Fundamentalism and the Limits of Modern Rationalism* (Princeton, N.J.: Princeton University Press, 1999), 49–92; see also Fred Dallmayr, "Islam: Friend or Enemy?" *International Studies Review* 3 (2001): 171–74.

4. See Hannah Arendt, "What Is Freedom?" in *Between Past and Future* (New York: Penguin Books, 1980), 164–65; Jean Bethke Elshtain, *New Wine and Old Bottles: International Politics and Ethical Discourse* (Notre Dame, Ind.: University of Notre Dame Press, 1998), especially chapter 1, pp. 6–24 ("Sovereignty at Century's End"). Compare also Daniel Ergester, *Divine Sovereignty: The Origins of Modern State Power* (DeKalb: Northern Illinois University Press, 2001).

5. See Claude Lefort, *Democracy and Political Theory*, trans. David Macey (Minneapolis: University of Minnesota Press, 1988), 17–19; Jacques Derrida, *The Other Heading: Reflections on Today's Europe*, trans. Pascale-Anne Brault and Michael B. Naas (Bloomington: Indiana University Press, 1992), 76–78; Martin Heidegger, *Besinnung*, ed. Friedrich-Wilhelm von Herrmann, *Gesamtausgabe*, vol. 66 (Frankfurt-Main: Klostermann, 1997), 189–91. Compare also Fred Dallmayr, "Heidegger on Macht and Machenschaft," *Continental Philosophy Review* 34, no. 3 (September 2001): 247–67.

🌓 CONCLUSION

Sovereignty after September 11:
What Has Changed?

ERIK C. OWENS

IT WAS SAID WITH SOME FREQUENCY in the days following September 11, 2001, that "everything has changed" in light of the terrorist attacks that brought carnage to Washington, New York, and Pennsylvania. This sentiment has some truth, particularly for those living in the United States, because in so many ways the uncertainty, fear, and suspicion that gripped the nation that day were unprecedented in American history. To be sure, just six years earlier domestic terrorists had murdered innocent civilians on American soil (in Oklahoma City); Americans had endured attacks against the homeland by armed forces both foreign (Britain in 1812, Japan in 1941) and domestic (during the Civil War); and they had been gripped by fear of imminent danger during American involvement in numerous wars both hot and cold. Nevertheless the events of September 11, 2001, were unparalleled: In a few short hours, fewer than twenty foreign terrorists had succeeded in shutting down the entire American civil aviation system, sending American political leaders into secret bunkers, creating chaos of apocalyptic proportions at the center of the nation's largest city, and—most horrifically—killing nearly 3,000 innocent civilians.

These suicide hijackings, combined with the mail-borne anthrax attacks that followed, made our domestic and quotidian activities appear fraught with danger and uncertainty for the foreseeable future. The U.S. government announced that it had only limited ability to detect or prevent future attacks. Every piece of mail; every skyscraper or government office; every large public gathering; every train, bus, or airliner might be the next locus of disaster. The invisible enemy could be anywhere and seemed everywhere at once in light of vague government warnings to "be alert." In short, the United States as a nation was terrorized for the first time, and it is not an overstatement to suggest that this experience has changed the way we think about the world.

It also has been said (by President Bush, among many others) that the terrorist acts of September 11 irrevocably altered the course of international politics. In his address to Congress on September 20, 2001, the president recast global politics into two parties, declaring that "Every nation, in every region, now has a decision to make: either you are with us, or you are with the terrorists." (Who the "us" in that declaration was meant to be has been a matter of some contention. It is plausible that Bush intended it to mean "we who oppose terrorism," but many listeners around the world heard something different and bridled at the notion that all nations must be "with the United States" if they oppose terrorism.) Four months later, in his State of the Union address, Bush offered a memorable moniker for the group of states he deemed to be "with the terrorists": They formed "an axis of evil" in the world that must be prevented—preferably through "regime change"—from spreading weapons of terror and mass destruction. The ramifications of this presidential rhetoric will take years to unfold, but it is clear already that a coalition against terrorism must include states that otherwise oppose U.S. interests and that the world's states will not neatly divide themselves into "pro-American" and "pro-terrorist" alliances, however much they want to avoid the latter distinction. Nevertheless, the contours of a new international coalition against terrorism have emerged that may very well signal a new kind of geopolitical alignment. The challenge for the United States is to prosecute the long "war on terrorism" in such a way that existing tensions between Islamic and western nations are not hardened or exacerbated.

Yet notwithstanding the profound impact of September 11 on American and global political life, it also is clear that *not* everything changed on that terrible day. Terror was brought to American soil that day, but in too many other places around the world the mass murder of innocent civilians has been a gruesomely common feature of the past decade. Rwanda, Sierra Leone, Congo, Bosnia, Kosovo, Sudan, and East Timor provide the readiest examples of large-scale civilian murders, but one could also cite terrorist activity (on a smaller scale than September 11) in dozens of countries from Israel to Northern Ireland to Sri Lanka to Colombia.[1] Although stating the obvious—that violence and terror have been inflicted on other peoples around the world (including Americans traveling or working abroad) in recent years—does nothing to diminish the suffering Americans endured following September 11, it does place that suffering in a broader context. The sacredness of human life is always at risk of being violated, even on a large scale; regrettably but perhaps inevitably, Americans have rejoined the global chorus of lament for the sufferings inflicted by the wicked and malicious on the innocent.

Some of the lessons to be drawn from the terrorist attacks of September 11 will require more information and a longer historical perspective than we have at present. For example, much of the testimony given during congressional hearings on the failure of American intelligence agencies remains secret for reasons of national security, and we do not yet know the full extent of al-Qa`ida's presence in the United States before or after the attacks. Even at this early point, however, we can discern some important lessons about the relationship between the sacred and the sovereign in international politics after September 11. Most important, although the modern (Westphalian) archetype of sovereignty faces many challenges today,[2] September 11 teaches us that we ought to resist this trend and focus on *strengthening* the sovereign states system. In a nutshell, this means that the international community should force states to uphold the positive requirements their sovereignty entails—which is to say, we need more *responsible* sovereign states.

Sovereign Rights and Responsibilities

Despite the anarchic nature of international relations (in terms of the absence of supra-state authority), the Westphalian system is predicated on the notion that states will maintain order within their boundaries. Sovereignty entails both rights and responsibilities, and states that fail to fulfill their basic responsibilities jeopardize their sovereign rights. Traditionally, the rights of sovereignty include recognition of both internal supremacy (meaning that the state is the final arbiter of domestic disputes and the highest law and authority within a territory) and external independence (meaning that the state has the right to be free from interference by other states, assuming that it does not act aggressively toward them).[3]

Recognition of a sovereign state's rights is contingent, however, on fulfillment of the correlate responsibilities of sovereignty. These responsibilities—the normative dimension of the Westphalian tradition—have been codified in a wide range of covenants, charters, and international laws that partly constitute what Daniel Philpott calls the "constitution of international society."[4] The most prominent such code is the United Nations (UN) charter, Article 2 of which states, "All members, in order to ensure to all of them the rights and benefits resulting from membership, shall fulfill in good faith the obligations assumed by them in accordance with the present Charter." In their relations with other states, each member state of the UN has a duty to settle disputes by peaceful means; refrain from "the threat or use of force against the territorial integrity or political independence of any state"; and provide assistance to the UN when it takes "preventive or enforcement action." Within their own borders, states have an obligation to maintain peace and order, protect innocent citizens from harm, and respect the basic human rights of all persons, including the right of self-determination.[5] As Pope John Paul II has noted, "The state is firmly sovereign when it governs society and also serves the common good of society and allows the nation to realize its own subjectivity, its own identity."[6]

The extent to which states that fail to fulfill their basic responsibilities jeopardize their sovereign rights is a matter of some contention. International lawyers and political theorists often disagree about whether the concept of sovereignty admits degrees.[7] The former usually argue that there are no degrees of sovereignty in international law—an entity is either sovereign or it is not, and the existence of sovereignty is purely a result of recognition by a critical mass of other sovereign states. The latter, by contrast, often present sovereignty as a characteristic of which states can have more or less. This is the view I employ here because the concept of degrees of sovereignty carries special relevance in the context of a state's rights and responsibilities.

When sovereignty is considered as admitting degrees, we may say that almost every state's sovereignty has been eroded in recent decades by a cluster of related "revolutions" in technology and communication. Globalization has made it impossible for a single state to completely control the flow of ideas—not to mention capital, pathogens, pollution, and weapons—across its borders.[8] (Indeed, the very notion of globalization implies the erosion of national boundaries—a fact that takes on new significance after September 11 because porous national borders are now considered more of a national security threat than a boon to commerce.) The result, argues Susanne Hoeber Rudolph, is that the "monopoly sovereignty" that states have long enjoyed is "thinning out," giving up and sharing space with many transnational religious and political organizations and activities that overlay the territorial map.[9] Other scholars of religion and politics, including Robin Lovin and Nicholas Onuf, agree that the state can no longer fully and consistently meet all the responsibilities that sovereignty requires of it, so citizens must look to other institutions—nongovernmental (e.g., human rights organizations), intergovernmental (e.g., various UN agencies), transnational (e.g., corporations and religious institutions), or subnational (e.g., local terrorist groups or gangs)—to provide some of their basic needs. (See chapter 7 for more on this point.)[10]

These institutions are formidable, and likely permanent, challenges to states' control over their domestic affairs, but it remains the case that there is no substitute for state power. Although nongovernmental organizations (NGOs), intergovernmental organizations, transnational groups, and substate actors play an increasingly important role in the world, they continue to rely on the regulatory, enforcement, and civil mechanisms of states.[11] Much has changed since Josef Stalin cynically asked, "How many divisions has the pope?" but his question still has resonance—not just for the Vatican but for the UN as well. The UN may send peacekeepers or aid workers into war-torn regions (it currently has fifteen active peacekeeping operations around the world), but its famous blue helmets are worn by soldiers from national armies. These peacekeepers can be withdrawn at any point at the will of their leaders, as President Bush threatened to do in July 2002 in a flap about immunity from the International Criminal Court (ICC). When states oppose the activities of trans-, sub-, or supranational organizations, it is the state (or a coalition of states) that generally wins the day. The "war on terrorism," after all, is primarily an *international* war against transnational, substate terrorist organizations; the UN and other nonstate actors such as corporations will assist the process, but capturing or otherwise thwarting terrorism requires the unique powers of states.

Furthermore, the aforementioned weakening of state sovereignty does not constitute a complete failure of sovereign responsibility. Clearly, there are distinctions to be made between a general weakening of sovereignty across the international system and the troublesome status of "weak" and "failed" states. Weak states (also called "semi-failed states" or "quasi-states")[12] are those that lack sufficient development, infrastructure, political culture, civil society, or enforcement ability to fulfill their responsibilities as a sovereign state. Weak states usually are impoverished, but there remains a government with limited authority and some semblance of order among the citizenry; present-day Colombia provides an example. The term "failed states" usually is reserved for states that cannot or will not safeguard minimal civil conditions (peace, order, security, rule of law, etc.) within their borders. The chaos, lawlessness, and corruption that reign in failed states are largely self-inflicted (i.e., not brought on solely by natural disaster, poverty, or military occupation by another nation), and their citizens suffer mightily as a result. In short, failed states "are hollow juridical shells that shroud an anarchical domestic condition."[13] Domestic anarchy is fertile soil for a host of problems with international consequences, including terrorism, money laundering, and illegal trafficking of weapons, drugs, and people. By most accounts, failed states of the past decade include Rwanda, Somalia, Afghanistan, Sudan, Sierra Leone, and, arguably, Yugoslavia.

The existence of failed states is partly the result of the post–World War II globalization of the norm of sovereignty itself.[14] As Robert Jackson has argued, until the mid-twentieth century sovereignty carried with it normative civic dimensions that forced states to be responsible members of the international community; thus, the "burdens of empire" were placed on "civilized" nations to supervise peoples who could not sustain a robust independent civic culture. Jackson called this a regime of "positive sovereignty." By the 1960s, however, colonialism had been largely discredited, and the remainder of the century would see the establishment of dozens of new sovereign nations. These new norms of sovereignty that accompanied the rejection of colonialism legitimized all states as sovereign; "negative" sovereignty, as Jackson called it, merely entailed exclusive control of a territory with internationally recognized borders. States clamored to assume the rights of internal supremacy and external independence but neglected or failed to affirm their responsibilities—notably to their own citizens. By making negative state sovereignty the global norm, the international community has recognized the creation of many states that are too weak to protect their citizens' interests.[15] It is largely the failure of states to live up to their responsibilities— to meet citizens' most basic needs and to create policies and regimes with which citizens can identify—that has strengthened support around the world for substate and transnational actors such as al-Qaʿida.

Failed states have always been a concern for diplomats and policymakers, especially those who represent the great powers, because an internally lawless or externally aggressive state destabilizes—and thereby defeats the purpose of—the sovereign states system. The terrorist attacks of September 11 have placed these concerns near the top of the U.S. foreign policy agenda. Although al-Qaʿida is thought to operate "cells" in dozens of countries around the world, including those with functioning governments and strong civil societies, the terrorist organization's leaders have located their primary bases in Afghanistan (a failed state until the recent "regime change" by American-led forces) and Yemen (a weak state in which the government does not control wide areas that are under tribal control). Terrorism experts have speculated that the next sanctuaries for al-Qaʿida leaders, presumably routed from Afghanistan, will be Pakistan and Somalia—another failed state, and thought to have been the planning site for the 1998 bombings of U.S. embassies in Kenya and Tanzania.[16]

What, then, should be done about these weak and failed states that may become the next home to terrorist cabals plotting a follow-up to September 11? Ignoring the problem by refusing to assist failed states is no longer an option; if the U.S. foreign policy establishment once doubted the relevance of failing states and their domestic struggles to American national security, that attitude clearly is not predominant any more. In post–September 11 America, we are unlikely to hear a reprise of former Secretary of State James Baker's statement about Bosnia: "We have no dog in this fight." Covert or overt attempts at "regime change," as executed in Afghanistan and currently contemplated for Iraq, are likely to require sustained military action with uncertain political results.

Neither policy—avoidance or conflict—is likely to create long-term regional or national stability, and neither policy addresses the underlying injustice that citizens of weak and failed states usually suffer.

One systemic approach to the problem of failed states would entail making the rights of sovereignty harder to obtain in the first place. In other words, we could strive for a reinstatement of a regime of positive sovereignty—to require, in essence, that a state be strong in a civic sense before it is granted the privilege of political sovereignty by the world community. Yet this shift, however well-intentioned, is unlikely to occur, in part because rejecting sovereign statehood to peoples who seek self-determination runs counter to the anti-imperial impulses that came to dominate international relations in the past half-century. Making existing states more responsible—more accountable to the norms of sovereignty—is possible, however, through the measured use of carrot and stick. The stick is the threat of economic sanction, diplomatic isolation, or military intervention designed to encourage states to uphold basic conditions of order and justice. John Kelsay draws on a variant of this argument in chapter 5 of this book; he contends that military intervention is legitimate when a state fails to uphold its responsibility to establish and maintain a just social order within its borders. "The sovereignty of states and the integrity of borders," writes Kelsay, "are in some sense related to, even dependent upon, adherence to standards of justice."[17]

By definition, however, weak and failed states lack the political culture, civil society, and government authority required to sustain a just social order. A long-term solution therefore requires much more than threats of economic punishment or military intervention; it demands the sustained engagement of developed nations with weak and failed states that currently cannot fulfill their obligations as sovereigns. Such engagement would marshal the vast economic, diplomatic, and technological resources of the developed world to help build a self-sustaining civil society in states that could thereby earn the prerogatives of sovereignty. This strategy will entail building roads; monitoring elections; training policemen, politicians, and soldiers; opening schools; encouraging free trade; and perhaps even helping to draft a new constitution (as several Americans did for the world's newest sovereign nation, East Timor). In short, as Sebastian Mallaby has noted, only "the much-maligned process of nation-building" can make a long-term difference for weak or failed states.[18] Because of their intellectual expertise, practical experience, or political neutrality, NGOs can be important partners in such nation-building efforts, but states remain best equipped to begin the process by ending existing violent conflicts (through military or police action) and financing the work of the nation-builders.

There is a certain irony in the fact that George W. Bush, who dismissed nation-building during the 2000 presidential campaign as both dangerous (for the American soldiers often charged with the task) and wasteful (for the American taxpayers), now finds himself in the business of building a new Afghan nation. Whether he and his advisors will apply the lesson to other weak or failed states remains to be seen, though his comments in June 2002 about the future American role in building a sovereign Palestine are hopeful.[19]

It is important to note that the difference between nation-building and imperialism can be extremely thin. Mallaby argues that effective nation-building *must* be imperialist: "The logic of neoimperialism is too compelling for the Bush administration to resist," he writes.

> The chaos in the world is too threatening to ignore, and existing methods for dealing with that chaos [viz. economic aid and non-imperialist forms of nation-building] have been tried and found wanting. . . . The question is not whether the United States will seek to fill the void created by the demise of European empires, but whether it will acknowledge that this is what it is doing. Only if Washington acknowledges this task will its response be coherent."[20]

Weak and failed states are problematic (from a foreign policy standpoint), however, primarily because they are chaotic and threaten the international system of states, not because they fail to mirror the political and cultural values of Western democracies. Mallaby surely is correct that to strengthen failed states, would-be nation-builders must begin by creating (or reviving) local political institutions that make economic development possible. These institutions, however, need not become outposts of a new American empire that thrusts its political and cultural values upon the traditional tribal societies that predominate in most failed states. Disestablishment of religion, for example, is a central principle of American constitutionalism, but it is not a necessary component of all stable and just states (as many European nations demonstrate), and it need not be a goal of nation-building in Islamic societies.[21]

I have suggested in this chapter that the terrorist attacks of September 11, 2001, highlight the dangers of failed states for the world community. Failed states not only spill chaos into neighboring countries and regions, they also serve as safe havens for terrorists, arms dealers, and drug kingpins. Therefore it is essential, in my view, that the community of "responsible" sovereigns—states that earn the *privileges* of sovereignty by fulfilling the *responsibilities* of sovereignty—agree to undertake a concerted effort to establish and promote justice, order, and the rule of law in failed and weak states around the globe. This effort, of course, will require many forms of nation-building and a massive commitment of many kinds of resources (economic, diplomatic, and technological), but it will be much more effective and less costly than confronting the scourges of failed states for decades to come.

Notes

1. For descriptions of acts of genocide, war crimes, and crimes against humanity perpetrated in these nations, see Samantha Power, *"A Problem from Hell": America and the Age of Genocide* (New York: New Republic/Basic Books, 2002).

2. The challenges to sovereignty I have in mind arose during the twentieth century and include decolonization, humanitarian intervention, globalization, and the growing influence of transnational organizations. For a discussion of these challenges and an account of the "modern archetype of sovereignty," see the introduction to this book.

3. Much has been written about the rights enjoyed by sovereign states. See notes 1 and 22 in the introduction to this book for a sampling of helpful resources, especially Robert Jackson, "Sovereignty at the Millennium," *Political Studies* 47 (1999): 425, and Daniel Philpott, "Sovereignty: An Introduction and Brief History," *Journal of International Affairs* 48, no. 2 (winter 1995): 357–58.

4. See chapter 2 ("The Constitution of International Society") of Daniel Philpott, *Revolutions in Sovereignty: How Ideas Shaped Modern Institutions* (Princeton, N.J.: Princeton University Press, 2001).

5. United Nations Charter, Article 2, paragraphs 3–5. As Gene Lyons and Michael Mastanduno have noted, these are significant limitations on the exercise of sovereignty. These limitations are qualified, however, by paragraph 7 of the same article, which states, "Nothing contained in the present Charter shall authorize the United

Nations to intervene in matters which are essentially within the domestic jurisdiction of any state or shall require the Members to submit such matters to settlement under the present Charter." See Gene Lyons and Michael Mastanduno, "Introduction," in *Beyond Westphalia? State Sovereignty and International Intervention*, ed. Gene Lyons and Michael Mastanduno (Baltimore: Johns Hopkins Press, 1995), 8.

6. These remarks were made in a homily the pope delivered in Poland in 1983. Quoted in Jean Bethke Elshtain, *New Wine and Old Bottles: International Politics and Ethical Discourse* (Notre Dame, Ind.: Notre Dame University Press, 1998), 22–23.

7. Thomas Weiss and Jarat Chopra, "Sovereignty under Siege: From Intervention to Humanitarian Space," in Lyons and Mastanduno, *Beyond Westphalia?*, 99–100.

8. Anne-Marie Slaughter, "The Real New World Order," *Foreign Affairs* 76 (September/October 1997): 183–97.

9. Susanne Hoeber Rudolph, "Religion, States, and Transnational Civil Society," in *Transnational Religion and Fading States*, ed. Susanne Hoeber Rudolph and James Piscatori (Boulder, Colo.: Westview Press, 1997), 11–12.

10. In chapter 7 of this book, Robin Lovin contends that international organizations must acquire some of sovereignty's original trappings—including the ability to generate a sense of awe and emerge as a source of identity and loyalty among those who otherwise lack power within the nation-state—if they are to be effective. *Cf.* Nicholas Onuf, "Intervention for the Common Good," in Lyons and Mastanduno, *Beyond Westphalia?*, 43–58.

Stephen Toulmin offers a memorable literary analogy of the constraints that states now face in trying to fulfill their responsibilities. Whereas Thomas Hobbes' conception of the nation-state required overwhelming force concentrated in one sovereign ruler (the Leviathan), in Jonathan Swift's Lilliput, power and influence—not brute force—carry the day. Today we live in a Lilliputian world, Toulmin writes: "If the political image of Modernity was Leviathan, the moral standing of 'national' powers and superpowers will, for the future, be captured in the picture of Lemuel Gulliver, waking from an unthinking sleep, to find himself tethered by innumerable tiny bonds [of NGOs such as Amnesty International, the Catholic Church, the UN, etc.]." Stephen Toulmin, *Cosmopolis: The Hidden Agenda of Modernity* (Chicago: University of Chicago Press, 1992), 198.

11. International legal theorist Anne-Marie Slaughter often has made this point, though she argues that state power is being disaggregated by the forces of globalization. That is, the specific functions of states (e.g., judicial, legislative, regulatory, military) are fusing across state boundaries in a process she calls transgovernmentalism. See, for example, her seminal essay "The Real New World Order."

12. See, for example, Robert H. Jackson, *Quasi-states: Sovereignty, International Relations, and the Third World* (Cambridge: Cambridge University Press, 1990).

13. Robert H. Jackson, "Surrogate Sovereignty? Great Power Responsibility and 'Failed States,'" Working Paper no. 25, Institute of International Relations (Vancouver: University of British Columbia, November 1998), 2–3.

14. See Sebastian Mallaby, "The Reluctant Imperialist: Terrorism, Failed States and the Case for American Empire," *Foreign Affairs* 81, no. 2 (March/April 2002): 2–7.

15. In *Quasi-states*, Jackson distinguishes between positive and negative conceptions of sovereignty—the former granted only to nations with robust political cultures, the latter offered *pro forma* to practically any state with exclusive control over a territory. For a concise summary of this distinction, see John Kelsay's discussion of Jackson in chapter 5 of this book.

16. Ewen MacAskill, "Other Countries Could Face U.S. Military Action," *The Guardian* [London], 17 November 2001; Mike Williams, "What Next for al-Qaeda?" BBC News, 27 November 2001, available at http://news.bbc.co.uk/hi/english/world/south_asia/newsid_1678000/1678467.stm.

17. John Kelsay, "Justice, Political Authority, and Armed Conflict: Challenges to Sovereignty and the Just Conduct of War," chapter 5 of this book, 129.

18. Mallaby, "The Reluctant Imperialist," 4. On nation-building and American imperialism, see also Michael Ignatieff, "Nation-Building Lite," *New York Times Magazine*, 28 July 2002; Mark Danner, "The Struggles of Democracy and Empire," *New York Times*, 9 October 2002; Fareed Zakaria, "Our Way: The Trouble with Being the World's Only Superpower," *The New Yorker*, 14 and 21 October 2002, 72–81; and Stephen G. Brooks and William C. Wohlforth, "American Primacy in Perspective," *Foreign Affairs* 81, no. 4 (July/August 2002): 20–33.

19. See "President Reiterates Path for Peace in Middle East," White House press release, 26 June 2002; available at www.whitehouse.gov/news/releases/2002/06/20020626.html.

20. Mallaby, "The Reluctant Imperialist," 6.

21. Established religions exist in many states around the world, from the United Kingdom to the United Arab Emirates, with little effect on their political stability. Although many of the world's weak and failed states have primarily Muslim populations (e.g., Somalia, Afghanistan, Yemen, Sudan), others have been primarily Christian (Rwanda) or a mixture of several religions (Sierra Leone, Yugoslavia, Liberia).

Confessions of a Former Arabist

JOSHUA MITCHELL

WERE I A YOUNGER MAN, I no doubt would feel the sort of rage that is appropriate to youth over the terrorist attacks on the United States. To be sure, I would still offer prayers for the victims, their families, and the future. Sadly, however, the human animal is not long sustained by prayer and sympathy, least of all young men who dream of glory and revenge. Before September 11, 2001, it was long unthinkable to speak of glory and revenge, and perhaps in the distant future we will again think such ideas are archaic; we have heard much about them in recent months, however, and we will continue to hear much more in the years ahead. For now, the liberal peace of which we have dreamed has been deferred. The End of History, it seems, has been postponed.

In my youth—when I was too young, in fact, to know anything of glory and vengeance—I lived in countries that most of my friends in the United States did not know even existed until a decade ago: Kuwait and Yemen. It is always difficult to reconstruct the memories of one's youth because fact and fiction intermingle, and the angle of events is always acute. My father had emerged from World War II, like so many others, with a grand optimism that the world could be made a far better place than the one he had witnessed. A dozen years later, with a Ph.D. from Princeton in hand, he found himself a representative of the United States in a region of the world he knew through long nights of study and the fortune of family lineage—the latter serving him as a sort of intuitive compass during his years at Princeton and beyond. In Yemen, we were one of the first families to represent the United States—a fact that so irritated the Soviets that they suggested to the government officials there that we might be members of the intelligence community. Six months into our stay, we were given twenty-four hours to burn our documents and leave the country. I departed with dim but durable memories of lazy, bumpy treks along steep mountain paths, securely snuggled next to my four-year-old twin sister in a saddle on the back of a donkey, escorted only by kind but impoverished guides, in whom my parents had unwavering trust. It was the age of martinis and Kent cigarettes, when U.S. citizenship brought honor—and more than a little envy, too—in a world still digging out from the destruction of a world war.

The Kuwait of my youth was not without a measure of quiet stability. Our life was sheltered by compound walls, beyond which lay a vast ocean of sand into which new roads to the embassy had to be cut each time we ventured out. Beyond this shimmering granular ocean was the Red Sea, where we would spend hour after spectacular hour body surfing on waves that broke gently on beaches that seemed to stretch without interruption to even more mysterious lands without names to the south. Twenty-five years ago I returned in search of a past I thought could be retrieved, or at least confirmed—only to discover that forty-story skyscrapers now occupied my beaches. I have not gone back again.

After our two-year stay in Kuwait, my father took a position as a professor of modern Middle Eastern history at the University of Michigan in Ann Arbor. The year 1963 was a momentous one in the United States: confusing to those firmly interwoven into its social fabric, bewildering to a little boy of eight who still dreamed in Arabic and who had no firm recollection of a country that was his own by law but foreign by any other measure. My father's book on Muslim fundamentalism, *The Society of the Muslim Brothers*,[1] so long in coming, was finally published in 1969, in no small part because his doctoral advisors—and, at times, even he—did not believe that fundamentalism of any persuasion could withstand the overriding power and logic of modernization. That, of course, was two years after yet another great Arab-Israeli war. Although I dimly recall my father talking about any number of public debates in which he had participated at that time (as well as during the 1973 war), my only tangible recollections are of packed meetings at Hillel House, the local Jewish Community Center, where whatever convergence of the minds that had occurred between the two sides was always brought to an abrupt halt by the testimony of a teary-eyed survivor of the Holocaust. Properly speaking, there is no possible response to such testimony because its warrant to authority was the horror of the event itself. My father knew this but sought, without success, to find a balance between the two sides.

I have indicated that I am a former Arabist. That is true, though not in the strictest, vocational, sense. That was my father's labor; I absorbed his sentiments and sympathies more by osmosis than by study. I received my instruction through his numerous travels, the innumerable guests, the late-night meetings and parties with bright-eyed graduate students at our home near campus. His views were less opposed to Israel than in favor of a kind of civilized respect, which he thought would have to be the precondition for any stable resolution of a problem that seemed long-standing even after the 1973 war. I concurred then, as I do now.

The anniversary of my father's death, nearly two decades distant, occurred the day after the worst attack on the United States in its nearly 400-year history, from colonial times to the present day. I could not help but wonder, on that horrible day, what he would have said if he were still alive. (The labors of his life were brought home in an even more poignant way when the first videotape released by Usama bin Ladin after the attack revealed an elder associate, seated to bin Ladin's left, who had been a member of the Egyptian fundamentalist group that my father had studied so long ago, and perhaps even interviewed.) Sons do not always follow their fathers, however, so speaking on their behalf often is a hazard. Yet like my father I am a professor, and in a field not wholly unrelated to his: the history of political thought as it has developed in the West. I retain my deep affection for the peoples of the Arab world, but it is trumped, decisively, by what I have gleaned in my own long labors as a scholar of the political achievements of the Anglo-American world. It is in that capacity that I offer my thoughts here, though with a debt to all that I learned in another lifetime so long ago in the Middle East.

There has been talk recently that a war has been waged not on the United States alone but on civilization itself. This assertion, I think, is only partly correct. To cast the matter in this way invites us to speak in terms of a "clash of civilizations," which is an unhelpful and horribly dangerous way to couch the problem. The *direct* issue before us is not the fate of civilization but the fate of nation-states. More specifically, the question is whether nation-states are to be the political institutions that will carry civilization forward in this century. The great accomplishment of the West in the past half-millennium has been the development of the nation-state. For all of its problems, which are legion, the nation-state remains our best guarantee against the alternatives of individual anarchy, tribalism, or a global universalism without content—all of which are being entertained today, in one form or another.

In the Middle East, the nation-state does not have a long historical pedigree and for that reason is a fragile affair, susceptible to greater instabilities than we in the Anglo-American world imagine. We now stand, however, on a historical precipice: For civilization to survive, the nation-state cannot be allowed to be threatened by men who are given cover by other nation-states, in the Middle East or elsewhere, who want it both ways. That is, a nation-state is a responsible world actor, whose rights of sovereignty are coterminous with its obligation to play by the rules that emerge in times of relative peace. To consent, even tacitly, to harboring men whose intention is to destroy other nation-states is to renounce, entirely, the right to sovereign integrity; it is to declare war, without firing a shot, on the very idea of the nation-state as the carrier of civilization; it is to announce to the agents of commerce around the globe that there shall be no security of contracts, no rule of law, no rights of property. It is to declare, to citizens within its borders and without, that trust means nothing and that power here will be arbitrary.

Our new century will be, I fear, a sober test of our willingness to defend the nation-state—not, I hope, in the name of "nationalism" but because the alternatives are far worse. Let us not speak about "defending civilization" because that will surely lead to an escalation of conflict beyond its true bounds. Nation-states within all of the distinct world civilizations are threatened by what happened in New York, Washington, and the farmlands of Pennsylvania. Yet it also is undeniably the case that all of the nations of the Middle East, whatever their disposition toward, or complicity in, terrorist acts of war, will now be tested. And they will be evaluated by the world community not on the basis of the beauty of their culture, the dignity of their history, or their manner of bearing suffering with equanimity but by whether they are able to achieve, perhaps before the long period of gestation that otherwise would be necessary, the substance and form of a nation-state that will be required for civilization to endure.

For the nation-state to take hold in the Muslim world, however, it will be necessary to go far beyond institution-building and international philanthropy. Evidence suggests, for example, that the men involved in the terrorist attacks of September 11, 2001, had their own "fathers" in mind. I use this term loosely, of course, but it is not off the mark to see in the actions of terrorist "sons" a rebellion against those who have maintained their hold on power in the Middle East. Through a twofold strategy the "fathers," on one hand, cater to Western power in the international community while on the other hand they condemn the West in internal politics as a way of placating—but not including—"militant Islam" at home. Egypt and Saudi Arabia may be the best examples. Although Islam may well be a religion of peace, the sad fact remains that no nation-state has been able to retain its fidelity to Islam and simultaneously become a stalwart defender of the nations. We may squabble about exceptions (Turkey comes to mind), but the fact that they *are* exceptions is reason enough to pause. Not by accident, then, did these "sons"—whose own "fathers" back home had adopted the corrupt strategy I have mentioned—set about their business in Afghanistan, a place that in effect had no "fathers" or state rulers. The terrorist "sons" want nothing of the trappings of their "fathers." They want nothing of the nation-state. The "sons" want a "nation of Islam" that transcends national borders, which are the only evidence they need of the hegemony of the West.

It is no accident, moreover, that the terrorist "sons" had glory on their mind. Glory is a "manly" virtue, the psychic fuel of empire and dominion—as Augustine pointed out a long time ago in *The City of God*.[2] Whenever the "sons" get it into their mind that their "fathers" have betrayed them, it will not be long before they dream of glory—even of glorious deaths. This lust for glory is powerful indeed, yet monotheism, in each of its three branches, has declared that glory belongs to God and does not accrue to His creatures. In this regard, talk of the terrorists' "courage" is quite misguided. Courage, Plato tells us in *The Republic*, requires wisdom, which involves knowing what is worth dying for and why. Courage therefore cannot involve any psychological dynamic that touches on the betrayal or perceived weakness of the "fathers." Some observers have said that the terrorists were courageous. This claim is erroneous, I think. Courage is deliberative. The desire for glory is *genetic*, as it were, in that it has as its reference point the generative relationship between the sons and the fathers.

Beyond the betrayal of the fathers and the motivation of glory, there is yet another problem that may be even more ominous: the relationship between science and religion. Islam, it will be rightly said, advanced the sciences while Europe lapsed into barbarism. Must it not therefore be able to accommodate science? This formulation, however, misunderstands what is at issue. The question is not whether at any given period Islam and science were compatible but what Islam's response was when scientific advances no longer comported with the cosmology set forth in its holy teachings. The West had such a crisis at the time of Galileo, and Christianity survived it. Islam did not emerge similarly undamaged. In *Democracy in America*, Tocqueville suggested that Christianity—unlike Islam—proffers only *general* specifications about the relations between the Divine and the human economy, but not a scientific cosmology against which the advances of science would clash. The First Article of the Nicene Creed—*I believe in God the Father, Creator of Heaven and Earth*—is mute with respect to the features of the cosmos and their respective relationship one to another, as well as the manner in which, together or in part, they can be known; thus, it can accommodate a vast array of scientific and technological advancements. To be sure, there is ongoing tension between Christianity and science, which Darwin's work only heightened. Yet whatever theoretical difficulties there are, it remains a bald fact to be reckoned with that the United States—the most religious nation in the world, with the possible exception of Iran—also is the most scientifically advanced. Although one can imagine saying that about the Persia of a different age, no present-day Islamic nation can make anything remotely resembling this claim. This long-standing problem has been brought into relief in the Muslim world in direct proportion to the scientific advances in the West. It predates the ascent of Israel as a nation-state and directs our attention to a far deeper source of acrimony within the Muslim world than does U.S. foreign policy toward Israel, which is so often invoked as the primary source of Muslim "grievances." A Palestinian state is surely needed, and U.S. foreign policy in the Persian Gulf region must be recalibrated to a post–cold war world, but let us be good doctors and diagnose the disease at its root.

The achievement of stable nation-states in the Muslim world will require, above all, political representation of the sort that renders commerce not only possible but also a desirable end of life. This need not be crass commercialism of the sort that our pundits suggest is the only possible outcome of such a view. The great lesson of early-modern Europe was that the real alternative to commerce was glory through warfare. For all of the limitations of commerce, the discovery of the West was that commerce saved us from glory, which was worse. Commerce can become a vehicle for glory, to be sure; at its best, however, it defangs the desire for glory that originally animated it. The terrorist "sons," as I have noted, have chosen glory to avenge the impotence of their "fathers." The discovery of the West was that the "fathers" needed less to be avenged than to be periodically replaced through a system of political representation that ousted them when their hold on power betrayed their charge. Replaced they were, by "sons" who thought they could do better—and by "daughters" as well.

Commercial republics are the great achievement of the West today—the fruit of many centuries of trial and error, a great deal of rumination, and no small amount of spilt blood. At their best, they guard against inept or tyrannical "fathers," redirect the passion of glory toward commerce, and use the advances of science to secure that ephemeral but worthy objective: well-being.

I do not put forth this solution without great hesitation because I well know that the formulation I have offered is a distinctly Western one, which emerged out of battles that were waged *within* Christianity itself. So understood, it is not at all clear that similar conclusions can be reached about the importance of the nation-state from *within* Islam. I do know for certain, however, that *if* the nation-state is to take hold in the Muslim world—without being a cloak behind which the corruption of the "fathers" can be masked to both the international and the domestic community—it is going to have to do so from within, so to speak. Prompted by the terrorist attacks, Islam stands on the threshold of this event.

For our part, then, let us not allow the rage of youth to confuse and misdirect our attention from the very real and credible threat we now face. The issue is whether the Muslim world, *on foundations of its own*, has the wherewithal to participate in the community of nations. The alternatives are that it will encounter the world as a supposedly universal "Nation of Islam" or as particular tribes of ethnic communities that speak the language of universalism without being able to coordinate the sort of society that makes even a modicum of well-being possible. The seventeenth century first ushered the era of nation-states into the West. The twenty-first century, I fear, will either witness the global advent of the nation-state or the suffering of us all.

Notes

1. Richard P. Mitchell, *The Society of the Muslim Brothers* (London: Oxford University Press, 1969).

2. See Augustine, *City of God*, trans. Henry Bettenson (New York: Penguin, 1984), bk. 5, ch. 15, pp. 204–5: "[The Romans] subordinated their private property to the common welfare, that is, to the republic and the public treasury. They resisted the temptation to avarice. They gave their counsel freely in the councils of state. They indulged in neither public crime nor private passion. They thought they were on the right road when they strove, by all these means, for honors, rule, and glory. Honor has come to them from almost all peoples. The rule of their laws has been imposed on many peoples. And in our day, in literature and in history, glory has been given them by almost everyone."

Index